T0287967

GRANT AT VICKSBURG

GRANT at VICKSBURG

VICKSBURG

The General and the Siege

Michael B. Ballard

Southern Illinois University Press
Carbondale and Edwardsville

16   15   14   13   4   3   2   1

Library of Congress Cataloging-in-Publication Data
Ballard, Michael B.
Grant at Vicksburg : the general and the siege /
Michael B. Ballard.
     p.   cm.
Includes bibliographical references and index.
     ISBN 978-0-8093-3240-3 (cloth : alk. paper)
     ISBN 0-8093-3240-X (cloth : alk. paper)
     ISBN 978-0-8093-3241-0 (ebook)
     ISBN 0-8093-3241-8 (ebook)
1. Vicksburg (Miss.)—History—Siege, 1863. 2. Grant,
Ulysses S. (Ulysses Simpson), 1822–1885—Military
leadership. I. Title.
E475.27.B356 2013
973.7'344—dc23
2012032501

Printed on recycled paper.♻
The paper used in this publication meets the mini-
mum requirements of American National Standard
for Information Sciences—Permanence of Paper for
Printed Library Materials, ANSI Z39.48-1992. ♾

To the memory
of
JOHN Y. SIMON
pioneer in documentary editing
scholar, gentleman, friend

Contents

Illustrations

Preface

Grant at Vicksburg: *The General and the Siege* grew out of an original plan to publish a single volume on the siege of Vicksburg. Amazingly, no scholars or any other writers have published a study solely on the siege. However, having written two chapters on the siege in my book *Vicksburg: The Campaign That Opened the Mississippi*, I decided I was not ready to take the plunge into a full-length examination of that epochal military operation.

After much contemplation, I realized that I knew very little about Ulysses S. Grant's personal activities throughout the forty-seven-day siege. (Actually, the siege proper lasted forty-three days, beginning after Grant's failed assaults of May 19 and 22, 1863.) After examining numerous biographies and campaign studies, including my own, I found that the siege was in a historiographical void. So I moved forward with the project. This decision was made before the U. S. Grant Association moved the Ulysses S. Grant Presidential Collection (now Library) to Mississippi State University. Having these papers sitting in file cabinets a few feet from my office door in Mitchell Memorial Library was beneficial to say the least, but the presence of the papers had not figured in my decision to write this volume. But their proximity certainly helped.

When I began this work, I was not sure how to approach it, nor did I have any idea that the study would take shape as it did. I wanted to address the Yazoo River drinking episode, but I had no idea it would turn into a chapter. Likewise, I had become well aware of racial issues from my previous works, but I did not realize the scope was so broad. The military issues, the obvious focus of a siege, proved to be much more complex than I expected. I decided I must rely on the papers of those persons who were present, logically and especially focusing on Grant's multitude of correspondence. The story of Grant and the siege that emerged went well beyond any parameters I anticipated, and, as I always hope will be the case in all my Civil War journeys, I learned much more than I thought I knew. I have tried to be fair to Grant, pointing out his weaknesses and strengths, his trials and tribulations. He must emerge as the hero because, after all, he won. But his siege days proved to be challenging, and I trust that Grant, the man, the human being, will emerge from these pages as he should be known. He had on-the-job training of the most challenging kind, and he was the better for it. Having taken Vicksburg, he left with a confidence he had not known before, and he would take that confidence and lead the Union to victory.

In large part, I have let the letter writers, including Grant, speak through their written words. The misspelled words in their quotations are original. I have avoided the use of *sic* as much as possible, and where necessary to improve clarity, I have added punctuation, letters, and words between square brackets. Grant was a notoriously poor speller, but he had plenty of company. In the midst of a siege and all the concurrent situations in the Vicksburg vicinity, writers were not all that concerned with grammar or spelling, nor need they have been. Their words paint a vivid portrait of what they experienced, and through their writings, we can feel the essence of that long-ago siege that changed the course of the Civil War.

As with any book, there are those who make contributions that facilitate an author's journey. Elizabeth Joyner, Vicksburg National Military Park archivist and preservationist, has been a long-time friend, and she patiently helped me retrace my previous steps through the voluminous archival holdings at the park. My focus this time was narrower and required fewer primary sources. Yet, her patience was the same: congenial and cooperative. Terry Winschel, who is one of my best friends, offered his usual insights and suggestions, which, without fail, are always invaluable. Terry, a historian at the Vicksburg National Military Park, has moved his office to the John C. Pemberton headquarters home, which makes my visits and our conversations all the more intriguing and fun. David Slay, a ranger at Vicksburg National Military Park, shared with me invaluable research data he has gathered on racial issues.

My friends associated with the Ulysses S. Grant Presidential Papers and Grant publishing projects have also provided valued assistance, especially my assistant Ryan Semmes and my former major professor John Marszalek, the new head of the Ulysses S. Grant Association. They both pointed out materials that proved to be very useful on this project, and I am deeply appreciative for their help and even more for their friendship.

I am thankful to have two friends, Larry Hewitt and Bruce Allardice, who went out of their way to help find a photograph of Sylvanus Cadwallader. Larry, who had scoured the Chicago area, suggested getting in touch with Bruce, who found a photo of Cadwallader in his obituary in a

San Diego newspaper. There may be another photograph of Cadwallader in existence, but if so, it is well hidden.

Thanks to my "cousin-in-law" Dale Jordan, a graphic arts specialist at Mississippi State University, for composing an excellent siege map. He endured, despite all the names I penciled in, and the final product is outstanding.

I am also very grateful for the encouragement and patience of another friend, Sylvia F. Rodrigue, of Southern Illinois University Press. When I first talked with her about this project, she expressed immediate interest, and she continued to be unfailing in her support. I have never worked with anyone more gracious. I appreciate her professionalism in guiding me through all the processes of the press and her selection of the two readers for the manuscript; both offered valuable suggestions and insights.

My wife, Jan, as always, has patiently endured this project. No matter how much time I spend in front of a computer or going through notes scattered all around our joint office in our home, she rarely complains, and when she does, she certainly has cause. But she is always encouraging, most especially when I need a boost to my morale. Writing is a lonely pursuit, but it is easier when you have someone who loves you standing by during the difficult periods. I am most fortunate and blessed to have her as my mate.

GRANT AT VICKSBURG

⁓1⁓

Long Road to Vicksburg

On May 22, 1863, at 8:30 P.M., Major General Ulysses S. Grant sat in his tent headquarters at Vicksburg and wrote the following message to Rear Admiral David Dixon Porter, commanding the Union fleet on the Mississippi River: "I had sent you a dispatch stating that the assault at 10 A.M. was not successful, although not an entire failure. Our troops succeeded in gaining positions close[d] up to the enemy's batteries, which we yet hold, and, in one or two instances, getting into them. I now find the position of the enemy so strong that I shall be compelled to regularly besiege the city." The same day, Grant wired Major General Henry Wager Halleck, commanding all Union armies: "Today an attempt was made to carry the City by assault but was not entirely successful. . . . The nature of the ground about Vicksburg is such that it can only be taken by a siege."[1]

Grant had not been forced to admit failure for some time. Since having his army ferried across the Mississippi River from Louisiana, beginning the morning of April 30, Grant and his army had won battles the next day at Port Gibson, then Raymond (May 12), Jackson (May 14), Champion Hill (May 16), and the Big Black River bridge (May 17). So in eighteen days, his army had defeated Confederate forces five times. On May 19 and again on May 22, he had ordered his men to charge Lieutenant General John C. Pemberton's Confederates, entrenched behind strong fortifications in a semicircle around Vicksburg from north of the city to the south. Both assaults had failed. Grant had no choice but to settle for a siege.[2]

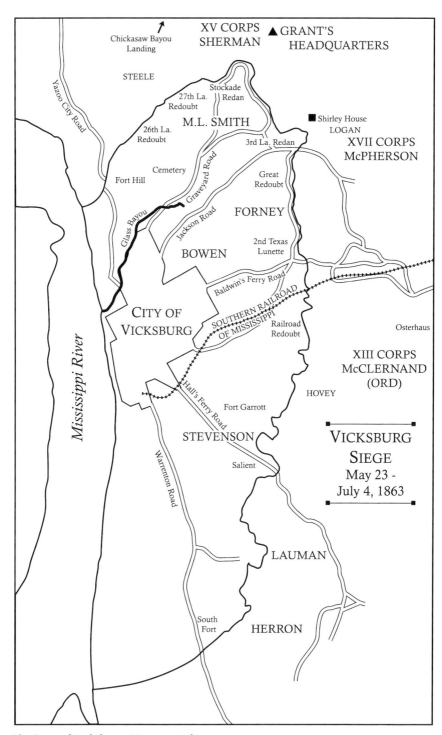

The Siege of Vicksburg, May 23 to July 4, 1863. Dale Jordan.

Grant had experienced failures before. His road to the outskirts of Vicksburg had not been easy. He started the Civil War shakily, but his leadership improved. His first action of note in the field had been the Battle of Belmont, Missouri, November 7, 1861, where he had been forced to withdraw his army to the safety on the Missouri-side shore of the Mississippi River. Yet, his attack had positive strategic results for it led to the withdrawal of Confederate troops from Kentucky. Grant had convinced Confederate leaders that their foothold in the Bluegrass State was tenuous at best. Grant's performance had not been remarkable; the West Point graduate had not experienced combat since the Mexican-American War (1846–48), and he had not led an army into battle before Belmont. Yet, he had not suffered a serious loss, and in the long view, he had accomplished something worthwhile.

After Belmont, Grant's next major role came when he led attacks from the Ohio River against Fort Henry on the Tennessee River and, more significant, Fort Donelson on the Cumberland. The two rivers allowed penetration into Tennessee, and with the help of the Union navy and with no Confederate navy to offer opposition, Union forces could potentially go up the Cumberland all the way to the Tennessee state capital, Nashville. Grant captured both forts, Henry on February 6, 1862, and Donelson, February 16. When the Confederate commander at Donelson approached him for surrender terms, Grant made himself a national hero when he responded that the only term he would accept was unconditional surrender.

So, thanks to his initials, he became known as "Unconditional Surrender" Grant. Considering he had been known as "Sam" Grant at West Point, due to his initials "U. S." being used for "Uncle Sam" by fellow cadets, the paperwork error in his West Point appointment papers turned out to very convenient. His true name, Hiram Ulysses Grant, had been printed as Ulysses Simpson Grant, and, fortunate for him, Grant made no effort to correct the mistake.

At his next great battle, Shiloh, April 6–7, 1862, Grant's success continued, but his victory was tainted. His forces, camped near Pittsburg Landing on the Tennessee River, were surprised on the first day of battle and driven nearly all the way to the river. Union gunboats and darkness helped stop the Confederates. Next day, Federal reinforcements under Major General Don Carlos Buell helped force the Confederate army south to Corinth, Mississippi, which had been Grant's target. Grant's losses during the two-day fight totaled slightly over thirteen thousand, the largest casualty count of any Civil War battle up to that time. Grant's immediate superior, Halleck, came down from his Saint Louis headquarters and took command. Grant's mismanagement of the first day's fight infuriated Halleck, who made Grant second in command of the combined armies, a title tantamount to Grant being relieved. Major General George Thomas took charge of Grant's Army of the Tennessee, while Buell continued to command the Army of the Ohio.

With the arrival of additional reinforcements, Halleck led one hundred thousand troops toward Corinth. Having no command and nothing to do, Grant grew very depressed and strongly considered resigning from the army. Only the intervention of Major General William Tecumseh Sherman, who had become a close friend, convinced Grant to stay. Eventually, Confederates, heavily outnumbered, evacuated Corinth, and Halleck occupied a nearly empty town. The railroad crossing there made Corinth an important prize for Union forces in the western theater. Within a few weeks, Halleck received his reward by being called to Washington to become the new commander of all Union forces. Grant had his command back, but it was greatly depleted when Halleck, before he left, sent troops to Tennessee and Arkansas.

Grant acted with temerity for months, running his command as though he must do everything not to lose rather than make decisions to assure victory. The shadow of his post-Shiloh experiences hovered over his headquarters, and his sluggish behavior belied the image he had created at Donelson as an aggressive, decisive general. His army managed to win a battle at Iuka, east of Corinth, on September 19, 1862, though Union tactical coordination proved to be nonexistent. Confederate commander Major General Sterling Price managed to escape, taking his army south, removing it from between Grant's two wings, one of which never got into action. Two weeks later, a violent fight erupted at Corinth, October 3–4, when Major General Earl Van Dorn led his Confederate army, combined with Price's, against Major General William Rosecrans's troops occupying Corinth.

Prior to the battle, Grant went on leave to Saint Louis, though he had feared throughout the Iuka operation that Van Dorn might attack. Grant returned in time to coordinate the sending of reinforcements to Rosecrans, but few of them arrived in time to make a difference. Rosecrans managed to beat back Van Dorn on the second day of the battle, and Grant refused to let Rosecrans continue pursuit of the Confederates, seemingly afraid that such a move would be too risky. There would have been little risk, and Rosecrans might well have captured Van Dorn's entire force, but Grant had no intention of making a mistake and being sidelined again by Halleck. Halleck thought Grant wrong to call off Rosecrans's pursuit, but Grant convinced him that he had made the right decision, and Halleck in his new role reacted as became his habit. He deferred to the general in the field.

After firming up control of the Mississippi–west Tennessee border, Grant looked to attack Vicksburg, the heavily fortified Confederate bastion to the southwest on the Mississippi River. Delays resulted primarily from Grant continually requesting reinforcements, for he was convinced that the Rebels in his front either had equal or superior numbers. This was not true, but his fears of failures continued to dominate his thinking. Halleck sent him more men, and Grant by December at last felt his force was strong enough to invade Mississippi.

Grant marched the major portion of his army southward along the Mississippi Central Railroad. Meanwhile, Sherman led a detachment from Memphis on a southeasterly course, close to the route of the Mississippi and Tennessee Railroad, which connected Memphis with the north central Mississippi town of Grenada. Grant intended to add Sherman's troops to his to increase the size of Union forces and continue all the way to the Mississippi capital, Jackson, and then turn west and attack Vicksburg.

He made two mistakes, both of which came back to haunt him. First, by marching south, he extended his supply line that was based in Holly Springs, a short distance from the Mississippi-Tennessee state line. On December 20, Van Dorn led a cavalry force behind Grant's lines and destroyed tons of Union supplies piled around the Holly Springs railroad depot and in nearby buildings. Grant had no choice but to order his army to retreat north to the Tennessee-Mississippi state line, for the countryside in winter could not provide enough food for his men.

Before Van Dorn's raid, Grant heard rumors that Major General John A. McClernand, an Illinois politician who had served with Grant at Belmont, Fort Donelson, and Shiloh, had managed to get permission from Washington to lead his own army down the Mississippi River to attack Vicksburg. McClernand believed that President Abraham Lincoln, Secretary of War Edwin McMasters Stanton, and Halleck had given him the freedom to operate independently. McClernand soon learned that was not the case.

Grant, infuriated by the news of McClernand's plans, sent a message to Washington to Halleck, demanding to know what was going on. Grant received assurances that any force in his district would be under his command, including McClernand's. Grant decided to send Sherman back to Memphis and then downriver with a large force to attack Vicksburg from the north and after three days of fighting had to retreat, having suffered numerous casualties. Grant had intended to continue south to Jackson as planned and attack Vicksburg from the east, but Van Dorn had ruined that part of the plan with his raids.

After arriving at Memphis from Illinois, McClernand went downriver and found no sign of Grant, who had retreated back to the Tennessee-Mississippi state line. Sherman had heard about Grant's setback, but he had his army trnsported up the Yazoo River and attacked Confederate forces at Chickasaw Bayou, a few miles north of Vicksburg, and was repulsed. Meanwhile, Grant had chosen not to meet McClernand's boat, a clear sign of his anger at McClernand's interference. Sherman had taken his forces back to the Mississippi by the time McClernand arrived. McClernand took command, being senior to Sherman, and led a successful campaign into the Mississippi against Fort Hindman on the Arkansas River, which empties into the Mississippi north of Vicksburg. The Union victory on January 11, 1863, made it easier to block Confederate supplies from Arkansas intended for Vicksburg.

Grant traveled downriver and took command of all forces, and McClernand was incensed when he found out how Washington had betrayed him. The situation led to hard feelings and occasional insubordination on McClernand's part. Yet, Grant ignored McClernand's impudence, though his later explanations for doing so sound hollow. He had fought with McClernand, and he knew that, being a politician notwithstanding, McClernand had shown ability as a combat commander. Could it be that Grant thought McClernand more competent than he would ever admit? Time would tell.

During the early months of 1863, Grant set in motion several attempts to bypass attacking Vicksburg to find some way to get to the city without resorting to a suicidal assault on the bluffs hovering above the Mississippi River. He put men to work digging a canal across a neck of land on the Louisiana side of the Mississippi. The idea was to divert the course of the river, leaving Vicksburg without a river port, thereby making the city less consequential to Grant's determination to clear the Mississippi of Confederates. The canal idea had been tried in the summer of 1862, and it did not work, nor did it work in 1863. The river's current refused to cooperate, but Grant had to try because President Lincoln wanted him to.

Other equally doomed measures followed: the Lake Providence expedition, an attempt to get south of Vicksburg via connecting waterways on the Louisiana side of the Mississippi; the Yazoo Pass expedition, which came to a halt north of Vicksburg at the town of Greenwood, where a fort, named after Pemberton, was armed well enough to prevent the descent from the north by Union vessels coming down the Tallahatchie River; and the Steele's Bayou campaign, which almost cost naval commander Porter some of his ironclads due to Confederate resistance and narrow waterways that constricted maneuverability. The last failure came when the so-called Duckport Canal operation failed to allow supply barges to get downstream below Vicksburg.

Therein was the dilemma: How could Grant get his army past Vicksburg via Louisiana and move his troops across the Mississippi River into the state of Mississippi? Grant claimed in his memoirs to have had the idea of moving his troops down the Louisiana side of the river for some time, and others also took the credit. Lieutenant Colonel James Wilson, one of Grant's aides, said he had heard McClernand mention such a plan before Grant said anything about it. The idea could have come to anyone familiar with the situation. Every other effort to get at Vicksburg had failed, and outflanking the city to the south seemed the only viable option left. Grant had to make the final decision, and he most likely felt the right to take credit for it.

Grant talked with Porter, and the two agreed that Porter would pad his boats with cotton and otherwise protect them as well as he could and attempt to run ironclads and transports downriver right in front of the Vicksburg batteries. Tactically, he intended to move his squadron from one side of the river to the other, depending on the abilities and accuracy of Confederate gunners. He hoped by hugging the eastern shore that Pemberton's artillery could not be depressed (barrels pushed downward) enough to hit the Union vessels. Porter suffered minor losses, and Grant felt enthused enough to have Porter make a second run, which also succeeded. Now Grant would have the means downstream to transport his men from the Louisiana shore into Mississippi.

McClernand's XIII Corps led the march down the Louisiana side of the river. An interesting question that can only be answered by implication is whether Grant trusted McClernand more than he ever admitted or whether he simply took advantage of the fact that McClernand's men were in a prime location to lead the army. If Grant indeed not only disliked McClernand, and there is little doubt that he did not like him, but also did not trust him, why would McClernand have been given the important assignment of being in the van? McClernand's location could have easily been a nonfactor as Grant laid out his operational plans.

There are several possible reasons. Major General James B. McPherson had never led a corps in battle; his army experience had been primarily as an engineer. Grant, and Sherman also, thought very highly of McPherson, and Grant likely did not want to risk the inexperienced McPherson performing poorly in the attempt to cross the Mississippi. If Grant lost his first encounter with the enemy in Mississippi, his campaign might end, and though Grant would be the one in trouble, he did not want to torpedo young McPherson's career.

What about Sherman? Grant and Sherman's friendship continued to blossom, but there was a problem. Sherman did not like Grant's plan, and he had said so. Grant aide Wilson wrote after the war that Sherman's opposition to the operation was a factor that kept Grant from putting his friend into the lead position. Being a Grant staff member, Wilson was at the planning table and certainly could have heard Grant make such a comment. In an April 23 letter to his wife, Sherman himself seemed to confirm Wilson's story: "McClernands corps had moved down—McPhersons will follow and mine come last—I dont object to this for I have no faith in the whole plan." Whether Grant further considered Sherman's failure at Chickasaw Bayou is not known.[3]

Though speculation about Grant's choice will continue, the fact is he trusted McClernand enough to take the lead, and McClernand had to do well or the campaign indeed might be doomed. Grant had much at stake; would he have put his military future into the hands of a general whose ability he questioned? Not only did McClernand lead the way into the first battle at Port Gibson but his corps also marched inland after victory at Port Gibson as Grant's left flank, as Grant directed the two corps, McPherson's being the other, north and northeast. Sherman and his corps would join them later. The left flank was the most dangerous, for Pemberton's Confederates shadowed Grant's march, and the Rebels were positioned along the Big Black River, which flowed along McClernand's left. Grant had to trust McClernand as a general, and the collapse of their working relationship that came later during the siege would cast an unjust pall over McClernand's significant role during the campaign.

Getting to the Port Gibson battlefield had not been easy. McClernand, followed by McPherson, marched and waded south until they reached a place called New Carthage. Porter took part of his fleet south from that point to see how much firepower the Confederates had at the town of Grand Gulf. He found they had quite a bit, and several of his boats took a pounding. Grant had hoped to cross the river at Grand Gulf, but, obviously, that plan had to be scrapped. Porter led his vessels farther downstream and found a suitable spot, Hard Times landing on the Louisiana side and a site called Bruinsburg, across the river in Mississippi. There had once been a settlement there, but it was gone; nevertheless, it was perfect for Grant's lead corps, McClernand's, to disembark from the army transports escorted by Porter's boats. Confederates had not fortified the place.

McClernand's corps quickly moved inland into rugged country west of Port Gibson. A portion of McPherson's followed in time to join in defeating Confederates at Port Gibson on May 1. Sherman led his corps downstream to catch up. He had stayed behind to demonstrate against bluffs north of Vicksburg. The diversion had not fooled the Confederates, and now he rushed downstream. Grant led his troops toward the Southern Railroad of Mississippi, which connected Vicksburg with Jackson and points east, McClernand on the left flank and McPherson the right. On May 12, McPherson met a Confederate brigade near the town of Raymond and showed mediocre leadership in taking several hours to defeat the vastly outnumbered Rebels. Sherman, whose corps had come ashore from the Mississippi a few days after the fight at Port Gibson, and Grant were concerned that Confederate troops under General Joseph E. Johnston, newly arrived in Mississippi and sent by Confederate President Jefferson Davis, had been gathering in Jackson. Grant ordered Sherman to march to the capital city from the south while McPherson attacked from the west. McClernand stayed in the area between Raymond and Bolton, a small town to the west near the Big Black River. Johnston chose to give up Jackson, and little fighting occurred there on May 14, resulting in another Union victory.

By this time, Pemberton had moved his Vicksburg army, less two divisions left in the city, east beyond the Big Black to Edwards. Johnston and Pemberton had communication problems, compounded by Davis's direct orders to Pemberton to hold Vicksburg and Johnston's belief that the city should be abandoned. Pemberton took his army toward Raymond in an attempt to cut Grant's supply line; Union supply wagons with military escorts had followed Grant's army inland for several miles. He eventually realized, especially after leaving Jackson and heading toward the Big Black, it would be difficult to continue protecting them, so he sent orders to keep the wagons at Grand Gulf, where a Union supply depot had been established.

En route, Pemberton received a message from Johnston; Johnston wanted the armies to merge at Clinton, west of Jackson, and the town from which McPherson staged his march east to Jackson. Johnston was nowhere near Clinton; he had taken his army to the northwest to Canton. Pemberton tried to obey, but as he ordered his army to reverse its course, Grant, who had received a copy of Johnston's message from a

Union spy, attacked on May 16 along a ridge known as Champion Hill. After a long day of bitter, hard, and bloody fighting, McPherson and McClernand, plus Major General Frank Blair's division from Sherman's corps, defeated Pemberton's three divisions and sent the Confederates retreating to the Big Black. (Sherman and the rest of his corps had stayed behind to destroy Confederate war matériel in Jackson.) One of Pemberton's divisions was separated from his army during the retreat from Champion Hill. Pemberton waited along the Big Black for the missing troops, which had to bypass Grant's army to the south, turn north, and go to Canton to join Johnston. On May 17, McClernand's corps smashed Pemberton's line at the Big Black, and the Confederates retreated into Vicksburg. Davis's firm orders for Pemberton to hold Vicksburg ultimately doomed the city.

Grant found out soon enough, however, that victory would not come easily. He had won five battles, and he felt confident he could easily take the city. He thought Pemberton might swing to the northeast and unite with Johnston, thus giving up Vicksburg. Johnston advised Pemberton to do that very thing. Pemberton, however, obeyed Davis's instructions that Vicksburg must be held. Pemberton had two fresh divisions that remained in the city during the fighting at Champion Hill and the Big Black. His chief engineer, Major Samuel Lockett, had done a good job planning defenses around Vicksburg. The main Confederate strongholds, connected by infantry entrenchments, ran in an arc facing east from north of the city to the east and around to the south. Grant at the time did not have enough troops to stretch the length of the Rebel defenses. At the time, he gave that little thought, partly because he did not know the span of the enemy line. More important, he believed he could whip Pemberton's forces irrespective of the length of Rebel lines. The Mississippi River, dominated by Union boats, would be a factor as Union naval firepower along the waterfront would be dangerous to the Confederate rear.

The key defenses, beginning from north of Vicksburg, consisted of Fort Hill, a high bluff overlooking the river and practically impregnable from infantry attacks. East of Fort Hill stood the 26th Louisiana Redoubt. Other significant works included Stockade Redan and the 27th Louisiana Lunette, both blocking Graveyard Road; nearby stood Green's Redan, which provided cover fire against any Union attacks down Graveyard Road. The entrance of Jackson Road into Vicksburg proved to be a key point. A strong Confederate defense, the 3rd Louisiana Redan, stood on one side of the road and not too far away the Great Redoubt on the other. Union soldiers often erroneously referred to this position as Fort Hill, and its prominence on high ground made the name just as appropriate as the actual Fort Hill. South of the Great Redoubt stood the 2nd Texas Lunette, a strong defensive position blocking Baldwin's Ferry Road, a route into downtown Vicksburg. Just south of this lunette, the Southern Railroad of Mississippi entered Vicksburg. On a bluff south of the railroad, the impressive Railroad Redoubt had been constructed. South of the redoubt stood Square Fort (eventually renamed Fort Garrott) and a position called Salient Work, which blocked Hall's Ferry Road. Inside South Fort, south of Vicksburg, Confederates had a field of fire against enemy approaches from Warrenton, a community just south of Vicksburg. The fort marked the termination of the Confederate right flank.

In addition to Lockett's carefully engineered works, the Confederates had a tremendous terrain advantage. The ridges and steep slopes of the hilly area made approaches hazardous for Grant's army. The Rebels had increased the difficulty by felling trees toward Union lines, intertwining branches, and sharpening the ends of branches, in effect making an obstructions of chopped-down trees, called abatis. In addition to the abatis, tangled wire and cane poles, plus piles of tree limbs, blocked potential approach points. Lockett placed cannon at strategically significant places between the various anchor points of his line. To defend these lines, Pemberton had approximately thirty-three thousand troops, but many of those who had been involved in fighting at Champion Hill and Big Black would not be able to enter into combat right away. Grant had thirty-five thousand men when he approached Vicksburg, and his troops were in much better shape to fight.

Grant's three corps approached Vicksburg with Sherman on the right, McPherson in the center, and McClernand on the left. Porter's gunboats and mortar boats in the Mississippi along the Vicksburg waterfront waited to assist Grant as soon as the opportunity arose. Grant had no idea of the severe challenges his men faced trying to overcome the Vicksburg defenses, but while his soldiers were elated with their successes, he reasoned that Pemberton's men had to be depressed. Of course, Grant did not know about the two fresh Confederate divisions ready to help man the city's defenses. It likely would not have mattered to him because he was convinced that a strong charge would defeat the Rebels, and Vicksburg would fall.

If Pemberton had any notion of trying to escape, which he did not, Sherman's corps would likely have stopped the Confederates. The obvious route of escape lay to the northeast, where Pemberton could join with Johnston and carry on the battles with Grant without being tied to Vicksburg. Pemberton also could have pushed southward; McClernand did not have enough troops to reach the river, so there was, at least temporarily, a passage for the Confederates to escape Grant's army. Pemberton would consider this option much later, but he did not at the time. He believed and he continued to believe far too long that Johnston would come to his aid.

Grant did not care what options his opponent had; the fact that Pemberton had retreated into Vicksburg made it clear the Confederates intended to fight. Yet, they would not put up much resistance, or so Grant believed, and he would not give them time to rest. On the afternoon of May 19, Grant ordered three artillery shots to signal an attack. Grant had problems he had not considered or was not aware of. Sherman's corps was the only one close enough to the Confederate defenses to attack effectively. McPherson's corps was one thousand yards east of the Rebel line, and McClernand's men continued to fight through rugged terrain and could not attack en masse from their position.

The situation made the carnage of Sherman's troops inevitable. The attack of the three Union corps broke down into scattered shooting that in no way resembled coordination. Only part of McPherson's corps managed to do any fighting at all, though his men did edge closer to Confederate lines. McClernand's corps, likewise, made some forward progress but did no harm to enemy positions. Sherman's men, being the closest to Rebel works, engaged in heavy but unsuccessful fighting. Without either McPherson or McClernand applying pressure along Confederate fronts, the Confederates focused on Sherman.

Colonel Kilby Smith's brigade of Blair's division made it within about 150 yards of Stockade Redan, but Smith found that he did not have sufficient cover for his brigade. He stopped and sent word to Sherman, and Sherman basically responded that Smith should do the best he could. Colonel Giles Smith's brigade made better progress and reached the north face of the Stockade Redan stronghold, but concentrated Confederate fire grew so heavy, the men had to fall back and find whatever cover they could. The most effective charge came from the 13th U.S. Infantry; these professional soldiers survived crossfire and got closer to Stockade Redan than any others in Sherman's corps. The 13th, too, had to fall back to keep from being annihilated. The 13th's assault impressed Sherman enough that he authorized the regiment to put "First at Vicksburg" on its flag, which survived riddled with fifty-five bullet holes. The remainder of Blair's division experienced similar fates as Rebel Louisianans swept the attacking lines with a steady, withering fire. As evening approached, Sherman had to accept the repulse, and the fighting ended. Union casualties tell the story of the day: McClernand lost 7 killed and 93 wounded; McPherson, 16 killed and 113 wounded; and Sherman, 133 killed, 571 wounded, and 8 missing. Of Sherman's casualty totals, Blair's division accounted for 120 dead, 485 wounded, and 8 missing. Confederate reports are scant, and the only accounting lists 8 dead and 62 wounded. A complete list would not have raised those numbers significantly higher because they were shielded by earthworks.

In his memoirs, Grant looked back on the May 19 failure and put the best face on it he could: "It resulted in securing more advanced positions for all our troops where they were fully covered from the fire of the enemy." He admitted that he did not think the enemy would make much of an effort to defend Vicksburg. He also underestimated Pemberton's numbers, though he never admitted it. Army gossip was that the Rebels only had about eighteen thousand men. If Grant had known about Pemberton's two fresh divisions, he might not have been so rash. The fact was that he did not have his whole army in position to make an attack. He did not know how close McClernand and McPherson were to the main line of Confederate works. He knew Sherman was reasonably close for he was with Sherman, and Grant would make his headquarters in the rear of Sherman's corps. Grant had not inspected his line, so he had no appreciation of terrain challenges that faced his army. In effect, Grant made a poor decision, based more on his own adrenalin and the victorious attitudes of his men than a knowledge of factors involved.

He saw no reason that his string of victories could not continue: "Accordingly, at two o'clock, I ordered an assault. It resulted in securing more advanced positions for all our troops where they were fully covered from the fire of the enemy." Grant's tone indicated he considered the May 19 action little more than a heavy skirmish that had produced positive results. His remarks in the official records, written at the time, exhibit the same attitude.[4]

Grant used the next two days to give his commanders time to solidify their positions, and he made sure Sherman's divisions established contact with Porter to set up a secure supply depot on the Yazoo River at the rear of Sherman's troops. Ironically, the supply depot would be along Chickasaw Bayou, the area where Sherman had suffered a beating a few months earlier. Roads were built to facilitate distribution of supplies.

On May 21, Grant wrote another order. He would try again, and this time his attack would be coordinated, or so he thought. Grant explained in his memoirs that his first consideration in ordering another assault "was—the troops believed they could carry the works in their front, and would not have worked so patiently in the trenches if they had not been allowed to try." There is no indication that all his soldiers agreed. One wrote long years after the war that the army had great confidence in Grant and would follow any orders. "As for myself," he contended, "I know I would not have been hard to restrain from running up against breastworks bristling with cannon and bayonets in the hands of brave soldiers."[5]

Grant detailed preparations for the second assault on May 22. First, he wanted his corps commanders to survey on May 21 all roads leading toward Confederate works by which the army could advance. As many artillery batteries as possible should be positioned to provide cover fire for the infantry. He ordered cannon and advance skirmishers to begin the fight. Then, infantry, arranged in columns of platoons or in flanking positions if the roads were not wide enough to accommodate platoons, would charge, all three corps moving at 10 A.M. Infantry should have bayonets fixed, and they should not fire until the Rebel outer line had been overrun. The men would carry only canteens, ammunition, and enough rations for one day. Skirmishers would follow the infantry and climb over whatever walls confronted. Grant demonstrated his optimism in his dictation to Assistant Adjutant General (Lieutenant Colonel) John Rawlins: "If prosecuted with vigor, it is confidently-believed this course will carry Vicksburg in a very short time, and with much less loss that would be sustained by delay. Every day's delay enables the enemy to strengthen his defenses and increases his chance for receiving aid from outside."[6]

The men in each Union corps spent May 21 readying for tomorrow's fight. Batteries were placed in strategic positions; entrenchments were dug. Confederate cannoneers made Union preparations adventurous, and Rebel marksmen kept Grant's work parties uneasy. Blair strengthened his position by bringing forward twenty-seven artillery pieces to sweep Graveyard Road. Their shot and shell could easily reach Stockade Redan. Meanwhile, McPherson's corps crept along the Jackson Road, Major General John A. Logan's division in the lead, approaching the ominously strong-looking 3rd Louisiana Redan.

Along the way, Mrs. James Shirley's white house stood near the road. Mrs. Shirley, a Unionist, cowered inside against her chimney. A Federal detachment went to the house and convinced her to take refuge well away from the home. The Shirley house is the only such structure to survive the siege battlefield down to the present day.

Union officers who had a close view of the Confederate line realized that a line of entrenchments connecting the 3rd Louisiana Redan with the Great Redoubt would make their task more difficult. The rugged terrain made fields of fire difficult and compounded the problems of Union brigades and regiments reinforcing each other. The steep ravines slowed the massing of artillery along McPherson's front.

On the Union left, McClernand focused on artillery emplacements flanked by rifle entrenchments. He placed one division east of the Railroad Redoubt and one east by southeast of Square Fort and held one in reserve on the Baldwin's Ferry road. McClernand realized that potential flanking fire on his right from Confederates in the 2nd Texas Lunette could be a big problem. He ordered Major General Andrew Jackson Smith, whose division had taken position east of the Railroad Redoubt, to stretch his line southeast of the lunette. Still, McClernand's right flank would not be secured unless he could connect it with McPherson's left, a half-mile north with rugged terrain in between. Additional troops relieved Smith's the evening of the twenty-first, and the Federals continued to entrench to the point that infantry could confront the east wall of the lunette. McClernand, the incurable politician, loudly applauded the efforts of his men and intimated clearly that his men had done more than any others along the siege lines. His mouth did little more than continue the ever-widening gulf between him and Grant.

A blowup between the two was narrowly avoided on the twenty-first. Grant ordered a detachment from one of McClernand's divisions to return to the Big Black to make sure Johnson did not try to cross the river and attack the Union rear. Grant issued the order without notifying McClernand, and McClernand, infuriated, ordered the men sent to the bridge to return. The explosive situation cooled when Grant received assurance that two infantry companies and scouts had settled in at the Big Black bridge to watch for the enemy. The news did not totally satisfy Grant, who insisted that McClernand send a brigade to the bridge. The incident demonstrated that Grant could be as vindictive as McClernand. Grant never treated McPherson or Sherman in the same manner.

Grant also sent troops south of Vicksburg, an area left open by his current battle line. He made the move more as a diversion than to block any attempt by Pemberton to escape. If escape had been on Pemberton's mind, he would not have deployed his army inside Vicksburg to repel Union attacks. Grant asked Porter to have a gunboat lob a few shells to the south to further get Pemberton's attention.

Musket and cannon fire died down the evening of May 21 as darkness settled over the landscape. Grant ordered the attack next day to begin at 10 A.M. McClernand protested, perhaps to get back at Grant for the troops sent to the Big Black. McClernand argued that an attack from all across the Union front would not be as effective as massing each corps and delivering three hard blows against the Rebel lines. McClernand liked this tactic; he had used it well with his corps during the campaign thus far, both at Port Gibson and the Big Black. However, in this case, terrain made such a proposal ridiculous, and McClernand contradicted his own idea by spreading out rather than concentrating his forces. Sherman massed his troops along Graveyard Road, not because of McClernand's suggestion but because terrain forced Sherman to put all his attacking troops on the road. A concentrated attack on Stockade Redan might produce positive results. He found out soon enough the reverse might be the case. As May 22 dawned, small-arms and artillery fire echoed across the ravines and along the ridges of Vicksburg. Confederates may have thought the day would simply consist of more shooting at Yankees and watching them trying to get closer to their defensive works. The clock moved closer to ten. Blair put together a detachment of 150 men, dubbed the Forlorn Hope, a military term meaning the men involved would be fortunate indeed if they escaped death.

Ten o'clock arrived, and the Confederates soon realized the day would be memorable. Union soldiers, too, would long remember it but for different reasons. Watches had been synchronized, and the Union assault sprung as planned.[7]

Blair's 150 went forward toward Stockade Redan, with Union cannon and rifled muskets unloading a brisk, covering fire. The Confederates remained ominously quiet. Some 150 yards from the walls of the redan, the road dipped down slightly before rising up to more level terrain. From that point to Stockade Redan was an open field of fire. As the Forlorn Hope stepped into the open area, Confederate regiments aligned two deep rose from behind the redan walls and opened fire. The 150 did not turn and run, but many dove for cover, and a small number dashed forward into the ditch fronting the redan, some trying to climb the wall of dirt. One planted a flag that flew for some time; some Confederates tried to retrieve it, but most decided living was worth more than exposing themselves to Union firepower to try grabbing a flag. Rebel fire convinced Union soldiers that a straightforward attack down the road to the redan was suicidal.

Behind the 150 who led the way, Blair's brigades followed. Ohioans in the lead decided to stop rather than run headlong into the lead storm coming from the redan. The narrow road quickly became clogged, and Blair had no choice but to call off the attack. Other units in Sherman's corps fared no better as the Confederates in Green's Redan and Stockade

Redan spread their field of fire to cover Graveyard Road, appropriately named on this day.

Major General Frederick Steele's division on Sherman's right took hours just getting into position after ten o'clock arrived and passed. Steele's men had to negotiate the deep ravine through which Mint Spring Bayou flows. The Confederates had abandoned the position prior to the twenty-second, a wise tactical decision, but one that resulted in the loss of a water source.

On Sherman's left flank, McPherson's right wing had Steele's problems, spending more time moving than fighting. Some of McPherson's soldiers realized that attacking Confederate entrenchments would expose them to fire from Green's Redan. Brigadier General Thomas Ransom decided to wait for reinforcements before proceeding, but by the time Giles Smith's brigade showed up, it was mid-afternoon. Time for fighting quickly waned.

Logan, a Southern Illinois political general who, unlike McClernand, forgot politics when in battle, led McPherson's attack on the left. Logan, suspected at the beginning of the war of having Southern sympathies because he came from Southern Illinois where many sympathizers lived, had already proved himself a solid leader, most recently at Champion Hill. Destined to play a key role in the capture of Vicksburg, Logan found the going very rough as he faced off against Confederates holding the 3rd Louisiana Redan and the Great Redoubt. He sent one brigade climbing up the slope behind the Shirley house into Jackson Road and straight at the 3rd Louisiana Redan. Troops got to within about one hundred yards of the Confederate defenders, when men in the lead lost their nerve and left the road in desperate searches for cover. Another brigade followed, and some of the men reached the ditch fronting the redan, but there they remained, dodging lit cannon balls rolled into their midst by Confederates who could not risk standing up, a required position to shoot downhill at the Yankees in the ditch.

Logan sent Brigadier General John Stevenson's brigade against the Great Redoubt, and, initially, Stevenson's men made progress due to shelter a ravine provided. Stevenson ordered two columns, carrying ladders to facilitate climbing the outer walls of the redoubt, to charge forward without firing a shot until they got close. The charge began after the initial barrage by Union cannon fire ceased. Stevenson's men made impressive progress, running through a storm of bullets from the redoubt's defenders. He stopped the men long enough to break their column formation and form a long battle line. After a few rounds of friendly artillery fire hit the redoubt, Stevenson's soldiers charged, and two Confederate cannon loaded with canister greeted them. One of Stevenson's regiments got close enough to discover that the ladders were too short to reach the top of the redoubt. The loss of momentum gave Confederates time to concentrate their firepower, and Stevenson's casualties mounted. One of Stevenson's regiments mired in a hollow brimming with obstructions and waited while another tried to clear the way. Minutes, then hours passed as men did nothing but dodge enemy missiles and struggle with vines and felled trees.

On Grant's far left, McClernand's corps charged not only Confederate works but also fell headlong into controversy. McClernand's artillery, twenty-seven guns, fired from daybreak until the 10 A.M. attack hour. McClernand had three main targets; from his left to his right, they were Square Fort, the Railroad Redoubt, and the 2nd Texas Lunette. He sent Brigadier General Peter Osterhaus's division to attack Square Fort and Brigadier General Eugene Carr's to assault the Railroad Redoubt and the 2nd Texas Lunette, located with a few hundred yards of the Railroad Redoubt.

Smith's troops did well, and a few Iowans actually got into the interior of Railroad Redoubt before reinforced Confederates launched a charge to drive the Yankees out. Fighting grew fiercer as Union reinforcements also came forward. Some Confederates trapped within the redoubt surrendered, and a few Union soldiers surrendered to Rebels. The savage fight soon became a stalemate. Union soldiers who had reached the ditch at the foot of the redoubt flattened themselves against the earth but still had to watch for lit cannonballs rolled into their midst. The danger led to more Union surrenders.

While the attack on Railroad Redoubt sputtered, one of Carr's brigades attacked the left section of the front of the 2nd Texas Lunette. The Union soldiers fell as if cut down by a wide-swinging scythe. The Texans had built small steps inside the lunette so they could step up, shoot, then step back down to reload. A second attempted attack farther left met a similar fate. Two more Carr brigades came up, one getting close to the lunette before pausing to reform. Carr sent orders for the second brigade to take position between the lunette and the Railroad Redoubt. The order forced the brigade to divide its manpower, half to support the fight against the lunette and half to attack the redoubt.

The commander, Brigadier General Stephen Burbridge, protested to Smith, who told him he must talk to Carr. Carr refused to countermand the order, and McClernand would not override Carr. So Burbridge had to concede, no matter that absurd chain of command forced a ridiculous tactical error. His regiments sent to the lunette did a superb job, but they were simply overwhelmed by the compact firepower of the Confederates. Some of the Federals actually got to the top of the lunette wall only to be shot in the face. As Burbridge observed bodies of his men rolling down the outer lunette walls, he called off the attack, doing so without checking with anyone.

Burbridge must have laughed in disdain when he suddenly received a message from Carr giving him permission to use his own judgment. Burbridge reunited his brigade, and his troops charged the lunette, where they faced not only Rebel bullets but also cotton bales set afire and tossed into their midst. When the men stopped to push the bales out of the way, Confederate canister ripped into their ranks. While fighting raged at both the redoubt and lunette, Confederate reinforcements, freed by the relative inactivity on Sherman's and McPherson's fronts, raced in to support their comrades defending the two positions.

At Square Fort on the Confederate right, Union efforts fared no better. A deep, wide ravine fronted the fort, and the ground was cluttered with obstructions. After seeing many men shot down, Osterhaus ordered a halt, and though the fighting went on, Square Fort defenders knew the Yankees would come no farther. An hour after the full-scale attack had begun, Grant, reading reports and hearing first-hand that serious problems had developed, knew that everything had bogged down. He did not think there was any reason to continue. A message from McClernand challenged his attitude.

McClernand knew that Confederate reinforcements had blocked his advance, and he wanted McPherson to make some noise to divert the Rebels. McClernand had a point. McPherson's men had done comparatively little fighting, and his left-wing division would be very helpful in the fighting at the Texas lunette. Grant brushed off McClernand's request by telling his nemesis to use his own reserves. Grant assumed, without foundation, that McClernand had held back some of his corps. In fact, only one of McClernand's brigades had been held in reserve. McClernand's reports got Grant's attention. He believed his men had partially taken two forts and that Union flags flew over both of them. The truth was that the flag stuck on the bank of the Railroad Redoubt was the only one that waved. Some of his men had breached the fortification, but none had gotten into the lunette to fly a Union flag. McClernand could see battle flags flying all around, but he could not tell if they were atop Confederate works. McClernand's words made his attacks sound much more successful than they had been, but there is no evidence he deliberately overstated the situation. He believed what he wrote.

Suspicious of McClernand's report, Grant refused to order McPherson to send help. Instead, he told McClernand to bring up a brigade stationed on the far left of the Union line, near the town of Warrenton. The distance this unit would have to travel made it highly unlikely they could help McClernand. Sherman offered to renew his attack, at least enough to take pressure off McClernand. The fact that Sherman was willing to help says much about the effect of Grant's attitude toward McClernand. Sherman did not like McClernand either, but if he could positively impact the battle, Sherman was willing to take the chance. Grant let his personal feelings get in the way of his command responsibilities. Sherman's action impacted Grant's thinking to the point that he finally sent orders to McPherson to feint an attack. Another message from McClernand said that his men held Confederate entrenchments, asked if he should use all or part of the brigade coming from Warrenton, and said, falsely, that all his corps was engaged. The reserve brigade had still not seen any action. McClernand implied a stalemate had developed and without help he could do no more.

Shortly after 2 P.M., Sherman sent troops forward, with the same results, and all Sherman accomplished trying to help McClernand was to increase Union casualty lists. Sherman and McPherson's commander on his right, Logan, who was also adjacent to Sherman's left, wanted to attack again, but Grant refused. His fighting blood up, Sherman ordered other attacks, all ending the same way in a bloody repulse. The terrain voided any Sherman attempt to coordinate his attacks, so the Rebels, as they were doing to McClernand, were able to concentrate their fire very effectively.

Sherman had proven at Chickasaw Bayou, now at Vicksburg, and later in Georgia at Kennesaw Mountain that he was not a master of offensive tactics. His talent was maneuver, and he would, before the war ended, put that talent to good use. Perhaps Grant understood by this time that it was pointless for Sherman to keep up attacks where men were being shot down in droves. The diversionary efforts of McPherson's corps, more timid than Sherman's, Logan being the exception, produced nothing of note but kept his casualty figures low. McPherson finally did as McClernand had begged earlier. He sent his left division, minus one brigade left behind to keep the left flank covered, to assist at the Texas lunette.[8]

With reinforcements from McPherson and, he hoped, from Warrenton, McClernand grew delighted and promised Grant a massive assault. Then McClernand proceeded to make tactical blunders. McPherson's division, commanded by Brigadier General Isaac Quinby, was divided into three segments. Burbridge, when he saw more men coming up, decided he had been relieved, so he ordered his troops to pull back. Confederates watched the meandering enemy while dismounted Confederate cavalry on a quick sortie further confused the Federals. Rebel commanders also saw the reinforcements moving left and shifted troops to meet the threats. McClernand's mishandling of Quinby's troops, in part due to poor communication with his own commanders, forced a retreat. The men from Warrenton did not arrive in time to help at all. The May 22 assault that had begun with such high hopes ended with a whimper.

Grant's casualties put the attack in perspective. McClernand had fought longer and suffered more losses: 202 killed, 1,004 wounded, and 69 missing or taken prisoner. McPherson saw 150 killed, 880 wounded, and 36 missing or captured. Sherman lost 150 killed, 666 wounded, and 42 missing or captured. Grant's total casualty list was 502 killed, 2,550 wounded, and 147 missing or captured. Only scattered reports of Confederate casualties exist; they have been estimated at 500.[9] The bloody repulse convinced Grant that continuing such assaults would be pointless. He would have to settle for siege operations, though he felt optimistic that the Confederates would surrender within a few days. He was wrong.

~2~

A REGULAR SIEGE AND PARANOIA

WHEN GRANT NOTIFIED Porter that the 10 A.M. assault had failed, Grant had to admit that his only doable option was a regular siege. He needed Porter's gunboats and mortars to put additional pressure on the Confederates. Sherman had told Grant when they arrived outside Vicksburg on May 18 that the campaign had been a success, even though Vicksburg had not yet fallen. The goal of the campaign, however, had been to take Vicksburg, not just to reach its outskirts. The navy had proven in 1862 that it would take combined operations to force the city's surrender. Grant without the navy would be hard pressed to force Pemberton to capitulate, for the Confederates would be able to get supplies into the city via the river. Porter's presence negated that possibility, and Porter's guns would have the city and its defenders suffering artillery fire from the west and east.[1]

On May 23, Grant summarized his situation to Porter. He believed he would take Vicksburg, but now he had no idea how long it would take: "I intend to lose no more men, but to force the enemy from one position to another without exposing my troops." Union cavalry and other spies had informed him that Johnston's army retreated to Canton on May 14 after abandoning Jackson and was currently at Calhoun Station (present day Gluckstadt, north of Jackson) on the Mississippi Central Railroad. Reports indicated Johnston only had eight thousand men with another two thousand Confederates in the Yazoo City area. Grant wanted to know if Porter felt the enemy presence at Yazoo City posed any danger to the

Union fleet. He offered to send troops to chase the Rebels away, but he would prefer not to "until this job here is closed up." He emphasized he believed the Confederates could not last long.[2]

Grant sent an overview of the campaign thus far to Halleck. He did not tell the whole story of the failed attacks of May 19 and 22, but he did confess to heavy losses on the twenty-second. He blamed McClernand for misleading him: "He is entirely unfit for the position of Corps Commander both on the march and on the battle field. Looking after his Corps gives me more labor, and infinitely more uneasiness, than all the remainder of my Dept." Grant's remarks are disingenuous. If he felt that strongly, and McClernand was still in command, Grant had only himself to blame. He had opportunities to fire McClernand before May 22. Now that a siege had begun, he decided to be more blunt.[3]

Grant also made an effort to sound upbeat. "The enemy are now undoubtedly in our grasp," he claimed, and "the fall of Vicksburg, and the capture of most of the garrison, can only be a question of time. I hear a greatdeel of the enemy bringing a large force from the East to effect a raising of the siege. They may attempt something of the kind but I do not see how they can do it." Grant pointed out that Southern Railroad of Mississippi had been sufficiently wrecked at Jackson to the point that it would take a month for the Confederates to repair it. Thus, the Rebels would have a long march and logistical challenges. Grant maintained, "My position is so strong that I could hold out for several days against a vastly superior force. I do not see how the enemy could possibly maintain a long attack under these circumstances."[4]

On May 25, Grant issued Special Orders No. 140: "Corps commanders will immediately commence the work of reducing the enemy by regular approaches. It is desirable that no more loss of life shall be sustained in the reduction of Vicksburg and the capture of the garrison. Every advantage will be taken of the natural inequalities of the ground to gain positions from which to start mines, trenches, or advance batteries. The work will be under the immediate charge of corps engineers, corps commanders being responsible that the work in their immediate fronts is pushed with all vigor. Capt. F. [Frederick] E. Prime, chief engineer of the department, will have general superintendence of the whole work. He will be obeyed and respected accordingly." The challenge would be great; Grant's investment line extended fifteen miles from the north in a semicircle to the south. The Confederate line was seven miles in length, providing interior-line advantages of being able to shift troops to trouble spots at a quicker rate than Grant's commanders. Pemberton's problem was that he likely had all the men he would ever have, while reinforcements could and would be shipped to Grant.[5]

Wilson, a member of Grant's staff, noted that when siege operations began, six, and never more than eight, West Point officers were on hand, and none who had engineering experience needed to direct siege operations. Wilson exaggerated, for he had engineering expertise, so did Prime, and later, Captain Cyrus Comstock, another trained engineer, came on board. All three graduated from West Point, and Prime was a member of the Corps of Engineers. Grant credited the trio with leading engineering aspects of siege operations. Another important engineer was Lieutenant Peter C. Hains of McClernand's corps, who had been trained in the regular army. West Pointers, who had studied *A Treatise on Field Fortifications*, a text written by West Point professor of civil and military engineering Dennis Hart Mahan, should be, and most appeared to be, familiar with siege tactics.[6]

Hains planned approaches beginning May 23, but he did not have tools to distribute until May 30. Preparations for digging approaches were conducted in a deep hollow behind McClernand's line. Hains continued directing approaches for the XIII Corps for the remainder of the siege and, due to the McClernand-Grant feud, would be unfairly criticized for lack of progress after McClernand left the army.[7]

Common soldiers worked diligently to carry out orders regarding siege works. Grant's engineers chose a zigzag system of approaching Confederate works. The classical approach involved digging a trench on a straight line at enemy works, with horizontal entrenchments dug on either side of the main trench to be manned by infantry and artillery, which provided protection for those pushing forward the main trench. Vicksburg hills, narrow ridges, and ravines made straight-line advance difficult and in some areas impossible. The zigzag trenches provided better cover and could be adapted to terrain irregularities. Grant did conform to an extent, for horizontal trenches did branch out from the zigzag lines to cover troops at the heads of the lines.[8]

Grant's army learned the applications of an unusual vocabulary connected to siege warfare. A sap is a trench that had to dug in a certain way; sap rollers are cylindrical and large enough for men to hide behind while digging. The saps were generally stuffed with cotton to stop enemy bullets. Sometimes the cotton caught fire when Rebels tossed fireballs made of any kind of flammable material and ignited by powder. Gabions are baskets created from stakes and vines and positioned vertically inside works to assist in repulsing attacks by either side. Fences made of gabions are called revetments. Fascines are similar to gabions, except they usually were made from cane, which grew plentifully around Vicksburg. Soldiers cut the cane into segments and sharpened the ends. Grant's soldiers quickly learned that construction of siege materials required much more than shovels.[9]

Grant, continually concerned by the limited number of trained engineers on hand, frequently rode behind his lines to check on progress. Several soldiers noted seeing the general riding, pausing, pointing, and talking with corps commanders and other officers. Grant always seemed calm to those who observed him. Others noted his shabby appearance, which seemed to appeal to men in the ranks. Sometimes Grant worried his men when he rode by with members of his staff. They warned him that being on horseback exposed him to enemy fire. Grant would reassure them that he would not be shot, at one point stopping to ask a soldier to lift a campfire stick to light his cigar. The general joked with the men, telling some Indiana troops as the siege progressed that he was not the commanding general. The officer in charge, Grant said, was "General Starvation." Grant must have known that his visibility to the troops boosted morale. He had made them cheer earlier when they began shouting "hardtack" as he rode by, an indication they wanted other things to eat. He told them the road from the Chickasaw Bayou supply base was being constructed, and they would soon have plenty of food. He wanted them to know he intended to be active and share their experiences, rather than hanging around his headquarters behind Sherman's corps.[10]

James Wilson confirmed in his memoirs that Grant customarily rode the lines almost daily, with Wilson accompanying him. The rides sometimes led to chance encounters with local citizens. On Hall's Ferry Road, which connects the Big Black with Vicksburg, they met two elderly females walking to a neighbor's home. Grant and Wilson tipped their hats, and one woman, noticing Grant's ever-present cigar, asked him for one. He obliged by giving her several; Wilson remarked to the woman after Grant rode on ahead that she best make them last because Grant might not come her way again. The two rode on to Magnolia Hall, a mansion that burned shortly after war's end, which at the time was being used as a hospital. The home owner assured Grant he was loyal. Loyalty did not prevent him from becoming impoverished due to lack of compensation for caring for wounded soldiers and others who dropped by for medical care. Grant also instructed Charles Dana, an emissary with a journalistic background, who had been sent by Secretary of War Edwin Stanton to report on the Vicksburg situation, to ride the lines, and to talk with corps commanders or one of their staff about progress in digging toward Confederate lines. Certainly, had there been a regiment of engineers on hand, Grant could have spent more time taking care of other issues.[11]

Soldiers' descriptions of Grant varied little. Lieutenant Colonel Orville Babcock, a military engineer who came to Vicksburg during the latter days of the siege, described Grant as a short man, quiet and understated, with a cropped beard. A member of the 55th Illinois noted that with Grant's headquarters close behind Sherman's corps, he visited the siege lines almost daily, often accompanied by Sherman. "The one taciturn, smoking slowly, his impassive face telling no tales of any workings of the mind within—the other nervously chewing a cigar and voluble, his restless eyes noting everything within the field of vision." The two sheltered themselves behind large tree trunks while discussing situations.

A Rhode Island soldier wrote of Grant: "A man with no insignia of rank about his person, short of stature; wore a soft felt hat, army blouse and pants, carrying a cigar in his mouth. His appearance looked very little like the commanders of the Army under whom we had served in the East. But there seemed to be under that slouch black hat a something that inspired confidence to us who felt that there must be more than show and pomp in a military leader in order to win battles." Others noted the "very plain, common appearance," of the general, how he looked tall in the saddle compared to his short stature when standing. He looked like an "old farmer," as did Logan and McPherson. An Illinoisan wrote that those who knew him before the war would hardly recognize him in his dusty clothes, especially if they saw him "worming his quiet way through and along our trenches, carefully noting all the operations of our forces." Another soldier agreed that Grant did not appear to be a military officer, but his looks deceived those who might question his ability. Other officers could also be deceptive: "They look like military men but are not."[12]

An anecdote about Grant's interaction with one of his soldiers demonstrates that he enjoyed his preference to not be seen as a dressed-up, sparkling figure of a general. He stopped one day at an observatory built to provide an elevated view of Rebel lines. Most of the time, a guard was stationed at the base of the structure to keep unauthorized personnel from climbing it. The guard was apparently not paying attention that day and was furious when he saw Grant had crawled to the top. The guard began cursing and yelling at Grant, wanting to know what he was doing up there. Grant ignored him, and the guard threatened to shoot. Grant very slowly and deliberately began his descent, and the guard continued cursing him. Grant said nothing and began walking away. Another soldier nearby told the guard that his profanity had been directed at General Grant. The guard, flushed with embarrassment, ran after Grant to apologize. Grant turned and said, "All right my boy, but you must watch closely or some one will get shot there." Grant's calm, relaxed personality must have disarmed and shocked the soldier, who, no doubt, expected and would have received a much-harsher response from most officers. This was but one of many instances where Grant took the opportunity to build his troops' esteem for his generalship.[13]

Grant's headquarters initially was in an old wooden house, but he quickly learned that his soldiers needed boards for building works and pathways. They did not take time to ask about pulling boards from the home, so Grant relented and stayed in a tent for the remainder of the siege. His headquarters seemed to be a place of endless activities. Grant rarely spent daylight hours there; he kept himself busy riding and observing. All lived in tents, the higher-ranking staff officers having their own. A resident of the headquarters area described that the heat forced men to keep their tents partially open, especially at night as they sought some sort of breeze to make sleeping more bearable.

The headquarters site, on a bluff behind and overlooking Sherman's headquarters, doubtless received more wind than other locations, though, certainly, the hot air was miserable no matter what the location. The headquarters site was a comfortable place and did not lack for provisions or good water. Some residents, doubtless including Grant, had enough water to take baths, a war luxury in most army circumstances, especially during a military operation. Grant spent most of his time writing and riding unless he had appointments and/or conferences with his corps commanders and other field officers.

Rawlins took care of most paperwork, a clear indication being that Sherman and others often addressed written communications to Rawlins rather than Grant. Grant, however, clearly, wrote and responded to many messages himself, especially as the siege progressed. Rawlins sent many messages under his own name, but the context of what he wrote clearly indicated Grant's stamp of approval. Beyond the correspondence and occasional meetings, Grant generally used his headquarters, as a place to work and occasionally eat. Normally, he was as active as couriers constantly delivering and receiving messages.

Aside from his frequent riding forays to check the army approaches, Grant continued focusing his attention early in the siege on his left flank, still very thin compared to the rest of his line. He also became obsessed with taking steps to assure that Johnston could not seriously threaten the rear of Grant's army, especially via the Mechanicsburg

Corridor, that stretch of land between the Yazoo and Big Black rivers to the northeast. Grant demonstrated his concerns in the way he handled the deployment of troops.

His instructions to McClernand set the example. Brigadier General John McArthur's brigade, after a hard march that failed to get him to Mc-Clernand in time on the twenty-second, had to turn and go back toward the Mississippi to cover the Warrenton/Vicksburg Road crossing at Big Bayou; McArthur would report on any enemy activity south of the city.

Brigadier General Jacob Lauman received orders to take his division south of the city as close as he could get to the Confederate line and, hopefully, block any Rebel attempt to turn the Union left flank or try escaping via that route. Shortly afterward, Grant sent Lauman to the Hall's Ferry Road, which entered Vicksburg from the southeast. Lauman had to connect with McClernand's left and stretch his division to cover all other approaches to Vicksburg between his main position and the Mississippi. Grant knew at this point he did not have enough men to completely block any attempted Confederate escape to the south. Porter had warned him on the twenty-second that "all the left of Vicksburg is open for the enemy to go out or in as he likes." Yet, Grant understood that Pemberton having led his army into Vicksburg and having beaten back the two assaults had no intention of trying to escape, at least not for a while. Still, the investment of Vicksburg would not be complete until the Union arc from the right flank at Fort Hill to the left at Warrenton was made impregnable.[14]

McClernand complained about Grant sending detachments from the XIII Corps cavalry to Warrenton, Hall's Ferry, Baldwin's Ferry, Big Black River, and Perkins Plantation, all possible approaches for Johnston's army. McClernand complained his corps was "much diminished and weakened by the casualties of battle and fatigues of the campaign. It is hardly safe to weaken it further by detachments from it." Grant reminded McClernand that McClernand's supply base would be at Warrenton, the clear implication being that if he intended to keep the XIII Corps supplied, he needed to manipulate his troops to cover the region between his left flank and Warrenton.

Grant shifted some troops to assist, and he suggested that a regiment reduced by casualties and sickness could be used to partly fill the gap, which at the moment was not threatened by Rebels. Any stragglers should be rounded up and put on the line; Grant sent word to McPherson and Sherman to do the same. Grant reminded McClernand that whatever cavalry he still had on hand could scout the entire length of his line. McClernand replied that his cavalry was scattered, that several regiments were elsewhere guarding the Big Black, that McArthur or Lauman should set up a base at Warrenton to guard the place, a road could be built inland from Warrenton, and that any troops at the old Grand Gulf depot could be brought north to shore up the line. Grant replied that McArthur should solve some issues on his own, but the other suggestions could not be carried out right away. Grant, clearly, thought McClernand should seize the initiative and take care of his line with the men he had been provided. McClernand, however, aware of Grant's feelings toward him, could not be blamed for staying in touch with Grant about issues regarding his corps.[15]

Turning his attention to other problems, Grant sent word downriver to Major General Nathaniel Banks, who was besieging Port Hudson, a Confederate stronghold on the Mississippi just north of Baton Rouge. Authorities in Washington had wanted Grant to join Banks after the fight at Port Gibson, but Grant had no intention of giving up his momentum. To help Banks capture Port Hudson would take time, time for Pemberton's army to make Grant's inland march more difficult. Now Banks wanted Grant to send reinforcements. Grant had no intention of doing so, and he sent one of his staff, Colonel John Riggin, to Banks to discuss the Union situation on the river.

Grant told Banks about the situation at Vicksburg and that he hoped to block any Rebel attempt to escape the city. He admitted he did not know how many men Pemberton had, but finding the place "so strongly fortified," he had resorted to "a regular siege." Grant stated that his greatest concern lay in a possible attack by Johnston from the rear. This worry consumed Grant for many weeks, becoming an obsession. He did not feel he had enough cavalry to cover every possible approach from the east by Johnston, and he expected the Confederates would make "a desperate effort" to hold Vicksburg. Having stated his case, Grant made clear to Banks that the army at Vicksburg needed "as large a force" as could be assembled to force Pemberton's surrender. Grant had already begun calling in men from his district, mostly from Helena, Arkansas, and West Tennessee, though some would have to stay behind to secure those areas.

Grant added that he had intended to send troops to Port Hudson, as many as ten thousand, but while writing the message, he received word from a cavalry detachment that some of Johnston's force had marched as close as thirty miles away to the northeast, and an attack might be imminent. Could Banks send men to Vicksburg? Grant hoped Port Hudson would have been surrendered by the time Riggin arrived. Grant wanted Colonel Benjamin Grierson and his cavalry; Grierson had led his men to Baton Rouge after cutting a path of destruction from the northeast to the southwest through Mississippi. Clearly, Grant had no intention of aiding Banks, and he emphasized that if any reinforcing was to be done, Vicksburg must take precedence.[16]

Grant shared with Halleck his concerns over reports of Confederates gathering at the Big Black: "I have ordered all the force that can be spared from West Tennessee and communicated with Gen Banks asking him to come with all the force he can." Grant said he had fifty thousand men on hand, and he believed by calling in the majority of forces scattered around his district, he could increase his total to sixty thousand. Major General Benjamin Prentiss at Helena informed Grant that he was gathering reinforcements and would be sending the men and heavy siege guns to Vicksburg. Grant ordered Major General Stephen Hurlbut in Memphis to order cavalry scouts south to Grenada and to send to Vicksburg as many infantry as could be spared, including troops from western Kentucky.[17]

Brigadier General Grenville Dodge had set up a spy network operating out of Corinth. During the early days of the siege, Dodge tried to relieve Grant's worries over Johnston's so-called Army of Relief. Dodge sent additional operatives into central Mississippi to keep watch for reinforcements coming to Johnston. In addition to his male spy force, Dodge counted on pro-Union women. One major problem was getting information to Grant in a timely manner; usually Grant received news via Hurlbut in Memphis. If reports seemed especially urgent, Dodge ordered spies to go directly to Grant, but this proved to be dangerous because a few were captured and executed. The expansion of Dodge's operations also resulted in Confederate infiltration of his lines of communication, forcing him to be careful that he did not pay operatives who might be counterspies. Union spies were fairly accurate about numbers of reinforcements coming to Johnston, but Grant had no idea and would not for some time that Johnston would never use them. Grant worried more about potential enemy reinforcements than those already with Johnston. Yet, reconnaissance forays from north of Vicksburg found little evidence that Johnston intended to go on the offensive.[18]

Pemberton had reasons to be concerned about Union spies within Vicksburg. He knew many citizens had opposed secession, and many remained pro-Union. He could not be sure that deserters and black persons who surrendered or wandered into Union lines were not spies or informants keeping the Yankees up to date about the lack of food and supplies for his army. Some may not have in fact been spies, but their information served the same purpose. Once the city was completely hemmed in,

Confederate agents trying to reach Johnston or sent by Johnston would find the going difficult. Pemberton's chances of operating an intelligence network were practically nil. The most unusual example either of trickery or loss of morale occurred in late June when a circular from "Many Soldiers," Confederates, was distributed along Confederate lines. The words applauded Pemberton and his army but stated if the officers could not "feed us," it would be better to surrender than suffer the humiliation of desertion. How many copies of this paper were distributed is unknown, but it is known the Confederates had a shortage of paper. While the origin of the circular has never been established, it had the flavor of Union propaganda. If Grant knew anything about it, he never said.[19]

Grant continued to rely on Porter to do what the infantry could not. He expected Porter to keep the Confederate water batteries along the Vicksburg waterfront from enfilading the left and right flanks of the army. Steele had problems on the right quieting an upper Rebel water battery. Grant requested Porter to send a couple of gunboats to fire directly into the battery in conjunction with Steele's guns shooting down from the ridge at the river. Porter responded that he had only one boat available, and it could not do what Grant wanted. All Porter could promise was fire from mortar boats. Porter finally sent one boat, the USS *Choctaw*, but its machinery broke down, and the USS *DeKalb* leaked too badly to go into battle. Porter signaled that he expected a monitor from upriver at any time and that he intended to use the USS *Cincinnati* after he had covered the side of the boat facing the Confederate guns with logs. Rebel gunners sank the *Cincinnati* on May 27, the crew suffering forty casualties. It sank in shallow water, Porter believed it could be raised, and eventually it was after the siege ended. The event boosted Confederate morale, but in the larger view, it was a hollow victory for them.

Porter mentioned again that McArthur lost a good opportunity to overwhelm enemy batteries to the south, but now he understood McArthur had been sent to reinforce McClernand. Porter insisted that Sherman should send someone to point out the location of friendly and enemy batteries. Porter did not want to risk shooting long distance in the direction of Steele's batteries. Porter understood accidents could happen, and, indeed, his guns hit parts of Lauman's camp south of the city a few days later.[20]

Meanwhile, Porter sent an expedition up the Yazoo, and his more healthy vessels sank two Confederate rams and destroyed a battery on Drury's Bluff, a high eminence overlooking the Yazoo south of Yazoo City. Further, the small fleet burned the Yazoo City navy yard, which had produced the CSS *Arkansas* in 1862, an ironclad that had wreaked havoc on the Union navy. What they could not burn or otherwise destroy, Porter's sailors tossed into the river. The yard would produce no more vessels to threaten Porter or Grant. Porter believed he had the firepower to counter any artillery the enemy might place along the bluffs between the Union depot at Chickasaw Bayou and Yazoo City.[21]

The two prominent bluffs northeast of Chickasaw Bayou, Haynes's and Snyder's, were occupied by Grant's forces, and he wanted them held at all costs. He asked Porter to send the Mississippi Marine Brigade, a force of infantry that traveled by water, to help hold Haynes's until Grant could send other troops. Grant, clearly, considered the mariners a part of the navy, but the War Department eventually clarified that the men were part of the army. Porter assented and reported to Grant that big guns were gradually being put into place to increase pressure on the Rebels. Brigadier General Alfred Ellet, commanding the Marines, sent his boats back to Memphis to assist in transporting more troops to Vicksburg. While activities increased, Porter continued playing a key role in getting heavy artillery to Grant's army. Without Porter's transportation help, Grant's firepower would have been limited, and the siege no doubt prolonged.[22]

Reports continued to drift in to Grant's headquarters detailing rumors of Johnston's activities. Osterhaus, one of McClernand's division commanders, sent word that Union doctors and nurses left behind to treat wounded at a hospital in Raymond had been captured and paroled. Osterhaus thought, correctly, that no large enemy force occupied any territory in Grant's rear, meaning in this case terrain east of the Big Black River. Osterhaus heard a rumor that the Rebels had begun fortifying Jackson and using slave labor to build entrenchments. Otherwise, only a few Johnston scouts had been seen at Brownsville, a village between the Big Black and the Yazoo. Osterhaus read reports that Johnston was getting close with a large force and that a detachment of Confederates had been seen in the Champion Hill area, apparently to capture and parole Union sick and wounded still in the battlefield area. Osterhaus needed additional cavalry for scouting duties, something Grant already understood.

McClernand heard the 54th Indiana had been sent from Raymond to guard Confederate prisoners en route to Union lines where they would be transferred to riverboats for trips to Northern prison camps. McClernand urged Grant to send the Indianans back to the Big Black to join their brigade there. Osterhaus did not seem to take a Johnston threat seriously, but McClernand used the rumors to pressure Grant into building up Union presence along the Big Black, mainly to guard the rear of McClernand's corps.[23]

An immediate task greater than worry about Johnston proved to be the stench of dead bodies from the May 22 assault, which were rotting under the rays of the hot sun. Most of the corpses lay close to Confederate lines. Grant had refused to request a truce to allow burials, but a May 25 Pemberton message moved Grant to agree to cease hostilities. The two generals agreed that the truce would begin at 6 P.M. and last for two and a half hours. Grant notified his corps commanders, and the grisly task began. Grant allowed surgeons to go out to treat any wounded.

Why Grant allowed his wounded to lay unprotected from the weather is not clear. His correspondence and memoirs provide no hint. One possibility is that his army had retrieved all the wounded they could reach during the retreat to their lines. But he had no way of knowing if all wounded had been found, and leaving his dead to decompose under the heat of the sun demonstrated a harsh attitude. A Grant staff member later in the war, who wrote a three-volume history of Grant and the war after its end, based his writing on what he learned from those who were there: "The wounded suffered frightfully after every battle, and the party which is repelled is always unable to bestow attention on those whom it leaves on the field." The statement was true, but that factor did not excuse Grant waiting on Pemberton to initiate a truce.[24]

Perhaps, Grant became so consumed with worry over protecting his long front and threats from the rear he simply ignored the issue. Yet, surely the smell, though more a problem for Confederates than Grant's army, must have permeated the atmosphere and drifted into every hollow and ravine. Whatever his reasons for stalling, Grant's lack of action resulted in bodies becoming so distorted they could not be identified, and those that could be were badly swollen and blackened. How many wounded died before the truce is not known. Men in burial details persevered, despite the horrors they saw and the overwhelming odor. An Indianan summed his experience in a way that probably reflected the opinions of all involved: "I saw sights that I pray God I may never see again." Men on both sides not assigned to dig and bury visited and traded various items and, in general, had a nice social break, especially the numerous Missourians fighting on both sides. Once the work and truce ended, men returned to their positions, and the shooting resumed.[25]

Grant spent May 25 looking for reinforcements. He sent word to Prentiss to transfer cavalry to patrol the Union rear along the Big Black and the Yazoo. If Prentiss felt his command was secure, he should send infantry that could be spared. Hurlbut, commanding in Memphis, received orders to send out more cavalry, this time as far south as Grenada and along the Memphis-Corinth corridor, and to send infantry to Vicksburg. Grant told Hurlbut that he believed Johnston had six thousand to ten thousand men west of the Big Black, but Grant did not expect immediate trouble.[26]

While Grant pulled in more men, he received another call for help from Banks, whose army had assaulted Port Hudson defenses and been thrown back. Banks needed at least one brigade, though he believed that his situation was urgent. As in Grant's case, Confederate defenses were simply too strong. Grant responded that he was sending Charles Dana to confer with Banks. Dana, despite his mission to observe and report on Grant to Secretary of War Stanton, had become Grant's trusted friend and aide. Grant knew that befriending Dana was a good way to keep Stanton happy. Stanton eventually appointed Dana assistant secretary of war. Grant gave Dana information to supplement Riggin's earlier message delivered to Banks.

Dana had impressed Stanton with frequent and frank reports. On May 28, Dana wrote that siege operations thus far were "satisfactory," and he bragged on Sherman and the accomplishments of his soldiers digging to within eighty yards of enemy works. Yet, "[i]t is a mistake to say that the place is entirely invested. I made the complete circuit of the lines yesterday. The left is open in direction of Warrenton, so that the enemy have no difficulty in sending messengers in and out. Our force is not large enough to occupy the whole line and keep the necessary reserves and outposts at dangerous and important points; still, the enemy cannot either escape by that route or receive supplies." Dana's observations underscored Grant's concerns, but his words also indicated the left flank was not in great peril. Porter's boats could help thwart an escape attempt, as could McClernand by shifting troops to the left. And Dana was right about the Rebels getting supplies via the southern flank. It could not be done en masse other than by risking Porter's shells and McClernand's troops. The Confederates did not have the means to get supplies in, and Pemberton still had no intent of trying to break out.[27]

Dana's connection with Stanton proved valuable to Grant. When Dana wired Stanton about the need for additional men, he received the following response: "Everything in the power of this Government will be put forth to aid General Grant. The emergency is not underrated here. Your telegrams are a great obligation, and are looked for with deep interest."[28]

In the short term, Stanton's words meant little, and Grant warned Banks not to expect any assistance since Johnston's threat seemed to be gaining credence. Grant concluded by saying if he only had more men (a thinly disguised hint that Banks should send troops to Vicksburg), he could detach several thousand and defeat Johnston and then send help to Banks. Grant closed as previously with the hope that Banks had taken Port Hudson.[29]

Banks responded quickly that if he gave Grant men, he would have to give up his effort to take Port Hudson, and defending New Orleans would be practically impossible. Banks could send a few troops, but they could not be supplied for the trip, and he did not have the transportation to bring his entire army to Vicksburg. Banks argued that hard decisions must be made one way or the other. Gaining control of the Mississippi remained the top priority, and that depended on the Rebel surrender of Port Hudson. Banks repeated his plea for ten thousand men and indicated he could not spare Grierson, for he had no other cavalry.[30]

Grant reminded Banks that Vicksburg, not Port Hudson, was the most significant point on the river. Grant noted that it had taken much labor and risk to get his army to Vicksburg, and he would not risk his success by sending men to Banks. The latest scouting reports indicated Johnston was daily gaining reinforcements, estimates ranging from totals of twenty thousand to forty thousand, and Grant admitted that reports varied to the point that he did not know the facts. However, Grant concluded, if Johnston gained enough strength, then Grant must go after these Confederates and forget besieging Vicksburg. There would not be time. Sending Banks thousands of men would leave Grant "crippled beyond redemption." He had more than sufficient logistical support: "All I want now are men." He would not soon get a response from Banks.[31]

On May 26, Grant set into motion an expedition that he hoped would provide clarity to all the reports about Johnston's activities. In Special Orders No. 141, he stated that three brigades would be detached from both the XV and XVII Corps, and these brigades would be joined by the brigade stationed at Haynes's Bluff, making a force of twelve thousand. In temporary command would be Blair, a Missourian and a member of the politically powerful Blair family. Blair commanded the second division in Sherman's corps; the proximity of Blair and the brigades to the Mechanicsburg Corridor no doubt were key factors in Grant making his choices. The three brigades from each corps took different routes from their siege-line positions and converged at Sulphur Springs, a place south of earthworks along the Yazoo, where the Benton Road provided a route on the eastern side of the Mechanicsburg Corridor. Grant wanted the whole force "to move upon and drive out the enemy now collecting between the Black and Yazoo Rivers." The men were to carry seven days'

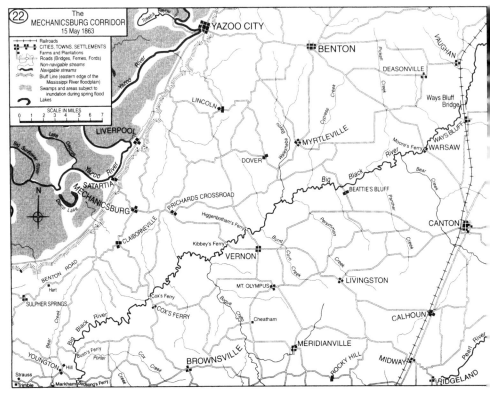

The Mechanicsburg Corridor, May 15, 1863. Map 22, Warren E. Grabau, *Ninety-Eight Days* (Knoxville: University of Tennessee Press, 2000).

rations, which meant Grant did not intend the column to get bogged down in battle but, rather, as he put it, to "drive out" any Rebels they encountered.[32]

On May 29, events kept Grant's attention on the northeast corridor. He heard from Blair that cavalry commander Colonel Amory Johnson thought the estimates of Johnston's numbers were much too high. A contingent of Confederate forces from Johnston's army had chased away Union cavalry patrolling the Mechanicsburg Corridor about thirty-five miles from the siege lines. This event precipitated Blair's expedition, designed to "clean out the enemy" in the Mechanicsburg Corridor and destroy the Mississippi Central Railroad over the Big Black. Grant hoped that the absence of the bridge would make Johnston think twice about sending troops across the Big Black at various ferry points, all of which were guarded by Union troops. In places, the depth of the river would hinder crossing by infantry and slow cavalry. Grant cautioned Blair not to take risks; certainly, he must not be cut off from Haynes's Bluff. He asked Porter to send one or two gunboats up the Yazoo to look for signs of Rebels while he waited for more news from Blair.[33]

Grant had already taken steps to block enemy activities along the Big Black before the Blair expedition began its march. On March 25, Johnson and his cavalry rode east to destroy the railroad bridge; their departure left Haynes's Bluff without a garrison, so Grant told Sherman to send one of his brigades to occupy the bluff. Grant, without informing Mc-Clernand of the order, ordered Osterhaus, commanding troops from McClernand's corps along the Big Black, to destroy the river bridge. Grant further wanted former slaves and a detachment of Osterhaus's command to tear up track and melt and twist the rails of the Southern Railroad of Mississippi, plus destroying any other bridges and track to the east as far as Osterhaus dare go. Osterhaus had already sent crews to Bolton, and his men had destroyed track and captured cotton and cattle. No Rebels had been sighted. Other detachments went all the way to Jackson, taking all supplies they found. They reported small groups of Confederates, but nothing to indicate Johnston was concentrating troops.[34]

Grant remained unconvinced that Johnston posed no imminent threat; he wired Hurlbut in Memphis on May 31 that Johnston surely had twenty thousand to twenty-five thousand men along the Canton to Jackson corridor. Another fifteen thousand were reportedly on the way to join the Rebel force. Grant strongly believed that as soon as Johnston received the additional troops, he would attack Haynes's Bluff. Pemberton and Johnston had, in fact, discussed the possibility of Johnston opening a path for Pemberton to escape Vicksburg via the northeast. The idea never seemed feasible, for it would only work if Grant's army stayed in their earthworks while Pemberton funneled his army through the passage opened by Johnston. Johnston was not an aggressive general, and unless he had twice the number of men he eventually would have, he would make no effort to crack the Union siege. Even if he had, Pemberton could not possibly have gotten his army out of Vicksburg while Grant's three corps sat and watched. Johnston would have to fight to open a passage; Pemberton's men would have to battle Grant's besieging army to reach any opening Johnston created. In effect, Grant worried about enemy strategy that could not be implemented. Grant did not understand Johnston's personality, or he would not have wasted time worrying.[35]

Grant elaborated his fears to Hurlbut. A Johnston attack might force giving up the siege, so Hurlbut must send every available man in his district, less the bare amount needed to secure the Memphis region.

He assured Hurlbut that the Memphis area would be safe until Johnston could be beaten. Until then, all parts of west Tennessee that lay north of the Memphis and Charleston Railroad could be abandoned if necessary. Hurlbut could pull troops from Kentucky, leaving only enough men to garrison the towns of Columbus and Paducah. In addition to infantry, Grant wanted two regiments of cavalry. He told Hurlbut that no boat should be allowed to go north up the Mississippi until all the troops coming to Vicksburg had been transported. Grant added a stern statement: "The entire rebel force heretofore against me are completely at my mercy. I do not want to see them escape by being re-inforced from elsewhere." Grant's paranoia about Johnston, obviously, had not negatively affected his determination to take Vicksburg. Sherman recalled, "Grant told me that he [Johnston] was about the only general on that side [Confederate] whom he feared." What Grant based his opinion on is not clear, but surely by the end of the siege, Grant realized such fears were baseless.[36]

Blair's command continued its adventure, expecting much but finding little. Johnson had received very erroneous information that one of Robert E. Lee's generals, A. P. Hill, had reinforced Johnston, giving the two a combined force of forty-five thousand. Also, Confederate Brigadier General States Rights Gist had arrived from South Carolina with several thousand men; this part of the report was true. The report further stated that Johnston had brought eight thousand men with him when he came to Mississippi, which was untrue. The only men Johnston had commanded after arriving in Jackson were the few thousand he had led to Canton after abandoning the capital city. Finally, the intelligence report said that stragglers from Pemberton's army, likely from William Loring's division, had joined Johnston, and they had. Supposedly, Hill had contacted Pemberton, which would have been remarkable because Hill was with Lee's Army of Northern Virginia marching toward Pennsylvania. Blair added that he thought the numbers "greatly exaggerated." He would confer with his generals about the route to be taken, and if he found Johnson's report to be accurate, he would turn to the Yazoo and rendezvous with Porter's boats.[37]

Grant grew more and more concerned about Blair. He cautioned more than once that Blair must not allow himself to be flanked. If he found he had to retreat, he should get a messenger across the Yazoo to get a message to Grant, who would do all he could to get Porter upstream.

Blair responded at one point with three messages to Vicksburg. From what Blair understood, a courier Grant sent had encountered Blair's cavalrymen, so there was no need to reiterate news that Grant would soon have in hand. Blair noted his advance had reached Mechanicsburg about 1:30 P.M. and encountered an estimated four hundred to five hundred Confederates, who offered light resistance and retreated across the Big Black. Union cavalry scouting along the Big Black had seen no more than a few Rebel stragglers, and the current situation seemed to be that Johnston was still concentrating at Canton. Blair assured Grant that no notable enemy force was on the west side of the Big Black and that Blair's men had destroyed enemy foodstuffs found along the way. Blair felt somewhat depressed by how the destruction affected local citizens, but he understood it had to be done to deprive Johnston's army of food.[38]

Grant urged Blair to return to Haynes's Bluff after wreaking as much havoc as he could: "You may rest at Haines Bluff with your entire command until you receive further orders from me. Such information may be received from the enemy, and sufficient reinforcements arrive here as to make it advisable to send out an army large enough to clean out Jo Johnston, and his party." Blair replied that it seemed clear most, if not all, intelligence Johnson had collected was false. Blair and Grant realized their messages were not being sent and received in chronological order, and this communication problem exacerbated the situation.[39]

On May 31, Blair reported his army had returned and taken position on Drumgould's Bluff, located south by southwest of Haynes's and Snyder's. He had received Grant's encouragement to return as his army already was marching back after the brush with Rebels at Mechanicsburg. Only a handful of Confederate cavalry had followed, but since the terrain was flat and open, the enemy had made no effort to fire at the rear of the Union column. Blair reported greater amounts of supplies and forage had been found and destroyed than he had indicated earlier. He claimed to have burned thousands of bushels of corn and a large amount of bacon and cotton and had driven back to the bluffs one thousand head of cattle. If he had had more time and greater numbers, Blair believed he could have cleaned out the countryside of horses and mules.

Blair shared his personal views about the strategic significance of the Mechanicsburg Corridor and in the process underscored and expanded Grant's own thinking. Blair thought Mechanicsburg to be the key strategic point between the Yazoo and Big Black. He based his analysis on the three roads that led from there to Vicksburg and the supply possibilities of boats on the Yazoo. The town of Satartia, on the banks of the Yazoo a few miles northwest of Mechanicsburg, could be used as a port. Other roads branching out from Mechanicsburg led to both rivers. Blair, like Grant, concluded that Johnston certainly would attack the corridor and that Pemberton only persisted in holding Vicksburg because he expected Johnston's help. Blair's thoughts were very logical, but he and Grant based assumptions on what they would do rather than knowing what Johnston might try. In the long view, their concerns proved to be empty.[40]

Blair's expedition had been, contrary to the rumor mill, a rather leisurely foray, according to the soldiers who walked and shuffled along in the stifling heat. The men encountered little more than skirmishers who usually fired one volley and ran. Good drinking water proved too scarce for many soldiers, and lack of water combined with the hot, steamy weather angered many of the men. An Iowa soldier was certain that if left to the private soldier's testimony, Blair would surely go to hell without any voice raised in protest.[41]

On June 2, Blair proposed another expedition. He believed he had enough cavalry on hand, about twelve hundred, to go back into the Mechanicsburg Corridor and destroy a bridge across the Big Black north of Canton. Such a mission could cripple Johnston's maneuverability. The cavalry, with infantry and artillery support, would ride in the direction of Mechanicsburg. While the cavalry moved, Brigadier General Joseph Mower's infantry brigade, with an artillery battery, would go by boat up the Yazoo and land at Satartia. From there, Mower's column would march east to Mechanicsburg. Johnson's cavalry should have a safe path to destroy the bridge since Mower's presence would drive off Rebel cavalry leader Colonel Wirt Adams, who did not have enough men to fight a much-larger Union contingent. Even if Johnson should encounter unexpected problems, many routes of retreat were open to him. Grant immediately approved Blair's proposal without suggesting any changes. Apparently, the realization that misinformation had caused unnecessary panic restored Grant's optimism.[42]

Grant thus ordered Mower to continue destruction of crops and anything else useful to Johnston. Mower should also block roads by any means necessary. Grant might be less concerned, but he, nevertheless, advised Mower as he had Blair: Retreat back to the Yazoo if necessary, and return to Haynes's Bluff. Grant promised Mower reinforcements, enough to make continual "excursions up through the rich Yazoo bottoms." On June 3, Grant ordered Brigadier General Nathan Kimball's division to Satartia via transports on the Yazoo, from where they would march to Mechanicsburg to reinforce Mower and the cavalry. This time, Grant did not intend a forward-and-back operation. He instructed Kimball, "The object of placing troops at Mechanicsburg is to watch movements of the enemy, who are said to be collecting a large force in the vicinity of

Canton." Kimball's cavalry must scout all ferry crossings of the Big Black and obstruct all roads leading west from that river. As for destruction and confiscation of property, Kimball should join in the destructive efforts of Blair and Mower. Any slaves who came into Union lines should be sent to Haynes's Bluff unless Kimball needed them. One gunboat and a transport vessel must be available at Satartia, not counting the supply boat that would be used to send food and ordnance from the Chickasaw Bayou landing to Satartia. Kimball could employ any spies he trusted and make sure they were paid through proper channels. Clearly, Grant's thinking had progressed from a raid by Blair to a potential occupational force.[43]

Kimball notified Rawlins that when he arrived on June 4 at Satartia, he found Mower moving east. As they stepped ashore, Kimball sent his men to join Mower in attacking Rebels deployed on high ground. Kimball and Mower pushed the small contingent of Confederates back to Mechanicsburg, where they again went into a line of battle. Kimball dispersed the Rebels with one brigade, and cavalry came up to chase others back toward the Big Black. Kimball told Rawlins that more artillery and the rest of the division were needed; scouts indicated that Johnston continued to build up a significant force at Canton. Rawlins passed along the information to Grant, and soon the 25th Wisconsin enjoyed boat rides to Satartia.

Grant notified Kimball that information had been received indicating Johnston was marching to Yazoo City. Any Union cavalry north of Yazoo City must be warned of the possibility of Rebels blocking routes south that would endanger the horsemen. Kimball could continue the effort to destroy the bridge over the Big Black above Canton, but he must take no risks. Grant warned, "The position of the enemy and his numbers must be well ascertained before going much beyond Machanicsburg." Grant also informed Porter that Johnston with "several" thousand men had gone to Yazoo City. Porter promised to send all the gunboats he had available up the Yazoo. Once more, Grant overreacted to exaggerated news from scouts.[44]

On June 5, Kimball sent a chilling message. He had reconvinced himself that Johnston posed a serious threat, and Kimball seemed to have proof. He had found Rebels in force at Liverpool, a bluff on the east side of the Yazoo City, ten miles above Satartia, and eight thousand Confederates had assembled at Liverpool, a bluff on the east side of the Yazoo. Kimball further stated that Johnston had moved a total of twenty thousand men into the Mechanicsburg Corridor west of the Big Black. Enemy reinforcements continued gathering at Canton. Kimball added on a positive note that his cavalry had ridden to the Big Black and destroyed several ferries east of

Satartia, and that Mower still occupied Mechanicsburg. Kimball then added an ominous note: "I am doing every thing possible to obstruct an advance should one be made by the enemy—Should it be desired to hold this place in such a case—more force will be required and more artillery. Should I not be able to beat or repulse them I shall hold to the very last."[45]

Grant promised, "I will renew my instructions not to run any risk of having your forces cut off from the main body. If Mechanicsburg is not safely tenable fall back to Oak Ridge Post Office or Hain's Bluff as necessity may dictate. Should you move back of course you will direct the transports and Gunboats at Satartia to fall back to such position as will be most advantageous to you. I am exceedingly anxious to learn the probable force of the enemy on the West side of the Black River. Keep me constantly informed of all you may be able to learn." Kimball decided to evacuate the Satartia-Mechanicsburg area based on a Rebel prisoner-deserter's reports of Johnston's strength. The Rebel convinced Kimball that Confederate General John George Walker had twelve thousand men, including two brigades sent by Braxton Bragg from Tennessee. Johnston had forty thousand at Canton. Apparently, all of Walker's troops were in the Mechanicsburg Corridor. These figures, like others, were gross exaggerations, and the prisoner likely was planted by Johnston.[46]

Grant reiterated his earlier message to Kimball, adding that cavalry should be used as a shield until the troops safely reached Haynes's Bluff. Kimball could use the works at the bluff to hold off any Rebel attacks. On June 6, Kimball sent word that he believed he faced at least fifteen thousand men, the river level was rapidly falling, which endangered the mobility of boats, and he intended to start for Haynes's Bluff as soon as possible. Grant seemed not to have heard that Kimball had decided to leave the Satartia-Mechanicsburg area. On June 6, Grant sent word to his corps commanders: "I am going up to Mechanicsburg[—]cannot be back before tomorrow night. Make all advance possible in approaches during my absence. Communications signaled to Haines Bluff will reach me."[47]

When Grant decided to go see for himself the situation at Satartia and Mechanicsburg, he made a fateful move that would haunt his postwar reputation for years, right up to the present day. He could hardly be blamed for going. The rash of contradictory, exaggerated, and false messages from the Mechanicsburg Corridor would have driven any commander to find out the facts, as best he could, by going to see for himself. The military consequences would prove to be inconsequential. He would not live long enough to know about the character assassination that would grow out of his fateful boat trip up the Yazoo.

❧3❧

River of Lies

On June 6, Grant readied himself for the inspection trip up the Yazoo River to Satartia. He asked Dana if he would like to come along, and Dana agreed to go. Grant addressed his plan to McClernand, but copies went to Sherman and McPherson. Dana sent a message about the trip to Secretary of War Stanton, and in the message, Dana noted that the boat carrying him and Grant was just departing. Dana's message was dated June 6 and the time noted as 7 P.M. The time is significant when considering the controversy that grew out of this excursion.[1]

Dana wrote in his memoirs that he and Grant rode horseback, accompanied by a cavalry guard, to Haynes's Bluff, where they boarded a small boat named USS *Diligence*, sometimes used as a mail boat and reserved for Grant's use if needed. Grant became ill and went to bed in an onboard cabin shortly after the trip began. The word *ill* in Grant's case could mean sick or that he had drunk too much liquor. In this particular episode, the assumption has been that he had imbibed too much, but Grant also had a problem with severe headaches. Vicksburg summers could make anyone sick with headaches or most any other malady. The heat and oppressive humidity, plus illnesses that abounded in military camps, did not produce healthy surroundings.[2]

The boat continued upstream to within a couple of miles of Satartia and met two gunboats coming downstream. When officers aboard the gunboats saw Grant's personal flag waving on the deck of the *Diligence*, they signaled to Grant's pilot to stop. The men came onboard to see where the general was heading. Dana told them, and they responded quickly that Satartia was not safe and that Kimball's division had retreated back to Haynes's Bluff. Confederates in the area might already be in Satartia. Dana responded that General Grant had become ill and was inside the cabin sleeping. The officers said Dana should immediately wake Grant, tell him the situation, and have him order the *Diligence* back downstream. Dana did enter the cabin, but he found Grant too ill to make a decision. The officers agreed that Dana could decide, though they, in effect, had made it an easy decision, and he ordered Grant's boat to turn and follow the gunboats.[3]

As dawn broke on June 7, Grant got up, put on fresh clothes, and came to breakfast. Dana described him as "fresh as a rose." Grant asked Dana if they had reached Satartia. Dana replied that they were back at Haynes's Bluff and related why the return was necessary. Grant seemed unperturbed, and since there were few officers in the area, he asked Dana to accompany a cavalry company and ride toward Mechanicsburg. Grant wanted more intelligence about Johnston's supposed advance from Canton to the Big Black, and he trusted Dana. The detachment scoured the countryside, not returning to Haynes's until the next day. Dana reported there was no indication of Johnston moving en masse at all.[4]

After the war, Dana became editor and part-owner of the *New York Sun*. In an article entitled "Gen. Grant's Occasional Intoxication" in the January 28, 1887, edition of that paper, Dana wrote a response to critics of Grant's drinking and why Lincoln and Stanton put up with his habit: "Gen. Grant's seasons of intoxication were not frequent, but occurring once in three or four months, but he always chose a time when the gratification of his appetite for drink with any important movement with perfect judgment, and when it was all over, no outsider suspected such things had been."

Dana went on to write that on the occasion of the June 6 trip, Grant did get as "stupidly drunk as the immortal nature of man would allow; but the next day he came out as fresh as a rose, without any indication of the spree as he had passed through. So it was on two or three other occasions that we happened to know of." Dana added that Grant's drinking never affected his generalship.[5]

James Wilson wrote in his diary on June 7, 1863, that he had seen Grant drunk. It is a simple sentence with no elaboration or context. Because the entry is June 7 does not mean Wilson saw him under the influence on that day. Thus, it is impossible to analyze the place, time, and circumstances under which he saw Grant, but none of that matters. As historian Brooks

D. Simpson points out, given the lateness of the hour when Grant arrived at Chickasaw Bayou, it is possible Wilson did not write the diary entry until after midnight, which would have been June 8. Dana made clear that Grant was sober when he awoke the morning of June 7 and does not mention Grant drinking any more during the day. Is the diary entry a lie or merely gossip, or did he see something no one else recorded seeing?

Wilson's role in the Yazoo story is, indeed, nebulous. In the draft of his biography of Rawlins, Wilson wrote of the Satartia trip that Grant got sick and believed a drink would help his feelings. However, the drink had the opposite effect. Would one drink have resulted in him being "stupidly drunk," as Dana indicated, or did it simply make him feel worse? Such nuances are difficult to decipher, but it is known that Dana's and Wilson's versions do not mention a news reporter named Sylvanus Cadwallader, who enhanced a mere incident into a remarkable episode. It is somewhat telling that in his published biography of Rawlins, Wilson's above comments do not appear.[6]

Giving some credence to the assumption that Grant was under the influence is an extract from a Sherman letter to John E. Tourtelotte dated February 4, 1887. Sherman was responding to a clipping Tourtelotte sent that contained the story of attacks by a former Union General Henry Van Ness Boynton, who, in his postwar writings, trashed Grant and Sherman. Boynton obviously hated both, and Sherman called him "a Coyote, or hyena, scratching up old forgotten scandals, publishing them as something new." Referring to Boynton's comments painting Grant as a common drunkard, Sherman wrote, "We all knew at the time that Genl Grant would occasionally drink too much. He always encouraged me to talk to him frankly of this & other things and I always noticed that he could with an hours sleep wake up perfectly sober & bright and when anything was pending he was invariably abstinent of drink." Sherman's description of Grant's condition upon waking up after drinking too much is similar to Dana's.[7]

Dana did not claim in his memoir that Grant was drunk, though his book was published after Grant's death, and he could freely have done so without incurring Grant's wrath. Since he wrote with some venom about it in his newspaper, it is not clear why he soft-pedaled it in the memoir. There is strong evidence that the memoir was ghostwritten by Ida Tarbell, known mostly for being a late-nineteenth-century muckraker, but surely the information came from Dana. Since Dana was in ill health, and he (or she) completed the book just a few months before his death in 1897, he likely decided not to include his "stupidly drunk" statement out of respect for the Grant family. Whatever the case, Dana's account is precise, straightforward, and matches in basic details the material appearing in the official records. Within a couple of decades after Grant's death, Cadwallader came forth with a fanciful tale about the Satartia trip. Cadwallader's story was nothing more than a lengthy, greatly embellished lie, but many historians have swallowed it without raising any questions.

Cadwallader, who had a midwestern background, having lived and worked in Wisconsin, was a war correspondent for the *Chicago Times* who had been sent to cover Grant's campaigns. The *Times* had a reputation as a "Copperhead" newspaper, meaning the paper espoused Democratic Party antiwar policies. Cadwallader also sent news to the *New York Herald*, another Democratic paper, and his stories always praised Grant. When Grant later moved on to the eastern theater of the war, Cadwallader openly reported for the *Herald* and was with Grant through the remainder of the war. Cadwallader, described as a "lone wolf of the Western correspondents" and "distant and unsociable," apparently got along well with Grant for reasons no one articulated. Assuming Grant did like Cadwallader, and there is no reason not to, Grant certainly had no reason to suspect that Cadwallader was anything other than a friend, so Grant had no idea how the reporter would blacken his name after his death. The oddity of Cadwallader's slander is that the newsman treated Grant as a hero and apparently thought of the general and later president as an icon.[8]

In the late 1880s, Cadwallader began writing his memoirs, and he finished them in 1896 at the age of seventy. They would not be published until 1955 under the title *Three Years with Grant: As Recalled by War Correspondent Sylvanus Cadwallader*. Respected historian Benjamin P. Thomas edited the memoirs, notably changing the original title "Four Years with Grant," to three, considering the change a more accurate reflection of Cadwallader's time with Grant. The publication of the book received much attention, and Thomas was praised for his fine editorial work. Yet, he, like so many others since, accepted Cadwallader's account of Grant's trip up the Yazoo on June 6 as gospel, rather than carefully analyzing the story.[9]

Cadwallader prefaced his story by applauding Grant's top aide, John Rawlins. Rawlins, loud, arrogant, and very profane by many accounts, came from a family in which alcoholism was a problem, so he took it upon himself to keep a tight rein on Grant's drinking. Cadwallader wrote that no drinking was allowed at Grant's headquarters, thanks to Rawlins, though the truth of such a ban is debatable. Rawlins may have had such a rule, but it did not stop Grant from finding an occasional opportunity to drink. One such time probably occurred on May 29. During Sherman's and Porter's visit to Grant on that date, mentioned in Sherman's June 2 message to Grant, Sherman found Grant "complaining of illness." Again, illness did not necessarily translate to drinking, but the implication is there.

On another occasion an officer of the 76th Ohio Infantry, Charles Dana Miller, recalled a Grant visit to the headquarters of Colonel Charles R. Woods, who commanded the second brigade of Frederick Steele's division. Miller happened to be at brigade headquarters the day Grant came by. Woods, according to custom, set out a bottle of whiskey and poured drinks. Grant picked up a glass, and when Miller declined an invitation to take a drink, Grant gazed at the Ohioan as if he had acted rudely. Grant asked Woods what sort of officers served under him that they refused a social drink. Miller thought Grant considered him a "curiosity." Clearly, Rawlins's attempt to control liquor had limitations.[10]

Cadwallader thought so highly of Rawlins that he named a son "Rawlins." Cadwallader also asserts, "To speak the whole truth concerning Gen. Grant's periodical fits of intemperance has required all the courage I could summon to my assistance." This has to be one of the most disingenuous sentences he ever wrote. He did not need courage to write the string of lies he wrote about a man long dead.

His story begins with a brief account of his trip up the Yazoo to Satartia; he is not specific as to the time except that it was "[d]uring the first week in June" but admits he cannot be precise as to the date. He rode in the *Diligence*, he claimed, the boat reserved for Grant's use. He named Captain Harry McDougall as the boat's commander. He then goes on to say that the next day, whatever day that might have been, the boat was returning to Haynes's Bluff when it met a boat carrying Grant and his cavalry escort, commanded by Colonel Embury Osband. Cadwallader claimed that because Grant knew McDougall, Grant decided to transfer to the *Diligence* and order it back to Satartia. Why would Grant want to change boats, especially since Dana claimed he and Grant were already aboard the *Diligence*? It is most noteworthy that Cadwallader does not mention Dana.[11]

Cadwallader said it did not take long to see that Grant had been drinking to excess, and not only that, but the general had a bottle in his hand and was continuing to guzzle. Grant had, Cadwallader claimed, already made several trips to the bar room of the boat. A question comes to mind: If Rawlins was so strict about keeping Grant away from alcohol, why would he allow a boat to be filled with it? Cadwallader was just warming up. He wrote that Grant "became stupid in speech and staggering in gait."

He had never seen Grant in such a state, "and I was greatly alarmed by his condition, which was fast becoming worse." Grant's aide-de-camp, Lieutenant Horatio N. Towner, H. N. Turner in Cadwallader's original manuscript, was Grant's only staff member available. Cadwallader's narration then becomes very narcissistic. He takes over, trying to urge the timid Towner to push Grant into the stateroom, using whatever excuse necessary, and then contain the general there until he sobered up. When Towner refused to cooperate, Cadwallader turned to McDougall, urging the commander not to allow Grant to have any more whiskey. McDougall responded that he did not have the authority to do such a thing. One can only wonder where Osband and the escort were during this time; they had definitely been on board, according to Dana.

Giving up on persuasion, Cadwallader cursed and threatened McDougall with dire consequences if the commander did not do as he asked: "I assured him that on my representations he would, and should be sent out of the department in irons if I lived to get back to headquarters." He suspected that McDougall well knew the possible ramifications of Rawlins's anger if he did nothing to stop Grant from drinking. So McDougall, by implication meekly giving in, closed the bar room and hid the key. Cadwallader then took charge of Grant, "enticed him into the stateroom, locked myself in the room with him (having the key in my pocket), and commenced throwing bottles of whiskey which stood on the table, through the windows, over the guard into the river." Again, one must wonder how such a stash escaped the notice of Rawlins's controlling hands.

When Grant realized what had happened, he ordered Cadwallader to leave, but the newsman refused. Grant then got mad and "ordered me peremptorily to open the door and get out instantly." Cadwallader refused "good-naturedly" to obey, remarking that he was the best friend Grant had in the Army of the Tennessee. After all, he was only doing for Grant what he hoped a friend would do for him in the same situation. After taking this firm stand, Cadwallader insisted that Grant start undressing due to the heat inside the room, and he aided the general in removing his coat, vest, and boots. Then he fanned Grant to sleep.

Cadwallader continues contradicting Dana's account of Grant's trip. The correspondent wrote that the boat did reach Satartia, and Grant determined to go ashore. Grant ordered Osband and the escort to disembark, so obviously they had to be on board while Cadwallader had taken charge of Grant. Osband, Cadwallader claimed, felt he "was now in a dilemma." The countryside was filled with Confederates and Rebel sympathizers, and Osband did not feel he had enough men to protect Grant. Once more, enter Cadwallader the aggressive savior, who told Osband he would accept the responsibility of having every horse shot or hamstrung to prevent anyone from the boat going ashore. Then Cadwallader went to see Grant and convinced the general not to go ashore that evening. Grant wanted to take his horse and ride back to his headquarters at Vicksburg, but Cadwallader again intervened, convincing Grant that to ride south without being familiar with the countryside might be suicidal. Meanwhile, the boat turned, no doubt so ordered by Cadwallader, and went back to Haynes's Bluff.

At that point, a somewhat sobered Grant sent a detachment from his escort to check on Kimball's camp and glean any worthwhile news, according to Cadwallader. The *Diligence* was tied up to wait for the cavalry. Cadwallader thought that was the end of the matter until an hour later when he found Grant had found more whiskey. Cadwallader retrieved the general, and after the cavalrymen had returned, the boat went farther down toward Chickasaw Bayou. Both Cadwallader and McDougall, according to the former, decided Grant must not be seen in an intoxicated condition, and McDougall "was now very willing to take orders from" Cadwallader. First, a campfire must be built, containing some green wood so as not to draw attention, and secondly, Grant must not be allowed to go anywhere without Cadwallader's permission. Cadwallader managed thus to delay continuing the trip until Grant seemed better.

Finally, McDougall docked the boat at Chickasaw Bayou near sundown, which would have had to have been on June 7 if Cadwallader's account was accurate. Cadwallader may not have been sure of the date, but the record is clear that Grant made only one trip up the Yazoo, and he left on June 6 and returned on June 7. The *Diligence* was anchored alongside a larger steamboat used for sutler supplies and commanded by "Wash" Graham. Graham kept a generous supply of whiskey and dispensed it freely, along with cigars, to officers. Cadwallader immediately asked Graham not to give Grant any liquor, and Graham promised he would comply. Cadwallader then rushed back to the boat to assist in getting the horses on dry land. Why Osband and his troopers would need assistance is not clear. Grant had already left the boat, so Cadwallader immediately assumed the general had made his way aboard Graham's boat. Grant could not be found, however.

Then Cadwallader heard a commotion among a crowd of officers, and he followed the sound and found Graham standing behind a table serving whiskey and champagne. Grant was working on a glass of whiskey when

Cadwallader arrived. Cadwallader wrote, "I was thoroughly indignant and may have shown rather scant ceremony in saying to him that the escort was waiting, and that it would be long after dark before we could reach headquarters." Grant did not act pleased, and the general turned to a horse named Kangaroo, which belonged to Grant aide Clark Lagon (the correct spelling is Lagow, a mistake editor Thomas did not note). Grant mounted the large animal and immediately spurred it. Grant sped away before the escort or Cadwallader had time to react. The road being very crooked and occasionally bridged to avoid swampy areas, the pursuers had trouble catching the general. Cadwallader noted that guards were posted at each bridge, but Grant paid them no attention. It is most likely that the guards, knowing that Grant was astride the horse, would have made no effort to stop him. Then, according to Cadwallader, Grant began riding through corrals, camps, campfires, creating a disturbance that brought noisy protests from soldiers. Cadwallader figured Grant had been lucky not to have been shot.

By the time Cadwallader caught up with the general, Grant was riding along at a slow pace. Cadwallader hand-wrestled Grant for Kangaroo's reins, and Cadwallader finally got the situation under control. Then he tried to figure out how to contact the escort, which was making its way along the trail, spread out in search of Grant. One of the riders came into sight, and Cadwallader told him to report to Rawlins at Grant's headquarters and ask for an ambulance to transport Grant. The cavalryman would guide the ambulance and its driver to Cadwallader's and Grant's location. When Grant became aware of his surroundings, he wanted to return immediately to camp, but Cadwallader managed to walk him around until the ambulance arrived. Grant resisted getting in the ambulance until Cadwallader promised to ride with him with their two horses tied to the ambulance. Cadwallader wrote, "On the way he confessed that I had been right, and that he had been wrong throughout, and told me to consider myself a staff officer, and to give any orders that were necessary in his name." There is no record of Cadwallader ever having issued even one such order.

Upon arrival at his headquarters, Grant soberly spoke to Rawlins and to staffer John Riggin and told them he was going to bed. Grant walked as if he had never had a drink, leaving Cadwallader dumbfounded. Cadwallader told Rawlins that he feared Rawlins would think he was the one drunk instead of Grant. Rawlins responded that he never suspected such a thing, he knew Grant well, and he wanted Cadwallader to tell him everything that happened. Cadwallader complied and admitted that he had usurped his power, and he knew Grant had the authority and the right to banish the newsman from his department. Rawlins assured Cadwallader that would not happen, but Cadwallader had a restless rest of the night.

There is no explanation by Cadwallader of why Rawlins did not become enraged as might be expected. Grant never mentioned the events, and Cadwallader noticed that from that point on, Grant treated him with much respect, often referred to him as a staff member, and went out of his way to make Cadwallader comfortable in the camp and to provide him with whatever he needed. It may have been so, but this assertion is no corroborating evidence that the fanciful tale happened. Grant had no idea Cadwallader would concoct such a story. Perhaps Cadwallader, being a pal of Rawlins and with Grant thinking him a friend, already had such privileges. Cadwallader had certainly exacted revenge for Grant's slight of Rawlins. That he did it long after both Rawlins and Grant had died illuminates his character.

The discrepancies between Dana's and Cadwallader's accounts are obvious and striking. An investigation of the situation using postwar and post–Grant death publications and correspondence among Grant staffer James Wilson, Cadwallader, and Dana sheds much light on who wrote the truth.

A significant part of the story is a message Rawlins wrote to Grant dated June 6, the time written, 1 A.M. This message has been used by many who accept Cadwallader's story as proof that the story was true. Though lengthy, it is instructive to quote the letter in full:

> The great solicitude I feel for the safety of this army leads me to mention what I had hoped never again to do—the subject of your drinking. This may surprise you, for I may be (and I trust that I am) doing you an injustice by unfounded suspicions, but if an error it better be on the side of his country's safety than in fear of offending a friend. I have heard that Dr. [Charles] McMillen, at Gen. Sherman's a few days ago, induced you, notwithstanding your pledge to me, to take a glass of wine, and to-day, when I found a box of wine in front of your tent and proposed to move it, which I did, I was told you had forbid its being taken away, for you intended to keep it until you entered Vicksburg, that you should have it for your friends; and to-night, when you should, because of the condition of your health if nothing else, have been in bed, I find you where the wine bottle has just been emptied, in company with those who drink and urge you to do likewise, and the lack of your usual promptness of decision

and clearness in expressing yourself in writing tended to confirm my suspicions. You have the *full* control of your appetite and can let drinking alone. Had you not pledged me the sincerity of your honor early last March that you would drink no more during the war, and kept that pledge during your recent campaign, you would not to-day have stood first in the world's history as a successful military leader. Your only salvation depends upon your strict adherence to that pledge. You cannot succeed in any other way. As I have before stated, I may be wrong in my suspicions, but if one sees that which leads him to suppose a sentinel is falling asleep on his post, it is his duty to arouse him; and if being seduced to that step which he knows will bring disgrace upon that General and defeat to his command, if he fails to sound the proper note of warning, the friends, wives, and children of those brave men whose lives he permits to remain thus imperiled will accuse him while he lives and stand swift witnesses of wrath against him in the day when all shall be tried. If my suspicions are unfounded, let my friendship for you and my zeal for my country be my excuse for this letter; and if they are correctly founded, and you determine not to heed the admonitions and the prayers of this hasty note by immediately ceasing to touch a single drop of any kind of liquor, no matter by whom asked or under what circumstances, let my immediate relief from duty in this department be the result. I am, General,

Yours respectfully, John A. Rawlins

Copies of the letter survived in private hands. Wilson, who included it in his biography of Rawlins, claimed the Rawlins family had Rawlins's copy, and that Rawlins had written on his copy that Grant did not seem to resent what Rawlins had to say. Wilson claimed that Rawlins told Sherman and McPherson about the letter, and after the deaths of Rawlins and Grant, it found its way into newspapers. Several people are known to have seen copies of the letter, so there seems no doubt about authenticity. There is some question as to whether Grant actually was given a copy of the letter; it has long been assumed that he did receive it. One question that has not been explored is why Rawlins wrote the letter. His relationship with Grant being so close, why not simply talk to the general and express his concerns? Did he simply want a written record, and if so, why?[12]

The most obvious question is what connection does Rawlins's letter have to do with Cadwallader's story? Certainly, it does not confirm it. At the time Rawlins wrote his missive, Grant had not left for Satartia. The internal evidence of the letter makes clears that Rawlins is referring to other incidents, possibly beginning with Sherman's and Porter's visits earlier. More likely he is merely referring to the empty wine bottle he found outside Grant's tent. The proximity of Sherman's and Grant's head-quarters made it easy for the two to interact; hence the wine at Sherman's camp. That Grant would set aside wine for a celebration when Vicksburg was surrendered should not have surprised Rawlins to the extent he in-dicates. Rawlins notes Grant's health problems, so perhaps historians again have been too hasty to assume "ill" means "drunk" in Grant's case. Regarding June 6, Grant could have been drunk, but his drinking may have followed whatever illness he may have had. At least Wilson thought so. There is nothing in the Rawlins letter to indicate a reaction to anything Cadwallader wrote or passed along to Rawlins. The timeline makes that impossible. Wilson ignored the timeline or was not aware of it, for in his memoirs he states that Rawlins wrote his letter in direct response to what had happened on the Yazoo. Neither Dana nor Cadwallader mentions Wilson; Wilson was not present and, therefore, he must have written what he had been told, which was erroneous, so those who point to Wilson's letter as proof of Cadwallader's story are pointing in the wrong direction.[13]

The root of Cadwallader's determination to write the story, to get back at Grant, was his disgust with Grant for writing so little about Rawlins in his memoirs. What did Grant write? Aside from mentioning Rawlins a few times, Grant in volume 1 of his memoirs penned the following: "Rawlins remained with me as long as he lived, and rose to the rank of brigadier-general and chief-of-staff to the General of the Army—an office created for him—before the war closed. He was an able man, possessed of great firmness, and could say 'no' so emphatically to a request which he thought should not be granted that the person he was addressing would understand at once that there was no use of pressing the matter. General Rawlins was a very useful officer in other ways than this. I became very attached to him."[14]

Cadwallader, and Wilson as well, did not object to what Grant had written, but what he did not write. They thought Grant would have been nothing without Rawlins. Cadwallader wrote Wilson in 1887 that he be-came furious when he read Grant's memoirs, angry "at the cold, hard, heartless fact that he could have written such a book at such length, and dismissed R from history (so far as he could do it) with a single common-place paragraph." If Grant still lived, Cadwallader fumed, he would have said that a man who would write such brief comments about Rawlins to whom he owed so much "deserved to be scourged from the face of the earth." Cadwallader then claimed that time had reduced his anger, and he believed that Grant's being so short-sighted must have been due to "human infirmity." But time, he said, could not restore the iconic image he once had of Grant. Cadwallader then went on in a somewhat ominous tone: "I now intend some truth be told, if I live long enough to accomplish the task, while there are still a sufficient number of living witnesses to back up all my assertions." The statement anticipates the tale he wrote in his memoirs about the Satartia episode. Since the memoirs were not published until many years later, Cadwallader could not count on living witnesses. However, at the time he released his story to Wilson, and via Wilson to Dana, Cadwallader found he could not count on those living at the time to back him up.[15]

John Y. Simon, noted Grant authority and editor of most of Grant's published papers, believed that Grant may not have given Rawlins more space because he tired of hearing about how Rawlins was his conscience, always shadowing the general, frequently speaking very profanely, and being cited by some as the genius behind Grant's success. One story exemplifies Grant's impatience; after he went to the Virginia theater of the war, and of course Rawlins went with him, Grant once asked Rawlins who exactly was running the army, Rawlins or him. Other Grant staff members may have disliked Rawlins's heavy-handed manner, and their attitudes may have influenced Grant. This is speculation, for there is no official or unofficial written record that anyone ever asked Grant about his relatively brief comments on Rawlins.[16]

Cadwallader seemed hypocritical in accusing Grant of short-changing Rawlins. In his own memoirs, Cadwallader mentions Rawlins several times, mostly citing Rawlins taking steps to protect Grant from liquor. He also implies that Rawlins deserved much credit for Grant's military successes due to his insightful advice to the general. Cadwallader did not write a laudatory commentary on Rawlins that would have made up for what he perceived as Grant's short-sightedness. In an 1887 letter to Wilson, who had contacted Cadwallader in the hope that the latter might have papers relevant to Wilson's proposed biography of Rawlins, Cadwallader wrote most glowingly of Rawlins in a way that is absent from his memoirs. At the time, Cadwallader did not anticipate writing a book but thought of writing articles for magazines. The absence of praise for Rawlins in the later memoir proves Cadwallader a hypocrite. Wilson agreed with Cadwallader that Rawlins made up half of Grant, but in his comments to the newsman about the Grant-Rawlins relationship, Wilson never resorted to the maliciousness of Cadwallader.[17]

Wilson's search for Rawlins's papers gained him nothing from Cadwallader, who blamed several Grant staff members and Grant himself for destruction of the papers. In his biography of Rawlins, Wilson noted that he found some Rawlins papers in private hands, and he thanked Cadwallader for the use of the manuscript that, as noted, was published many years later. If there was a large cache of Rawlins's papers anywhere, they never surfaced, and Cadwallader's accusation about those responsible for destroying them was never proven.[18]

The exchanges between Wilson and Cadwallader proved that Cadwallader's motive in writing the Satartia story was clearly to soil Grant and lift up Rawlins. In 1904, Wilson talked Cadwallader into sending him the eight-hundred-page memoir Cadwallader had written so Wilson could look for any information that would help him in his Rawlins biography. Cadwallader sent the manuscript and admitted that he had written too much and intended to cut a large section. In a very telling reaction to Cadwallader's account of Grant's drunken spree, Wilson responded, "Your description of Grant's drunkenness during the Satartia trip is more graphic, and more in detail than I have ever heard before." Wilson's comment is not surprising, but his words are an enlightening commentary on Cadwallader's tale, more so than Wilson thought at the time. Wilson was on Grant's staff at Vicksburg, and though he may not have been at Chickasaw Bayou landing when Grant returned, if anything of the sort that Cadwallader wrote had happened in the "detail" in Cadwallader's manuscript, Wilson certainly would have heard about and remembered the story.[19]

Wilson had written several years earlier when he read an earlier version of the Satartia story Cadwallader sent to him that he recalled the story "substantially" as Cadwallader had told it. Then he mentioned he had also heard it from Charles Dana, and Wilson asked Cadwallader who was with him. Cadwallader responded that Dana had not been aboard. Wilson responded that the published official records of the war demonstrated that Wilson was right about Dana being with Grant during the "celebrated" Satartia trip. The discrepancy led to letter exchanges among Wilson, Dana, and Cadwallader. Wilson wondered if there could have been two trips.[20]

Dana wrote Wilson that Grant may have made two trips up the Yazoo to Satartia, but Dana could only remember one. Dana mentioned that his was the one in the official records. He stated plainly that Cadwallader was not on the boat. Dana stood by the published record, noting that Captain John Grimes Walker, navy commander at Haynes's Bluff, was one of the officers (probably the commander) with the flotilla coming downstream who warned Dana about the danger ahead and offered to escort the *Diligence* upriver or to escort it back to Haynes's Bluff. Dana, of course, after realizing Grant was too ill to make the decision, decided to have the boat turned around. Dana continued, "Now Cadwallader speaks of having gone to Satartia beforehand, and of having met Grant and his party part way down, and turned back and then gone with him to Satartia on the boat in which he [Cadwallader] had come down upon, while Grant's boat returned to Haines's Bluff. I never had anything to do with such an expedition, and cannot remember that such as one ever occurred." Dana, who worked almost as closely with Grant as Rawlins, would have known if Grant had taken an earlier trip. When Cadwallader received the Dana letter that Wilson sent him, he penciled in under Dana's signature that Cadwallader's trip was a week before Kimball's cavalry took possession of Satartia. So, according to Cadwallader, there had to have been two trips, Cadwallader knowing about the first and Dana only about the second.[21]

On January 20, 1890, accompanying Dana's letter to Cadwallader, Wilson wrote the dates of Dana's account and enclosed copies of dispatches as printed in the official records. Again, Wilson noted, "It seems probable therefore that there were two such expeditions, though I cannot find the slightest clue to, of any except the one mentioned in the enclosed dispatches. Of course it is possible that a more careful reading of the whole record might reveal another. It is possible that there could have been two such trips, between the first occupation of Mechanicsburg & Satartia, and the withdrawal of the troops from that region. Your own data or memoranda ought to fix the date of your trip, and with the light I have give you, reveal just where the discrepancy arises between your story & Dana's and how they are to be reconciled." Wilson, in a scolding manner, concludes that he was surprised that neither Dana nor Cadwallader had copies of the official records then being published. Little wonder in 1904, Wilson could not remember all the things Cadwallader had written. The written record and memories of those who would have known proved that Grant made only one trip up the Yazoo. His contemporaries, Dana and Wilson, had shot down Cadwallader's story, though both tried to soften the blow with speculation about two trips, though both knew better.[22]

Another much-larger body of evidence contradicts Cadwallader's story, and it, too, has been ignored by historians. A thorough examination of Union soldiers' letters and diaries does not reveal one mention of Cadwallader's tale. These sources include the many hundreds of letters and diaries in the Vicksburg National Park Archives, the Illinois State Library (now housed in the Abraham Lincoln Presidential Library in Springfield), the University of Iowa, the Wisconsin Historical Society, the University of Michigan Bentley Library, the Indiana Historical Society, the Indiana State Library, the Ohio Historical Society, the United States Army Military History Institute, and many more repositories. If such an incident as Cadwallader described had occurred, the news surely would have swept through the camps from the right flank all the way around to the left. When Grant, according to Cadwallader, joined in a drinking party after coming ashore and, even more so, when he rode wildly through soldiers' camps, there would have been no way to keep the story secret. These many documents demonstrate that most soldiers knew Grant by sight and with the aid of campfires certainly would have known that General Grant was riding through destroying campsites. Yet, there is no mention of such an event. If it had happened, letters sent home and diaries would have been filled with comments. The silence of the soldiers speaks volumes about Cadwallader's lies.

After the publication of Cadwallader's memoir in 1955, historians reacted to the volume as a whole and specifically to the drinking story. Civil War historian Bruce Catton questions the validity of Cadwallader's memory. Regarding the Grant spree, Catton wrote in *American Heritage Magazine* in 1956, "Cadwallader describes a spree of Gargantuan proportions, which he asserts that he himself witnessed and from which, according to his memoirs, he extricated the General with considerable difficulty. Is this account, then, to be taken as accurate, or should it simply be added to the mass of unverified legends about Grant?" Catton invited historian Kenneth P. Williams, a very vocal critic of the Cadwallader memoirs, and Benjamin Thomas, the editor, to write letters to the *American Heritage Magazine*, in which Catton's comments appeared, to air their differences. It is evident neither had read the Wilson-Dana-Cadwallader correspondence, nor, it would appear, had Catton. Williams slammed Thomas's entire editorial effort, and regarding the drinking story, he pointed out the disparities between Dana's and Cadwallader's published accounts. Williams's lengthy letter is followed by an even-lengthier rebuttal by Thomas. Thomas attacks Dana's memoirs, pointing out they had been ghostwritten by Tarbell. That did not, of course, make them any less accurate, for, as mentioned, the memoirs dovetail with the documents published in the official records. Thomas's rebuttal is as filled with holes as is Cadwallader's account. How much impact the exchange may have had is not clear, but many historians who wrote more about the story later accepted Cadwallader's tall tale without bothering to investigate.[23]

Catton elaborated further on his take of Grant's drinking in an introduction to Julia Grant's memoirs, which were published in 1975. He notes that Rawlins's letter to Grant and Cadwallader's story are not similar in any manner. Catton additionally points out that Rawlins had been an attorney, and he understood the significance of maintaining written records. Julia Grant, Catton wrote, thought the preservation of Rawlins's letter indicated "very much as if this devoted defender of Grant's reputation had been trying to make a record." This was Julia's take on why Rawlins wrote a letter rather than talking with her husband. Catton believed Rawlins did have a transparent agenda.

Catton wrote that in the fall of 1863, while Grant was in Chattanooga, Tennessee, Rawlins wrote a similar letter to Grant, claiming that if Grant had two more nights like the previous night, the general would be bedridden and unfit to carry on. This letter was apparently never given to Grant; it may have been intended as a memo for Rawlins's file on Grant's drinking. Was that Rawlins's intent at Vicksburg? Catton further demonstrates there is no doubt that Rawlins's words were lies. On the night in question, Grant had attended a conference on military strategy regarding the Chattanooga situation. "A drunken party," Catton elaborates, "had in fact been going on, at a lower level of Army headquarters; Grant found out about it, angrily broke it up, and blistered the staff officer who gave the party so thoroughly that the man resigned and left the Army." Would Rawlins have been aware of the incident? As Grant's top aide, he certainly should have. Known as Grant's "conscience," Rawlins seemed to build on that reputation, and keeping a file on Grant's drinking habits would be evidence.

Catton uses a well-known phrase that puts Rawlins's relationship with Grant in perspective: "With a defender like Rawlins, Grant had no need of any enemies." Julia would seemingly have agreed. Certainly, the Chattanooga incident places the pre–Yazoo trip letter in an enlightening perspective. There is no concrete evidence that Rawlins intentionally intended to undercut Grant's reputation, but the circumstantial evidence is intriguing and compelling. If Rawlins did indeed have such an agenda, why did he not write something about the Cadwallader story? If he did, no such document has been located. Assuming he did not, could that simply mean there was nothing to write about?[24]

Shelby Foote, the noted novelist turned historian, embraced the story with glee in the second volume of his three-volume *The Civil War: A Narrative*. Published in 1963, Foote's volume 2, like 1 and 3, reached a large audience. An unabashed Confederate sympathizer and a great admirer of Nathan Bedford Forrest, Foote placed Dana and Cadwallader on the same boat and proceeded to paraphrase and quote directly from Cadwallader's account of Grant's drunken spree. To make the story work, Foote and other historians had to have Dana and Cadwallader on the same boat, which clearly was not the case. Dana was definitely on the boat; Cadwallader doubtless had been and would be on boats but not the one that took Dana and Grant up the Yazoo on June 6.

Regarding Grant's alleged wild horseback ride, Foote added a personal touch: "The road was crooked, winding among the many slews and bayous, but the general more or less straightened it out." Foote made no effort to investigate the veracity of the story, and the sad thing is that his book sold so well, and the three-volume set is still on the market, that Cadwallader's bogus account has received wide readership through the years, thanks to Foote. A surprising number of scholarly historians cite Foote's volumes, though they are undocumented, and in this case, the source he obviously used was a fantasy.[25]

Another popular-style writer, Samuel Carter III, likewise accepted the Cadwallader account without question. In his book, *The Final Fortress: The Campaign for Vicksburg, 1862–1863*, Carter embraced Foote's solution to the conundrum that Dana's and Cadwallader's different accounts presented: He put them on the same boat. Unlike Foote, Carter was warned that the Cadwallader story had no substance and that it was not verified by any other sources. Vicksburg National Park historian Al Scheller told Carter not to include what amounted to fiction, but Carter determined to insert it anyway. At least he documented his book, though he made a gross error in his choice of Cadwallader's memoirs. He should have listened to Scheller.[26]

William McFeely, in his Pulitzer Prize–winning book, *Grant: A Biography*, likewise accepted Cadwallader's story. McFeely went so far as to claim that there had long been "a loyal conspiracy to protect Grant" from the drinking story. McFeely mourned that Cadwallader and Thomas were so "vilified." He noted that Simon did not accept the claim that Cadwallader was even present when Dana made the trip but that Simon did not deny drinking happened. Simon thought Cadwallader's story may have been based on camp gossip. McFeely cites the Dana editorial "Gen. Grant's Occasional Intoxication" in the *New York Sun*, January 28, 1887, as the source for much of the story, but Dana never embraced Cadwallader's wild account. Dana, postwar editor and part-owner of the *Sun*, had clashed frequently with Grant's presidential administration on political issues. Did that have anything to do with his vicious remarks in the 1887 article?

McFeely praised Foote's version, false though it was. McFeely admits that Cadwallader may have exaggerated: "However, he was not likely to have forgotten its essentials, and little about the story, including his claim to have been aboard, fails to make sense, unless one is flatly determined to refuse to believe that Ulysses Grant was ever drunk." McFeely was right about it not making sense, but he did not dig deeply enough to determine the reason: Cadwallader made it up. McFeely then proceeded to repeat the earlier solution of Cadwallader and Dana being on the same boat, utilizing Cadwallader's story, but he did note that Rawlins's letter to Grant was written before Grant's trip up the Yazoo. At least he got that part right.[27]

Simpson in his 2000 biography of Grant was the first scholarly historian to point out the flaws in Cadwallader's account. Simpson wrote that Cadwallader's story was "concocted," and he goes on to discuss the contradictions between Dana's and Cadwallader's stories and how the story of two trips thus evolved. Simpson also notes how Wilson and Cadwallader had come to similar conclusions that Grant was overrated and that Rawlins, as well as themselves, had not received due credit for Grant's success. Dana was "disillusioned" with Grant; certainly, this was true as indicated in the frequent attacks Dana in his newspaper made against Grant's presidency. Simpson further pointed out that previous scholars, and he might have added nonscholars, had blindly accepted the Cadwallader story without bothering to question it.[28]

As mentioned, in his introduction to a reprint of Cadwallader's memoir published in 1996, Simpson elaborated and did a marvelous job of tearing apart Cadwallader's story. To date, it is the most thorough debunking in print. An especially significant touch is what Simpson found in Hamlin Garland's research notes in the University of Southern California Library. Garland, a popular writer, who, like Foote, disdained documentation, wrote a biography of Grant in 1898, so he never saw Cadwallader's memoir. The significance of noting Garland's writing is that he interviewed many Civil War veterans who knew Grant. Among Garland's notes, Simpson found that Wilson told Garland he had never seen Grant drink. What an admission, given Wilson's role in the Cadwallader affair! The implication is clear: Cadwallader was not the only one who strayed from the truth.[29]

Warren E. Grabau, whose book *Ninety-Eight Days: A Geographer's View of the Vicksburg Campaign* (2000) is one of the most innovative books produced on the inland campaign and siege, ignores both Dana and Cadwallader. Grabau writes nothing at all about the alleged drinking episode, which demonstrates his disdain for the story and his wisdom in not addressing it.

In January 2005, Brian J. Murphy analyzed the Yazoo episode in an article originally published in *America's Civil War*. Entitled "Truth behind U. S. Grant's Yazoo River Bender," Murphy pointed out Grant's low tolerance for liquor, and that being the case, even a small drink could make the general appear drunk. Murphy also traces the history of the many stories that still abound about Grant's drunken tendencies dated back before the Civil War when Grant was in the U.S. Army on the west coast. Murphy then launches into a discussion of the Cadwallader account, pointing out many of the flaws mentioned previously. Murphy does, however, question whether Grant was drunk at all on the trip, noting the general's frequent bouts with headaches. The evidence that Grant was drinking is presented strongly by Dana; Murphy's view may be partially correct in that the Yazoo incident could have grown out of both illness and drink.[30]

Grant's most recent biographer, Jean Edward Smith, wrote about Grant's drinking problem, but he relegates Cadwallader's story to a footnote. Smith offers no comment on the story, but in omitting it from his text, he showed sound judgment, though he perhaps judged Grant too harshly when referring to him as a clinical alcoholic. Alcoholism is in many instances subject to perception. There are accounts by people who knew and spent time around Grant who state categorically Grant often turned down drinks, that even when he took one, he was never observed in a state of drunkenness. Many soldiers and officers who served with Grant during the war support the argument that whatever Grant drank or how often, he never allowed drink to get in the way of his duties. Did that mean he never got drunk? Of course not, but these testimonies do imply that if he wished, Grant could take it or leave it alone, hardly the behavior of an alcoholic, clinical or otherwise.[31]

Winston Groom, a novelist-historian à la Foote, published *Vicksburg 1863* in 2009 and, like Foote, accepts Cadwallader's story as written. Groom, like so many others, places both Cadwallader and Dana in the same boat and, like others, obviously saw no need to find out if that was true; in Groom's case, he ignored Simpson's work. Groom admits there is some controversy, but he writes condescendingly, "No one likes to discover that their idols have feet of clay, and several of Grant's biographers have attempted to discount or discredit Cadwallader's account, principally by citing a few known errors in his memoir, which he did not write until 1896, and which even then remained unpublished for another fifty-plus years." After all, Cadwallader continued to be a member of Grant's coterie after he went east. Groom noted that Cadwallader shared a home with Rawlins in Georgetown,

District of Columbia, after the war. By most accounts of those who knew him," Groom argues, Cadwallader was considered "a thorough and trustworthy journalist."[32]

Like Foote, Groom could not pass up a story that was a novelist's dream. Yet, Groom did not waste time looking for facts, and his argument that Cadwallader remained a member of "Grant's coterie" means nothing. Grant had no reason to suspect that Cadwallader would wield a penned account of lies about the Satartia trip. If Grant had had an inkling of what was to come, Cadwallader would have been run out of camp and sent North. Grant had no clue to suspect Cadwallader would betray him, and as for implied hints, including more than a hint by Cadwallader, that he was allowed to stay to cover up the story, there was nothing to cover up. Cadwallader's reputation during the war may well have been stellar, but that in no way guaranteed that he would be truthful in his old age.

Historians will continue to have differing perceptions about Grant's drinking, the extent of it, the mythology around it, and how much it matters. After all, the stories about Grant and alcohol are legion and have been for many generations. His record speaks for itself: the greatest Union general of the Civil War, and perhaps the greatest general period, and a good, if not great president. The malignant attitudes about his presidency are going through a revisionist stage, and his presidential legacy will be looked upon more favorably as time passes, assuming the current trends continue.

Why, then, should Cadwallader's story be given the attention it has received? Why does it matter? Why is it not just another Grant drinking story that can be taken seriously or not? Does it really detract from his role in the Civil War? The answers may be found in the extreme nature of Cadwallader's wild tale. Many people who encountered Grant during the war came away with a story of some sort about his drinking. Cadwallader's story goes beyond the norm, well beyond the pale. Cadwallader went much further than "stupidly" drunk; he turned Grant into an alcoholic inveterate idiot who had absolutely no control over himself. The length of the incident alone, as written by Cadwallader, makes it stand out. Historians who have naively accepted it have made it worse by spreading it to multitudes of readers.

The gravity of the story demands an investigation, and those who have dug into the documented details have discovered that Cadwallader's fairy tale is just that. Why did he do it? Why would he so viciously attack a man he claimed to admire? Was Grant's perceived slight of Rawlins worth such a story? Did the aged Cadwallader get several events radically mixed up in his mind? Questions like these that might have been answered by those who witnessed Grant's trip: The boat's crew, his escort, and men being transported downstream from Satartia could not respond due to the long delay in the publication of the memoir. That none left any known account that would verify Cadwallader's remembrance of the Yazoo voyage says much about Cadwallader's validity. Rawlins could not comment on it because he died before Cadwallader wrote it. Rawlins could have approved or not; we will never know. The evidence clearly shows that Cadwallader lied and lied in the extreme. The witnesses who could have legitimately responded would very likely have verified that conclusion. Cadwallader did nothing more than deepen the stain of gossip, rumors, and half-truths about a famous general and president. Those who have bought into the story have contributed to a caricature of Grant as a drunk. In doing so, they have perpetuated Cadwallader's prevarications, hardly a service to the truth of history.

Grant obviously did not and never would know about the controversy. When he returned to his headquarters from the Yazoo trip, he did not waste time feathering Cadwallader's nest. He learned about military action at Milliken's Bend where Union black soldiers had assisted in repelling a Confederate attack. Grant believed in black soldiers, but his overall record in race relations during the siege was very mixed and provided great challenges, greater than he could have imagined.

~4~

Rampant Racism

Though Grant maintained his obsession with the Mechanicsburg Corridor, he could not ignore other problems. On the Louisiana side of the Mississippi, Confederate Lieutenant General Kirby Smith ordered Major General Richard Taylor to attack two of Grant's bases, Young's Point and Milliken's Bend. Smith had in mind disruption of Grant's supply line, but Grant had moved his central supply depot to Chickasaw Bayou, and Confederate infantry, artillery, or partisan snipers could not stop Porter's navy from replenishing Union stores. When Grant crossed his troops into Mississippi, he took steps to firm up his supply line on the Louisiana side of the river. He had depots established at Young's Point, Milliken's Bend, and Lake Providence. The transfer of his main supply depot to Chickasaw Bayou landing did not lead to an abandonment of the Louisiana posts. They could be used by Union detachments ordered to fend off Rebel forays in Louisiana. Grant detailed troops to establish camps at Milliken's Bend and other points to keep track of Rebel activities. Also, the locations could be used for training and recruiting areas for black volunteers who enlisted to become part of the black regiments then on the drawing board.

Adjutant General Lorenzo Thomas has been called "one of the unsung heroes of the effort to create African American military units." Whatever Thomas's personal feelings about black men, he embraced wholeheartedly the concept of black units. Secretary of War Stanton gave Thomas the job of recruiting black men along the lower reaches of the

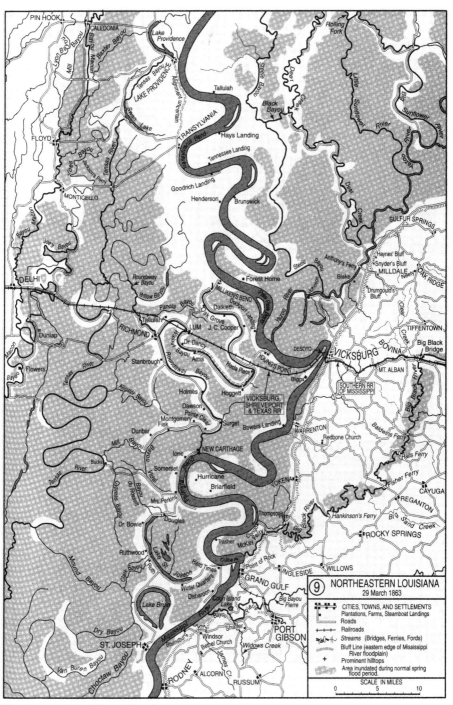

Northeastern Louisiana, March 29, 1863. Map 9, Warren E. Grabau, *Ninety-Eight Days* (Knoxville: University of Tennessee Press, 2000).

Mississippi, including, of course, Grant's district. Grant did nothing to hinder Thomas, and men encouraged by Thomas's evangelistic approach to convince Union troops that arming black men was a positive idea joined in his efforts. Thus, the establishment of a camp for black troops at Lake Providence came into being.[1]

On June 3, three days before he departed up the Yazoo, Grant received word from Brigadier General Jeremiah Sullivan that there were rumors of imminent Rebel attacks on the Louisiana side. Sullivan said nothing about what he had done or intended to do to thwart such offensives, nor did he seem to know any particulars about the Confederate presence. Grant sent Brigadier General Elias Dennis to take command.[2]

On June 7, the day Grant returned to Chickasaw Bayou, Confederate Major General John Walker attacked Milliken's Bend. June 6 began with a reconnaissance by Union troops, led by Colonel Hermann Lieb, toward the town of Richmond, south of Milliken's Bend. Along the way, Lieb ran into Walker's advancing force, and after a brief skirmish, Lieb decided he was outgunned and retreated back to Milliken's Bend. Lieb's detachment included the 9th Louisiana regiment of troops of "African Descent," one of several units of black troops organized in Grant's district during recent months. Two companies from the 10th Illinois Cavalry rode in advance of the black infantry.

On April 22, Grant had issued General Orders No. 25, in which he stated that all commanders must provide facilities for the ongoing organization of Negro regiments currently being organized. Commissaries and quartermasters must furnish whatever was needed in the same amounts as white troops required. All officers must be diligent in carrying out the policy of the Lincoln administration regarding the organization and sufficient training of black troops, and they should do all they could to stifle prejudices. The latter would prove difficult to implement; indifference to slaves and black soldiers during the Vicksburg campaign was rampant. Only time would tell how well the instructions regarding black troops would be carried out. By June, there had been little progress. Yet, with siege operations occupying his attention, Grant did not have time to focus personally on oversight.[3]

Innate racism among Union soldiers had been obvious throughout the Vicksburg campaign. Soldiers in occupied Memphis grew tired of the "drove of blackbirds" that came to the city. Others laughed about slaves playing banjos and doing the "nigger-dance." One white soldier hoped for permission to shoot slaves; eradicating blacks would allow white soldiers in the opposing armies to go home. There would be no reason to fight. Many resented the purpose of the war shifting from saving the Union to freeing slaves. One wrote, "I would rather have the union divided and let slavery alone where it is than to have the union restored and [slavery] abolished. . . . I don't think a white man was ever calculated to be shot at for the sake of a nigger." Many were bothered by the conditions of slaves, but their anger did not make them less racist. As for arming blacks, a Union soldier commented, "If there is fight in Sambo lets have it." An Iowan intoned, "The idea of arming and equipping Negro Regiments for the purpose of making them soldiers is, to my mind, worse than ridiculous nonsense. Blacks would only work *if you made them do so.*" He thought that out of a crowd of fifty thousand former slaves, there might be only a thousand who would not run away when they went into battle. Action across the Mississippi River in Louisiana would begin to change minds if not hearts.

Grant rarely commented on such events and was probably unaware of most of them. Certainly, he knew the racial attitudes of his men. He realized, however, that with the Lincoln administration pushing the idea of black troops, he had to make efforts he likely would have preferred delaying.[4]

Across the Mississippi, Union officers deployed on June 7 in anticipation of Walker's attack. The 23rd Iowa Infantry lined up by the side of the African Louisiana brigade, a total of just under eleven hundred men. They would be assaulted by Brigadier General Henry McCulloch's brigade of Walker's division, fourteen hundred troops. Walker's soldiers flew the black flag, indicating they would show no quarter, a gesture intended to warn black troops they could expect to be killed when opportunities arose. Upon learning of the situation, Admiral Porter sent the gunboat *Choctaw* to provide firepower from the river against McCulloch's force. At Young's Point, Walker's attempt to defeat Union forces fell apart due to delays getting to the battlefield. By the time Walker's men arrived, so had Union reinforcements. Thus, the proposed battle at Young's Point never materialized. After the Confederate withdrawal at Young's Point, Union troops reinforced the units at Milliken's Bend, but they arrived after the battle there.[5]

At Milliken's Bend, McCulloch's brigade charged Union defenders, many Rebels yelling they would give "no quarter," in case Union troops did not see the black flags. In his report, Dennis admitted some very telling facts about the Louisiana black troops: "The African regiments being inexperienced in the use of arms, some of them having been drilled but a few days, and the guns being very inferior, the enemy succeeded in getting upon our works before more than one or two volleys were fired at them." Bitter hand-to-hand fighting ensued, many soldiers using bayonets and guns as clubs in the close-quarter struggle. McCulloch's men managed to flank Lieb's position, forcing the Union line to fall back behind the levee that held back the Mississippi. The *Choctaw* took position, and the navy gunners, able to shoot well over the heads of their own men, opened fire on McCulloch's advancing brigade. McCulloch spread his line to the right, but more black troops, the 11th Louisiana Infantry being held in reserve, came forward and blunted the Rebel movement. The fighting continued until noon, according to Dennis, having lasted some eight hours, but after the initial Confederate success, the battle turned into a stalemate. The heaviest combat may have ceased before noon; official reports, other than Dennis's, make no mention of the time frame other than the early-morning start. Realizing he could do no more, especially against the big guns of the *Choctaw* and now the USS *Lexington* forced McCulloch to remain in position, and he decided to withdraw. His casualties numbered 185.[6]

Lieb's Africans and the 24th Iowa lost a high percentage of troops engaged: 101 killed, 285 wounded, and 266 captured or missing. The casualties made up over 60 percent of Lieb's force, an exceptionally high number. Some black troops were unaccounted for, though Dennis figured they would "probably return." He praised the black troops "deeds of valor." By his own admission, Dennis had said these men were not ready for battle, but their determination to fight anyway had earned some admiration from white troops. A Wisconsin soldier wrote home that he wanted all his kin to know "the nigger will fight," but he noted that on a hospital ship, the black wounded were segregated from the white. A Wisconsin artilleryman applauded the efforts of black soldiers, adding that previously, they were only "allowed to dig, to cook, to drive mules and do menial affairs." These men would fight and deserve the freedom they fought for. Charles Dana in a letter to Stanton told of how bravely the black troops had rallied after the initial attack. In his memoir, Dana commented that the battle "completely revolutionized the sentiment of the army with regard to the employment of negro troops. I heard prominent officers who formerly in private had sneered at the idea of the negroes fighting express themselves after that as heartily in favor of it."

Grant read reports of the battle and admitted that black troops at Milliken's Bend had "but little experience in the use of fire-arms. . . . Their conduct is said, however, to have been most gallant, and I doubt not but with good officers they will make good troops." He should have seen to it that these men were ready before being placed in harm's way. Certainly, the presence of Confederate troops in Louisiana was well known and the possibilities of attack obvious.[7]

Ramifications of the black flag led to rumors, some likely true, that Rebel soldiers had finished off wounded black persons, and black troops reacted in kind. How much of this may or may not have occurred is unclear, but David Porter reported that when the black soldiers saw their own being killed without mercy, they in turn "slaughtered" wounded Rebels "like sheep." Porter was not there, and since he was given to exaggeration, the extent of what he claimed must be considered with care. Dana also recounted to Stanton about how many men were found bayoneted and with cracked skulls, though he admitted that Dennis, also not there, did not know whether Rebels had murdered black soldiers. Like Porter, Dana had no first-hand knowledge, and they should have waited until all the facts were in before writing reports. Grant did not react in writing, but being close to Porter and Dana, he was aware of their statements.

Weeks later on June 22, Grant sent Taylor a message about the report of an unnamed white man that Taylor's troops had hung black soldiers and a white officer. Grant said that he had ordered Rebel troops captured to be treated as prisoners of war despite their fighting under the black flag. Grant had no intention to retaliate, but if this was the way Taylor wanted to wage war, Grant made clear he would "accept the issue" and respond in kind. Taylor vehemently denied any such events had occurred. No white officer had been hung, and Taylor reminded Grant of Confederate policy that any captured blacks, soldiers or otherwise, had to be turned over to civilian officials. Grant responded that he was "truly glad to have your denial." Regarding the treatment of captured black Union soldiers, Grant said, "In the matter of treatment of Negro soldiers taken prisoners, I do not feel authorized to say what the government may demand in regard to them, but having taken the responsibility of declaring slaves free and having authorized the arming of them, I cannot see the justice of permitting one treatment for them, and another for the white soldiers[.] This however is a subject I am not aware of an action having been taken upon." There Grant let the matter rest.[8]

Despite positive comments made about the efforts of the black soldiers at Milliken's Bend, the battle came, ironically, at a time when an official inquiry was being made of an ugly racial incident there. Grant, in ordering black troops and former slave civilians to various places, apparently did little to follow up on these people's living conditions. Contraband camps established for former slaves freed by Union armies had a deserved reputation for being squalid places where death rates were high. Grant did not and could not speak to such problems, for he had his mind mainly on military affairs regarding the siege. By ignoring the plight of freed slaves, including black soldiers, however, he at least stained his eventual success at Vicksburg, though the public would never know, and official Washington did not make race problems in combat operations a priority.

The story of the Milliken's Bend incident was rooted in early 1863 when General Frederick Steele made his diversionary campaign up the Mississippi River to Greenville and his brief inland sortie there. Among the participants in that campaign was Colonel Isaac Shepard of the 3rd Missouri regiment. Shepard had a northeastern pedigree, graduate of Harvard, Boston newspaper editor, member of the Massachusetts legislature, and devout Unionist and abolitionist. He came west at the beginning of the Civil War to Saint Louis, where he befriended Brigadier General Nathaniel Lyon and became one of Lyon's aides. When Lyon fell dead at the Battle of Wilson's Creek, August 10, 1861, Shepard became lieutenant colonel of the 19th Missouri, which was merged with the 3rd. Thus far, he had a positive, if not exceptional, record as a commander.[9]

Steele, who knew Shepard's background, asked the colonel to oversee the treatment of many freed men, women, and children who had followed Steele's withdrawal back to the Mississippi at Greenville. During this time, Thomas, in his role as adjutant general of the U.S. Army, started familiarizing Union commanders with the Lincoln administration's new policy of organizing blacks into army units. As mentioned, Grant and other officers in the west had followed suit by issuing orders to get the program underway. Such possibilities made Shepard anxious to be a part of turning former male slaves into soldiers, and he asked Sherman, his corps commander, to allow him to raise an "African Brigade"; Sherman told him to proceed. The initial excitement waned when Grant began his inland campaign, and Steele took his division and rejoined Sherman's corps to participate. Shepard, ill at the time, stayed behind at Milliken's Bend. Meanwhile, Thomas arrived at Milliken's Bend, and on May 9, as Grant led his army inland from Port Gibson, Thomas created the 1st Mississippi Regiment of African Descent, and on May 10, Shepard was named commander of a yet-to-be-organized African Brigade, to be recruited at Milliken's Bend.[10]

Shepard immediately saw that Grant's admonition to reduce bigotry had had no impact on the white soldiers at Milliken's Bend. His recruiting efforts brought scorn and hostility from Union troops stationed there. Shepard noted that black persons at Milliken's Bend, including women and children, many suffering from varying illnesses, were victims of anger and occasional violence. Shepard uses strong words in describing the situation; the living conditions of blacks were "squalid," the white soldiers' attitudes "were vicious and degraded." An outbreak of smallpox exacerbated problems, and though Shepard received some help in dealing with the disease, most white soldiers reacted with demands that the blacks must be kept segregated, and the "hatreds" and "perils" instilled in attitudes of white soldiers worsened. These soldiers might have opposed slavery, though many did not care one way or the other, but they did not consider blacks as equals.[11]

Out of this milieu arose the event that brought about an inquiry. Grant had been informed about the whole mess, and he certainly understood that while something must be done, the events at Milliken's Bend must not become national headlines. Neither he nor Lincoln could risk the backlash. The Court of Inquiry illuminated Shepard's situation and underscored the broad range of bigotry and violence that infested the Milliken's Bend area and that white violence extended beyond civilians to black troops.

At the time, Sullivan, commanding at Milliken's Bend, ordered Shepard's arrest on several charges, including initiating the whipping of a white soldier by blacks, and lying about his rank (calling himself a brigadier general) while ordering a white soldier to be punished. Like most white Union soldiers, Sullivan found Shepard's activities among blacks appalling and intended to use any opening to put Shepard out of business. There is no evidence that Sullivan ordered an investigation before having Shepard arrested. Sullivan had no interest in finding out how blacks had been treated, only how Shepard responded. Shepard asked for an inquiry, which convened on board the steamer USS *America* on June 4, two days before Grant left for Satartia. Grant must have been aware of the Milliken's Bend problems, though how much he kept up with the particulars of testimony is not known. In any event, he would not have given the inquiry more attention than the Mechanicsburg corridor. He really had no choice other than allowing the controversy to play itself out.[12]

Shepard started the proceedings by relating his version of what had happened, and he called several witnessed to back him up. Shepard indicated that Private John O'Brien, Company A, 10th Illinois Cavalry, had attacked a young black man, civilian. O'Brien and another soldier from Company A had wandered through the 1st Mississippi Colored troops' camp very late on a Saturday night. The two inebriated Illinoisans tied a black soldier to a tree and kicked him a number of times. The two white men then went to a "shanty" close by and attacked two black women, one of the soldiers carrying a hatchet "that was fortunately wrested from the brute and thrown away." It is not clear who took the hatchet from the drunken soldier; possibly, it was his friend who did not want to cross that line, not with a woman.

Nearby, a young black boy, said to be about fourteen years old, lay on the ground, probably hoping to be unnoticed. The two soldiers spotted him, cursed him, and the one with the hatchet ran threateningly toward him. The other stopped his fellow soldier and remarked that kicking the boy's brains out of his head would be sufficient. The hatchet soldier, apparently O'Brien, kicked the side of the boy's face, cutting a gash across the cheek. Putting his boot heel on the young man's face, O'Brien twisted his ankle until one of the boy's eyes was destroyed. Only when the youngster appeared unconscious did the attack cease. The man with O'Brien did nothing to stop him and, in fact, urged him on. Finally, an officer of the 57th Ohio stepped in and arrested O'Brien, who yelled that he would kill all the black people.

Escorted by a black soldier and a white sergeant, O'Brien wobbled to Shepard's quarters. His victim, remarkably able to walk, followed along. Shepard listened to an account of what had happened, and he was unable to get O'Brien to reveal the name of his drinking buddy, who apparently had slipped away during the excitement. Shepard ordered the sergeant to take O'Brien to his camp, but he had no intention of letting O'Brien escape punishment. The young victim's wounds disgusted Shepard, and he decided to set an example, hoping to put an end to such violence. Shepard testified, "I told the sergeant under his direction to let four or five black soldiers flagellate him and to tie him up." O'Brien was whipped, though most witnesses said it amounted to very little, certainly mild compared to the nature of O'Brien's assault on the teenager. Shepard, in fact, made sure the whipping did not go very far. He wanted to set an example, not to start a riot among the white soldiers: "[T]he whipping was slight, but the point I wish[ed] to make was gained, that the blacks ought to punish their own wrongs, and that was all I desired." The whips apparently were little more than small limbs off berry bushes, though O'Brien later insisted they were very large tree limbs. One witness said if O'Brien had bruises of a serious nature, they more than likely occurred when he, still quite drunk, lost his balance and fell back into the tree to which he had been tied.[13]

The court cleared Shepard of all charges, including the one that he had promoted himself to brigadier general, a charge that could have been vengeful, the result of Sullivan's and others dislike of Shepard's attempts to implement justice for blacks at Milliken's Bend. Shepard resumed his command, and Grant stepped in to be sure the transcript of the inquiry was not published. In a message dated August 29, 1863, long after the siege had ended, Grant commented regarding the transcript of the proceedings: "The General commanding . . . [sees] no good purpose to be served by the publication of the proceedings referred to at this time, and therefore withholds his consent. It should be always sufficient satisfaction for an officer of the army to know that the result of an investigation fairly made, meets with the approval of those above him, regardless of anything said by a partisan press."[14]

Grant understood that the outcry following publication of the grizzly details and aftermath would infuriate white people and black people, especially abolitionists. However, news of the incident did leak out, and stories and cartoons appeared in Northern newspapers illustrating black soldiers beating a white soldier. The cartoons did not noticeably raise ire in the North; perhaps, Northern whites considered them nothing more than cartoon characters. The mother of an Indiana soldier wrote her son about the story. He responded that no black man had whipped a white man. He said he knew one black had cursed a white soldier in the 124th Illinois, and the soldier walked into his tent, grabbed his rifle, and shot the black man dead. A "nigger" did not stand a chance in the department, so his mother should not believe what she heard. Shepard believed that if all the facts were made public, such anti-black reactions would be changed or at least become more temperate. The reverse might have happened, and Grant had no intention of gambling on what direction reactions might take. He understood that what happened at Milliken's Bend was a logical outgrowth of the racism that plagued his army. He could not afford to get bogged down with the issue. The siege came first; that was the bottom line.[15]

On July 11, after the fall of Vicksburg, Grant had to take time to address the incidents in a letter to Thomas. Thomas mentioned in a June 26 message to Grant that he had meant to recommend Shepard as a brigadier general to command the 1st Mississippi black troops. Thomas had heard that Shepard "is in serious difficulty—will you inform me its nature, and whether it should prevent his advancement."[16]

Grant responded carefully. He told Thomas that he had ordered an "informal investigation" into the Shepard matter, resulting in the clearing of Shepard and allowing him to resume his duties. Whether Grant sent Thomas the entire transcript of the inquiry is not certain but unlikely. If he saw it, did he read it thoroughly or depend on a briefing by someone like Rawlins? Grant proceeded to reveal his anger: "I will send the proceedings to your office for your information. I am satisfied that the whole difficulty arose from the outrageous treatment of the Black troops by some of the white ones, and the failure of their officers to punish the perpetrators when they were reported. Becoming exasperated Col. Shepard took the punishment in his own hands." Grant did not mention the attacks on black females and children of all ages and other sordid details. Since he did not, it is possible that he either did not send the entire report to Thomas or perhaps hoped Thomas understood that such details should be kept under wraps.[17]

Thomas investigated the matter personally and found out more than Grant had revealed. On October 5, he wired Stanton, detailing Shepard's background in the black troops' organizational period. He personally thought Shepard had done a fine job, and he would have recommended Shepard for promotion already. But, while in Washington, Thomas had heard that Shepard had ordered the whipping of a white soldier by blacks, "which caused great indignation against him in the army here." Thomas reminded Stanton that he had brought the case personally to Stanton's attention, and a decision had been made not to promote Shepard to brigadier general. Since then, Thomas had returned to the Vicksburg area, where he found upon personally looking into the matter that Shepard met the challenge of commanding black troops in proximity to white soldiers and had "acted with great judgment and forbearance, when the white soldiers committed acts of wantonness against the negroes and their families."

Thomas had not shared the white soldiers' atrocities in detail, but if he had not read them in the report, he, certainly, had heard about them on his fact-finding mission. Shepard's complaints being consistently ignored by his commanding officer, Shepard had acted in "the flagrant case . . . one calling for the severest punishment, even to the loss of life, he had the culprit tied up to a tree to be flogged." The result had been minor punishment, and Shepard stopped it after a short time. A Court of Inquiry had, indeed, found Shepard not guilty of wrongdoing, and Grant had considered the case closed without comment and restored Shepard to command. Thomas went on to cite how highly other officers in the area thought of Shepard and recommended his promotion to date from June 7, date of the battle at Milliken's Bend. Grant endorsed the recommendation, and Shepard received the appointment on paper, but his promotion was to date from October 27. The U.S. Senate, perhaps under political pressure from a bigoted military establishment, never acted, and the time allotted for approval of the appointment expired July 4, 1864. Thomas had done much to restore Shepard's reputation, but in the end, Shepard was denied a promotion he deserved.[18]

While Grant certainly, and correctly, placed taking Vicksburg as his top priority, he should have considered publishing the transcript at a later date, even after the war. Thomas had learned much from his investigation, but he had to learn from interviews with those willing to talk about the episode. However, given the reaction of military people in Washington as Thomas noted, allowing the Northern public to hear the full story possibly could have created a political disaster. If Grant had not tried to suppress the transcribed story, the Lincoln administration almost certainly would have. The testimony given during the hearing demonstrates the atmosphere of violence and criminal acts that permeated the actions of many white soldiers at Milliken's Bend.

One witness, a government commissioner assigned to observe the treatment of blacks, elaborated on the seemingly never-ending conflict between black and while soldiers. "The blacks are continually attacked," he noted, but he said in spite of these circumstances, black soldiers had, as far as he knew, acted subordinate to whites.[19]

The commissioner spoke further about the large numbers of black women and men who had complained to him about violence, especially against the women and their daughters. He stated, "It is my opinion that the black regiments can not be efficient while associated with whites under the same command." The blacks had no security. Another commissioner said that on one occasion, he begged authorities for a guard to go up that night to protect the women, and they declined. One officer claimed Sullivan had told commanders that they should only guard plantations, where many blacks had to work. But the men must not interact with the freedmen, unless there was a particular case to be investigated by Sullivan. Even a reference to an order issued by Grant, General Order No. 27, which seemed to allow such actions under particular circumstances, brought no response.[20]

The president of the commissioners for leasing abandoned plantations testified, "I would state generally that outrages against the negroes by white soldiers appear to be little noticed or attended to when complaints are made to commanding officers, [so] that I do not pretend, except in very heinous instances, to report them. The planters generally inform me that they are treated with ridicule when their complaints are entered. I know of no case where grievances have been redressed."[21]

Complaints by black women that white soldiers were raping their daughters became commonplace, and the rapes often took place while mothers were forced to watch. No doubt many of the mothers also were victims of unbridled assaults. Attacks on black men also became common, and the attackers needed no provocation. A white officer of the 1st Mississippi Infantry of African Descent reported that when he ordered the arrest of five white soldiers for rape, they did not deny their actions: "*They are only niggers.*" The provost marshal released all five the next day. Murder was rare, but it happened, and whites who committed the acts were not punished.

As for Shepard, the O'Brien incident endangered him, for reactions by white soldiers were predictably harsh. He received many death threats, some very openly. There is no record that Grant made any effort to protect Shepard. The affair did seem to make white officers of the 10th Illinois cavalry more aware of the problem of controlling their men. They thwarted any mass attacks by their men on black camps, but incidents still occurred. One drunken soldier who brought terror to an entire family was said to have remarked, "You d——d niggers think you are free, and you are not as well off as you were with the Secesh!" The blacks who endured the unspeakable at Milliken's Bend must have shared that thought. Certainly, if this was a place of freedom, they found the price of that freedom was very high and disgracefully demeaning.[22]

Shepard did manage to break one barrier during the course of the inquiry. The fact that black men and women were allowed to testify signified a step forward in military—and American—jurisprudence. Whether he realized it or not, Shepard not only was acquitted but he also broke previously unplowed ground.

Grant allowing the case to be played out had backfired. Whatever particulars he knew, and he likely knew them all, he certainly had access to the commissioners' reports. It did not necessarily follow that he read them word for word. The stream of insidious news obviously did not reflect well on his district, the siege notwithstanding. He finally decided to do what ordinarily Thomas and official Washington would not be pleased to see. He wrote Dennis on June 11 that in managing his troops, Dennis should keep black and white soldiers apart as much as possible: "All the Black troops should be got as much to themselves as possible, and required to fortify. Milliken's Bend will be the proper place for them." Grant's resort to segregation foretold attempted solutions to racial issues far into the future. In another message to Dennis, written on the fifteenth, Grant reemphasized, "Negro troops should be kept aloof from White troops, especially in their camps, as much as possible." However, Grant cautioned Dennis that if Rebel activities required a concentration of Union forces, "bring them together without regard to color." Interestingly, for Grant, military action could erase color lines, and he would gamble on potential consequences. Whatever official Washington thought, military necessities must come first.[23]

On August 1, Grant issued a strongly worded message, General Orders No. 50: "Conduct disgraceful to the American name has been frequently reported to the Major General commanding, particularly on the part of portions of the cavalry. Hereafter, if the guilty parties can not be reached, the commanders of regiments and detachments will be held responsible; and those who prove themselves unequal to the task of preserving discipline in their commands will be promptly reported to the War Department for muster-out. Summary punishment will be inflicted upon all officers and soldiers apprehended in acts of violence or lawlessness." This was a clear reaction to Milliken's Bend, given Grant's mention of cavalry. Making such a statement was noble; enforcement continued to be a problem.[24]

In the midst of the Shepard case, Grant took a step to reassure Lincoln that steps had been taken to protect black civilians. On June 11, he sent Lincoln a report prepared by Chaplain John Eaton Jr., general superintendent of contrabands for the Department of the Tennessee, which was an overview "of what has been done for, and with, this class of people within my command to the present time."

> Finding that negroes were coming into our lines in great numbers, and receiving kind or abusive treatment according to the peculiar views of the troops they first came in contact with and not being able to give that personal attention to their care and use the matter demanded I determined to appoint a General Superintendent over the whole subject and give such Assistants as the duties assigned him might require. Mr. Eaton was selected for this position. I have given him such aid as was in my power by the publication from time to time of such orders as seemed to be required, and generally at the suggestion of the Supt. Mr. Eaton[']s labors in his undertaking have been unremitting and skillful and I fear in many instances very trying. That he has been of very great service to the blacks in having them provided for when otherwise they would have been neglected, and to the government in finding employment for the negro whereby he might earn what he was receiving, the accompanying report will show, and many hundreds of visiters and officers and soldiers near the different camps can bear witness to. I commend the report to your favorable notice and especially that portion of it which would suggest orders regulating the subject of providing for the government of the contraband subject which a Department commander is not competent to issue.

Eaton had, in fact, begun assisting Grant in dealing with freedman in the fall of 1862 in North Mississippi. Eaton later married Alice Shirley, daughter of James and Adeline Shirley, whose white house, the Shirley house, became a siege landmark.

Eaton's report demonstrated that Lincoln was quite pleased with Grant's handling of contraband problems and that, in fact, Lincoln was enthralled with Grant's successes that led to the siege. Grant, no doubt, felt pleased that he could turn such matters over to Eaton, who was well respected in Washington. Eaton's letter also indicates that Dana at some point claimed Grant had said he would not have captured Vicksburg without the Emancipation Proclamation. There is no evidence to support Dana's assertion, if he made it. President Lincoln did not necessarily be-lieve Dana had said any such thing since he suspected Grant would not have made "so strong a statement." In any event, the rumor could not and cannot be confirmed. Ironically, in a postsurrender letter to Grant, Lin-coln wrote that Dana understood Grant believed "that the emancipation proclamation has helped in your military operations—I am very glad if this is so." Lincoln most likely thought Grant might have made a milder comment. The Dana rumor faded away, and Dana in a conversation with Lincoln raised Grant's stature in the eyes of the president.

Grant expanded Eaton's duties. Near the end of the siege, he sent word to Lieutenant Colonel Samuel Nasmith, leading a foray up the Yazoo: "Bring away with you all negroes disposed to follow you, and teams of rebels to haul them, and their plunder[.]" Grant understood that taking slaves away from Confederate citizens continued to be a priority, despite the challenges of caring for the freedmen. The freedmen, after all, gave Grant options for increasing his manpower, whether they dug ditches or became soldiers.[25]

Problems did come up about how to deal with the freed black popula-tion. Grant's policy seemed to be that wherever black labor was needed, commanders did not need permission to send them there. If these men had families with them, the families could accompany the men but were given no special considerations.

At one point during the siege, Major General E. O. C. Ord received orders to send black troops in his corps (Ord had taken McClernand's place after Grant fired the latter) to the Chickasaw Bayou landing. Along with the troops, all women and children should also be sent there, and the men would "furnish such details for fatigue duty as may be required in the Commissary, Ordnance and Quartermaster's Department at that place." Their duties included the care and feeding of mules. This would also provide time for the black troops to be organized. The black civilians, obviously, were not intended to congregate solely at Chickasaw; they were also to work at Haynes's Bluff. Later, these people learned their camp was being broken up, and the "old men, women and children" would be moved to "the most valuable of the abandoned plantations within our lines, and put . . . to work cultivating the Crops growing on said plantations." This concept dated back to December 1862, when Grant ordered women and children to be excluded from the crowds of freedmen who followed his army. They would be placed in contraband camps.[26]

As for "able bodied" black males available during the siege, enlisted or not, they would work on the Haynes's Bluff defenses, and "when their services are no longer required for that purpose, those not enlisted will be put out to labor on the plantations, and those enlisted will be subject to such orders as their Commanding Officers may receive from Dept. Headquarters."

At Haynes's Bluff, Brigadier General Cadwallader Washburn complained about "a very large Negro Camp occupied mostly by women & children at Snider's Bluff & very near where I wish to encamp smiths Division. The presence of so many women must be very bad—can they not be removed to millikens Bend or some other point." Washburn, obviously, assumed that having women in a camp, whether black or white men were tempted, was a situation that should be avoided. Grant, no doubt, had the same concern in 1862. During the siege, he normally left such problems in the hands of Rawlins, who knew Grant's policies and acted accordingly.

Black persons newly arrived at Warrenton had to be sent to Young's Point. Some "2500 Negro women &children [had] arrived at Warrenton . . . from Grand Gulf," and the person responsible for their transportation had refused to take them to Young's Point since reports indicated the presence of Confederates there. A commander at Warrenton complained that these people had to go somewhere, for if they stayed, "they will soon eat us out of everything." So the herding of freedmen continued: "They cannot be kept at Warrenton." If it was not safe to get them directly to Young's Point, "let them go around by Chickasaw Bayou, travelling at night."[27]

The herding mentality of Grant's commanders, acting of course with parameters Grant set, must be viewed in the light of military necessities. Yet, the freedmen had to wonder if such treatment improved their situations. Black men yearning to fight for their freedom likely felt they would endure whatever they had to for the opportunity, even though their weapons were shovels. In the case of older men, women, and children, they could be forgiven if they viewed their plights as little better than slavery. Often quartered in squalor when they were not being moved around, many probably had better day-to-day living conditions when they were enslaved on plantations. They were free now, and they were willing to endure humiliation, rape, various diseases, and death to stay that way. Too many of Grant's men went out of their way to make that endurance barely possible.

For the "able-bodied" males, they learned to expect physical labor, which commanders ostensibly used to free up white soldiers to do other chores. Such was not always the case, for often black and white men worked side by side, depending on the urgency of digging trenches or other earthworks. After the surrender of Vicksburg, black manual labor was vital to destruction of Confederate defensive lines. Grant's view of the masses of freedmen as manual laborers filtered through the ranks.

Duties varied. In one case, a call went out for a "detail of Negroes" or white soldiers to drive teams of horses and mules pulling coal wagons to be loaded on naval vessels. Osterhaus requested more black men, about a hundred, from organized regiments of black troops to help dig. If they could be spared, "the men had to bring tools along."

During the siege, working parties of black men in forward positions made it possible for Union troops to get closer to Confederate defenses. Many of those doing the digging were in black regiments, and white commanders became irritated when these men were withdrawn from place to place. One officer complained that about eighty men in one regiment had been organized as workers, and that though they absorbed into the 3rd Mississippi black infantry, the understanding was that they would remain and continue their work. Giving an indication of how happy white soldiers were to sit by and watch the black men work, the commander commented, "It is a hard case to require the [white] soldiers to do heavy military duty and also heavy fatigue duty." Work often had to be periodically suspended due to such military duty.[28]

General McClernand asked that the 1st Mississippi Regiment [of] African Descent, stationed at Grand Gulf in the early stages of the siege, be transferred to Warrenton, the extreme left flank of McClernand's Corps. These one thousand men could be used at Warrenton to fortify the location, and they would have more opportunities to drill. However, the whole truth included McClernand's desire for manual labor to distribute supplies from the river inland to his entire corps.[29]

Blacks dug rifle pits continually along various sections of Grant's siege lines and Haynes's Bluff and Big Black River until the surrender. By law, the black laborers were supposed to be paid ten dollars a month, though how strictly this law was applied is open to question. Workers on the abandoned plantations were likewise due wages, but corruption in the white ranks surely made such payments rare. In fact, black men were often robbed of money or anything else that suited white troops. After the surrender, a white Union drill instructor entertained Rebels with his actions against black recruits. The man kept a big stick close at hand that he used to whack the black men on their rear ends. Each time this happened, he would look at the Confederates and wink, resulting in a loud Rebel yell. Many freedmen, filled with self-confidence after the Vicksburg surrender, happily volunteered for duty despite the bigotry they were bound to face. Having endured slavery, they were willing to risk becoming soldiers in the white man's army.

Compounding Grant's concerns about social problems, under the shadows of the Milliken's Bend affair, some white soldiers found black girlfriends, which likely did not please many of their comrades. It is probable that most of these instances were mere sexual liaisons. As one historian describes, "Few of the liaisons between white soldiers and African American women were long-standing nor did they represent a lasting commitment for white men. The majority planned to return North and marry a woman of their own class and race." In many cases, white soldiers considered black women, and at times local white women, prostitutes. Whatever their views, it is quite likely that when surviving Union soldiers who had had sexual contact with black women returned home, they kept their history secret.

Some Union soldiers were ostracized by their comrades. Sexually transmitted diseases had become a fact of life due to prostitutes who made themselves available to both armies, and Union soldiers feared the problem would worsen when black women became available because they would have agreed with Eaton, who detested white soldiers who sought out black women, for he feared black men would be angered and/or demoralized. Due to the widespread racial bigotry in the Union army, officers never encouraged their soldiers to go so far as to marry their black lovers, but legal unions of black men and women were emphasized. Whatever the cases of individuals' circumstances, racial bigotry remained alive and well among Union troops at Vicksburg, and the city's surrender, which led some white soldiers to flaunt their liaisons, did not mean Union troops as a whole were less racist.[30]

The underlying currents of racial issues must have disturbed Grant, both for the possible negatives impacts on morale and for the dismay back home if soldiers' activities with black men and women could not be kept secret. Yet, the general did not back off from promoting the use of freedmen as soldiers. Despite the trauma and abuse suffered by many black people in and around Vicksburg, positive military results did emerge in the Vicksburg area both during the siege and thereafter. The ill-trained black troops who fought bravely at Milliken's Bend represented a trend for additional organizations of freedmen troops. Many black units developed in the Vicksburg area after the surrender, and Grant promoted the transitions from slavery to freedmen to soldiers.

The 1st Mississippi Volunteer Infantry [of] African Descent, which had fought well at Milliken's Bend, had been organized in May during the siege there and at Vicksburg, commanded by Colonel Watson Webber. In March 1864, these troops became the 51st United States Colored Infantry. After Milliken's Bend, the 1st Mississippi served in the Military District of Vicksburg through 1864. They became part of the 1st brigade, 1st division, U.S. Colored Troops, remaining near Vicksburg until February 1865. Reassigned to the 2nd brigade, 1st division, of Frederick Steele's command in the Military District of West Mississippi, the men remained a part of that unit until after the war ended. Transferred to the Department of the Gulf, they served until June 1866 when they were mustered out of the army in Texas. These troops participated in the siege and capture of Fort Blakely in the Mobile, Alabama, area in early April 1865.

Other black units that emerged from Grant's Vicksburg district included the 1st Regiment Mississippi Colored Cavalry, organized in October 1863. In March 1864, the cavalry unit became the 3rd U.S. Colored Cavalry. It was part of several cavalry brigades and divisions in Mississippi and west Tennessee. It remained on duty in the Vicksburg area until the end of 1864. During that time, the unit participated in several expeditions on the Yazoo River as far up as Yazoo City. Other Mississippi operations following the surrender of Vicksburg include an expedition to the Pearl River, Deer Creek, Rodney and Fayette, Natchez to Woodville, Issaquena and Washington Counties, Steele's Bayou, Rolling Fork, and the Big Black Bridge (rebuilt after the surrender). The men participated in Benjamin Grierson's 1864–65 winter raid from Memphis to Vicksburg on the Mobile and Ohio Railroad and through north central Mississippi. They continued to serve in Mississippi until mustered out in January 1866.

The 1st Mississippi Heavy Artillery African Descent, originating in the Vicksburg District, became the 4th U.S. Colored Artillery in March 1864 and the 5th Regiment in April. Becoming attached to the 1st Division U.S. Colored Troops in the District of Vicksburg, it later was unattached to any other unit and served in the Department of Mississippi and the

Department of the Gulf until May 1864. The men who composed this unit participated in operations south of Vicksburg and to Yazoo City, but a large part of their time was spent performing garrison duty in Vicksburg through May 1866, when they were mustered out.

The 47th, 48th, 49th, 50th, 51st, 52nd, and 53rd regiments of U.S. Colored Infantry were all organized on March 11, 1864. The 47th through the 50th emanated from African Descent Louisiana Infantry Regiments 8, 10, 11, and 12. All began their service in the Vicksburg District and were mustered out in January 1866. All were attached to the U.S. Colored Troops, 1st or 2nd Brigades, in the Vicksburg District. The 47th served in the Military Division of West Mississippi and the Department of the Gulf and was assigned garrison duty and participated in varying campaigns in Mississippi, Arkansas, and Alabama. These men fought in the Fort Blakely campaign and performed garrison duty along coastal Alabama. They were mustered out in January 1866.

The 48th served in the District of West Florida and the Department of the Gulf. They participated in scouting actions in Mississippi, Louisiana, and Florida and in the siege and capture of Fort Blakely. The unit remained in coastal Alabama for several months and was then transferred to Texas.

The 49th spent most of its service time in the Vicksburg District and the Department of Mississippi, being mustered out in March 1866. All of its military action came in various scouting trips within the district and the department.

Regiment 50 served mostly in the Vicksburg area, the Military Division of West Mississippi, and the Department of the Gulf, where the men were mustered out in March 1866. Aside from Vicksburg garrison duty and occasional marches to areas north and south of the town, the 50th served in Florida briefly and participated in the Fort Blakely campaign. After the capture of Blakely, the regiment continued to be active in the gulf region.

The 51st, 52nd, 53rd, and 66th Colored Infantry Regiments came from the 1st, 2nd, 3rd, and 4th of the 1st Mississippi Infantry African Descent. The regiments were absorbed into either the 1st or 2nd Brigades of the 1st Division of U.S. Colored Troops. The 51st served in the Vicksburg District from March through December 1864 in Vicksburg, a few other Mississippi locations, Louisiana, and Florida before joining in the Fort Blakely campaign. After additional Alabama coastal duties, they were sent to Texas and mustered out in June 1866.

The 52nd served in the Vicksburg District and the Department of Mississippi. The regiment's activities were largely confined to post and garrison duty in Vicksburg until June 1865. Thereafter, its scope expanded to other points in Mississippi and the Department of the Gulf. The regiment mustered out in May 1866.

The 53rd regiment served in the Department of Arkansas, in addition to the Vicksburg District and the Department of Mississippi. The men did post and garrison duty in the Haynes's Bluff area and made expeditions to Saint Charles, Arkansas, and several points in Mississippi. The unit mustered out in March 1866.

Attached to the Vicksburg District, the Department of Mississippi, and to the 7th Corps in the Department of Arkansas, the 66th Regiment performed most of its duties in Louisiana, Arkansas, and Issaquena County, Mississippi. The regiment was in the Department of Mississippi through March 1866, when it was mustered out.[31]

Grant's efforts did much to make the formation of the above regiments possible, but it was little noted nor long remembered after the war. Grant and Thomas laid the foundation for the development of black units during the siege. On June 24, 1863, Grant sent word to Shepard that trying to organize black regiments seemed "inexpedient." Regiments ordered by Thomas had not yet been filled with the proper number of recruits and had not been mustered in. A key factor in organizing black regiments was the word *authorized*. The authorized regiments must reach sufficient manpower before any more regiments were organized. Shepard responded to Rawlins, "I entirely approve of Gen. Grant's decision . . . to put a stop to the *quasi* formation of African Regiments by unauthorized parties." Shepard listed all the regiments Thomas authorized and noted that any others were "forming without *proper* authority, and it seems to me the men *should be ordered* to units not yet filled." Recruiting officers should be ordered back to their companies. Some of these procedures had been followed, Shepard said, but not in all instances.

Once the authorized regiments had been filled, recruiters could commence their efforts to build more regiments. Some black men had shied away from joining certain regiments by "direct prejudice," and Shepard thought such practices were "all wrong. . . . No one of the *authorized* Regiments is yet full," and battle and disease casualties had compounded the problem. Thousands more troops would be needed to fill the Colored regiments as they "*ought to be filled.*" If troops could be sent for "*general distribution*," Shepard pledged to "see them equit[a]bly disposed. . . . I regret to trouble you, but am very anxious to get these troops ."[32]

Clearly, Grant and his staff worked to establish organizational policies that worked properly in putting together black regiments. Grant understood these soldiers would free up white troops to be sent elsewhere once the siege ended and Vicksburg was in Union hands. Treatment of black persons during the siege had at times been inexcusably horrible, but Grant, focused on forcing Vicksburg to surrender and on keeping Johnston at bay, simply did not have time to concentrate on abuses of freed slaves. He also had very limited means to battle the innate racism in most of his army. When he turned to Eaton and employed segregation as a strategic necessity, situations began to improve. Grant's record in dealing with racial matters during the siege was not stellar; after the surrender, he made a determined effort to put black men in Vicksburg to work on converting Confederate earthworks to Union defensive positions. Yet, all circumstances considered, he did much to temper the tempest of racism. Whether he could have done more is both doubtful and debatable.

Aside from race-related issues, Grant had one problem that had loomed over him for many months. It did not involve the morality of racism, but it was much closer to home. He was finally able to solve it, and he was, no doubt, delighted with the solution. He had long hesitated to take any kind of action against McClernand, but when McClernand handed Grant a gift-wrapped way to fire the Illinois politician, Grant acted quickly.

Congressman and Coterie

The backgrounds and personalities of Ulysses S. Grant and John A. McClernand guaranteed personal conflict. Both had undeniable allegiance to the Union, yet their demeanors and approaches to the conduct of war could not have been more different. Grant, the West Pointer, embraced the club of West Point graduates, most of whom considered themselves superior to civilian officers necessitated by civil war. Grant the quiet, unassuming officer usually had a thick skin when interacting with fellow military professionals. He had considerably thinner skin when faced with civilian officers, especially those who sounded their own trumpets.

McClernand blared his personal horn often. Having a legal and political background, the Illinois Democrat had been welcomed by Republican President Abraham Lincoln into the pro-Union fold. When he volunteered to join the army, his connections made him a likely candidate for high officer rank. So when he and Grant both received brigadier general designations in the summer of 1861, the development was no surprise. McClernand was not the only inexperienced man to receive the rank early in the war, so West Pointers had to swallow their pride.

Some civilian generals turned out well; Grant would have one named John Logan serve under him. Logan, another Illinois politician, participated with distinction in several campaigns, including Vicksburg. Logan, however, did not have a McClernand-like personality. Frank Blair also had a strong political background, but the Missourian made a good soldier, without fanfare.

McClernand was bombastic, arrogant, a constant seeker of glory, profane, and, in general, had a personality that made it difficult for other officers to be around him or, more to the point, to serve with him. Yet, his combat record proved him a capable field officer, though Grant, William Tecumseh Sherman, James B. McPherson, and others in the Vicksburg campaign would never say so. McClernand's annoying persona so clouded their judgment that they could not find anything worthwhile in the man they grew to hate. Unfortunately, most historians through the ensuing decades agree and do so without checking the record. Is it correct to say that in the multilayered case of Grant and McClernand that Grant was right and McClernand was wrong? Evidence indicates complexities that cannot be explained with a black/white answer.

In their first battle of note, the two began their Civil War experiences at Belmont, Missouri, in late 1861. The conflict settled nothing except to make the Confederates across the Mississippi River abandon Kentucky. Grant, in command of all Union forces in Missouri, did compel a Confederate retreat, but he had to order a withdrawal himself. Yet, the fight received acclamation in the North, and McClernand, who had name recognition due to his political career, received most of the praise. Grant's top aide, John Rawlins, became infuriated and demonstrated his considerable cursing abilities: "God damn it, it's insubordination! McClernand says—McClernand did—After his great victory McClernand—The bastard! The damned, slinking, Judas bastard!"[1]

McClernand did receive much praise in Illinois newspapers, and he also received a letter of congratulations from President Lincoln. Did he give himself great credit for the performance of his troops and himself at Belmont? Indeed, he did, and he would continue to promote himself and his men. Not all the press praised him; clearly, Rawlins had overreacted, but the story goes that Grant did not. Grant had an ego but did not seem to care about credit, and he certainly didn't have the hunger and natural affinity for a celebrated reputation via the news media. McClernand, with his political background, was totally the opposite, as could be expected. The seeds of conflict between the two had obviously been planted; Rawlins's outburst makes that clear. Grant may have been quieter than Rawlins, and he may have been embarrassed by his aide's profane language, but he doubtless felt resentment. He actually praised McClernand's soldierly abilities, but he could not have been pleased with the latter's self-promotion.[2]

Grant's victory at Forts Henry and Donelson, a campaign that lasted from February 6–16, 1862, led him to great fame, as he earned the sobriquet

"Unconditional Surrender" Grant upon the occasion of the surrender of Fort Donelson. He would be rewarded with a promotion to major general of volunteers. McClernand would not fade into the background, however. He wrote a laudatory message to his men, and he must have smiled when others criticized Grant for not being on hand when the Confederate attack came. In his report, McClernand claimed Grant had approved a general Union attack all along the battle line. Grant denied it, and in comments accompanying a copy of McClernand's report sent to Henry Halleck, Grant wrote that McClernand's words were very biased as to Grant's command's performance, and he again denied he had ever ordered a general attack.

McClernand's report also lauded Grant as a "respected" leader of an army that had won a great victory. He stated his belief "that no stain will be found, no word of reproach or disparagement coupled with the record which shall bear the history of this great event down the stream of time, but that it will endure as an imperishable example of duty bravely, manfully, and nobly performed." These were words McClernand would very likely feel compelled to write to a fellow politician, but Grant was not a politician, and he expressed no gratitude. Whatever McClernand had to say, to Grant McClernand was still a pushy, loud-mouthed officer who proudly wrote such men as Illinois Governor Richard Yates and President Lincoln of his exploits. Grant had to bear McClernand's promotion to major general. Though they were on similar career paths militarily, and McClernand had proven to be a quick study in military arts, the early months of the war had shown they could never be friendly colleagues. The friction between the two would never go away, for their views of what a commanding general should be would never be compatible.[3]

At Shiloh, Grant blundered greatly when he underestimated the aggressive nature of General Albert Sydney Johnston's army at Corinth. Absent from the start of the battle, Grant was fortunate his army held on during the first day of attack, April 6, 1862. Reinforced the next day, Grant won the victory but at a high cost in casualties, and he incurred the wrath of Northern public opinion and of Halleck, who came from Saint Louis to assume command of the army.

During the first day of fighting, Sherman and McClernand had jointly done much to steady the fragmented Union line. Each bragged on the other, and McClernand noted how much he appreciated having the more experienced Sherman close by. Many Union accounts from those in a position to know told of McClernand being in the thick of the battle that bloody day. Whatever other adjectives might be used against him, no one could call him a coward. Grant later included McClernand when he began instructing commanders to exercise more discipline over their troops during the aftermath of the April 7 victory. McClernand, as he was prone to do, told Grant that other portions of the army were acting worse than his. On April 14, McClernand's friend and political ally, Yates, came to the battlefield. Yates, accompanied by hospital personnel and supplies, did his best to make political hay of the visit. McClernand and Yates talked, and whether they talked of McClernand's ambitious plans is not known.[4]

McClernand wanted an independent command, and he had earlier written President Lincoln, prior to Shiloh, about the possibility. There can be little doubt McClernand wanted a solo spotlight he would not have to share. He was doing well in the army, but he missed being the politician singled out for applause. After Shiloh, McClernand sent Lincoln another letter bragging on the conduct of his soldiers during the Shiloh fight, and he added that he thought it was a mistake not to pursue the retreating Rebels on the second day of battle, a clear swipe at Grant. His statement in military terms was insubordination; he had openly criticized Grant, his commander, and such words would not win him friends either within the army or in Washington. At the time, Lincoln was having to deal with an eastern theater trouble-making general named George Brinton Mc-Clellan, and he did not need McClernand kicking up dust in the west.[5]

Eventually, both Grant and McClernand became very dissatisfied with their plights: McClernand found himself commanding the reserve corps of Halleck's army making its way slowly south to Corinth, and Grant was second in command to Halleck, but Grant had no command authority and, in effect, was shelved. Grant thought about leaving the army, but Sherman talked him out of it. McClernand wrote Halleck that he was tired of having an inferior position, and Halleck, predictably, assured Mc-Clernand that his role was important, and he currently commanded many more men that he would have otherwise. Halleck had handled Grant's complaints in the same manner, pointing out that Grant had more responsibility as second in command than commanding his old army. Both responses were so much hogwash, but Halleck would have his way, and the two generals at the moment could do nothing about it. McClernand decided to do what he automatically would do when rebuffed: He resumed making political contacts. For the present, both McClernand and Grant would have to endure the campaign through the Confederate evacuation of Corinth and conflicting orders surrounding their activities thereafter.[6]

In late June, McClernand again appealed to Lincoln for a command and specified the southern part of Arkansas, the western section of Louisiana, and anywhere in Texas or the Indian nations. Finally, McClernand got his wish to leave, when Halleck sent him and his division to the eastern theater to help shore up Union defenses after McClellan had evacuated Virginia and the campaign to take Richmond. Yet, the reprieve was short-lived for Lincoln and Secretary of War Stanton did not want western forces weakened. McClernand had the same mind-set as Halleck, who believed the Mississippi River valley was more significant than forty Richmonds. McClernand, thus, continued contacting political friends in Illinois and Washington.

Halleck was called to Washington to take over as commander of all Union armies, and McClernand clashed with Grant on a number of issues related to the district lines within Grant's department and who commanded what. During this period, McClernand managed to make another enemy, McPherson, a young general highly regarded by Grant, who did not like the abrasive manner of the politician masquerading as a soldier. McClernand continued pressuring Lincoln and Governor Yates. Yates contacted Stanton about McClernand voluntarily wishing to come back to Illinois to help with recruiting. Halleck gave McClernand permission to do so in early August. McClernand could now work toward his wish for independent command by recruiting and training his own troops. The stage was being set for a major confrontation between McClernand and Grant.[7]

McClernand did a good job in Illinois, while all the time pulling political strings to get his desired independent command. Meanwhile, Grant suffered through a postdepression mood resulting from his Shiloh experience. He performed poorly at the Battle of Iuka in September, though his army won the day. He was not on hand for the October 3–4 Battle of Corinth, but a portion of his army, commanded by William Rosecrans, forced battered Confederates to retreat. Grant ordered Rosecrans to call off his pursuit of Major General Earl Van Dorn's Rebel army. The post-Shiloh Grant was uncharacteristically shy; he did not want to take any chances that might hurt him in Washington. He eventually began planning an overland campaign to take Vicksburg. During the planning process, he learned that McClernand was bringing an army down the Mississippi to attack Vicksburg. The news made Grant furious. He eventually learned that McClernand would have more reason to be furious.

Lincoln, Stanton, and Halleck, in effect, threw McClernand under the steamboat. He had proven he could raise and train troops, and that was fine. They did not stand in his way. But the orders he received contained a notable caveat. When he had built up a force that Grant did not need, McClernand could then organize what was left to operate against Vicksburg. However, all forces raised would be under Grant's command. In effect, McClernand would not have the independent command he thought he had, and he would not realize that he had been duped for some time to come. Meanwhile, when Grant heard about the McClernand expedition, he fired off a message to Halleck: "Am I to understand that I lay still here while an Expedition is fitted out from Memphis or do you want me to push as far South as possible? Am I to have Sherman move subject to my order or is he & his forces reserved for some special service? Will not more forces be sent here?" Halleck replied: "You have command of all troops sent to your Dept, and have permission to fight the enemy when you please."[8]

This should have completely relieved Grant's concerns, but a general he did not like was bringing troops down the Mississippi. McClernand would be going downriver, believing he would lead his own campaign against Vicksburg, when, in fact, he would be back under Grant's command. Grant understood this, but before McClernand arrived, he wanted to take Vicksburg to avoid potential problems of once more dealing with the pushy politician. There is no evidence that McClernand had specifically tried to undermine Grant. McClernand wanted independence, and he wanted unshared glory; those were his main motives. Grant probably thought otherwise, but to him, it did not matter why McClernand was coming. Grant wanted to act quickly so that when McClernand arrived, there would be nothing for him to do. If Grant could take Vicksburg, the McClernand problem would be solved.

So Grant sent Sherman on an expedition downriver, while Grant pushed south overland into Mississippi. He intended to take Jackson, turn west, and operate jointly with Sherman, who was to attack Vicksburg after he landed his troops along the Yazoo River. Van Dorn destroyed Grant's part of the campaign when he led Rebel cavalry against Grant's supply line, and Sherman attacked the bluffs north of Vicksburg along Chickasaw Bayou and was thrown back with heavy losses. Ignored by Grant when McClelland arrived in Memphis, McClernand went on downriver and, being senior to Sherman, took over the army there. The separate army McClernand expected to have was not there, so he took Sherman's force and made it his own. He led a successful expedition up the Arkansas River, capturing Arkansas Post on January 11, 1863. Grant disapproved until he found out Sherman thought it was a good idea.

In early 1863, Grant went downriver to let McClernand know who the real boss was, and McClernand, finally understanding that he had been hoodwinked, fought the situation by arguing with Grant at every opportunity and giving Grant many reasons to send him back north. But Grant did not fire McClernand, perhaps because he realized in looking at his commanders that the man who so disgusted him would be useful. Grant would have three corps in the field (a fourth under Stephen Hurlbut remained in Memphis), one commanded by McClernand; McPherson and Sherman led the other two. McPherson was inexperienced as a battlefield commander, and Sherman had proven that he was not especially skillful when going on the offensive. McClernand was a fighter, and Grant, however despicable he found McClernand personally, knew that.

So the Vicksburg campaign continued, and when Grant finally made the decision to march his army south through Louisiana and cross the Mississippi below Vicksburg, McClernand's XIII Corps led the way. Charles Dana complained about McClernand bringing his new wife along and ordering an artillery salute to honor Yates. Such an act was vintage McClernand, and as for his wife, circumstances would dictate that she could not remain close to her husband much longer. Dana, no doubt influenced by Grant, Sherman, and McPherson, had a low opinion of McClernand. He did not think McClernand worthy of commanding a regiment, much less a corps: "McClernand was merely a smart man, quick, very active-minded, but his judgment was not solid, and he looked after himself a good deal." Dana's hedging is humorous, and his judgment of McClernand's military ability was not based on personal observation or personal knowledge. Dana wrote, "[H]e was not a military man; he was a politician." Dana was not a military man either but a journalist with political connections.[9]

McPherson could have been in the lead as Grant sent his army down the Louisiana side of the river, but Grant would not risk failure by having a rookie out front. Sherman stayed behind to conduct a diversionary move against the Yazoo River bluffs north of Vicksburg. Sherman feinted against the Yazoo bluffs before heading downriver.

Grant caught up with McClernand's corps on May 1 after it had crossed into Mississippi the previous day, in order to keep an eye on him some would argue, but it is more likely that he wanted to observe McPherson, whose XVII Corps followed McClernand's troops. In fact, Grant spent much more time with McPherson and Sherman during the inland campaign than with McClernand.

McClernand used his numbers well, including a portion of McPherson's corps, and overwhelmed Confederate defenders at Port Gibson on May 1, and then as Grant moved his army north, McClernand's corps marched on the left flank where John Pemberton's Confederates would be most likely to attack. On the right, McPherson eventually ran into and defeated a Confederate brigade at Raymond on May 12. Of note is McPherson's position, further from imminent danger than McClernand.

Sherman eventually arrived, and he and McPherson successfully attacked Jackson on May 14, a job made easy by Joseph E. Johnston's planned withdrawal. While the other two corps occupied Jackson, McClernand's corps acted as rear guard, watching for any sign of Pemberton, who had led three divisions east across Big Black River, leaving behind two in Vicksburg. Johnston wanted to unite with Pemberton, but the plan never worked out, and Grant, with the benefit of an intercepted Rebel message, led McPherson and McClernand west, leaving Sherman behind in Jackson to destroy Confederate supplies.

Major General Alvin P. Hovey's division of McClernand's corps made contact with Pemberton's army on the Jackson Road as the Battle of Champion Hill developed on May 16. This would be the decisive battle of the inland campaign prior to action at Vicksburg. McPherson's corps also collided with Pemberton's divisions, and while McPherson battled Confederates on the Union right, McClernand came up on the left and the center of the Union battle line. Grant warned McClernand not to move too quickly and, yet, later criticized his nemesis for not moving fast enough. Grant, establishing his headquarters with McPherson, made little effort to maintain effective contact with McClernand. Grant won the fight, and McClernand moved fast enough to force one of Pemberton's divisions, William Loring's, to take a roundabout route back to Jackson, where Loring eventually joined with Johnston. The next day, McClernand swept Confederate resistance away at Big Black River bridge and led his corps across the river. McPherson came forward in the center of Grant's line, while Sherman took the right flank when he arrived from Jackson. Grant moved his three corps forward, and buoyed by his successes, he ordered his first assault on Pemberton's four divisions at Vicksburg on May 19.

McClernand's corps advanced to the top of a ridge eight hundred yards from the main Confederate line, which also lay on a ridge. In between was a smaller ridge about half way between, and between the ridges, small creeks trickled through gullies. McClernand aligned most of his corps and sent them down the slope in their front, across the gully, and to the top of the middle ridge, all the time under heavy fire from the Confederates. They could go no farther. Within four hundred yards of the main Rebel line, the corps stopped and held the position. The rugged terrain and undergrowth had disorganized many of McClernand's brigades and regiments, and the chaos as much as Confederate fire forced the withdrawal to the east side of the middle ridge to restore order in the ranks.[10]

Sherman and McPherson also made some progress, and the best that could be said for Grant's army was that it was closer to enemy lines than it had been at the start of May 19. Going farther would be a much greater challenge. McClernand's casualties were relatively light, indicating the corps had done more maneuvering than fighting. Seven were killed and 93 wounded. Sherman's corps had suffered the most, losing 133 killed and 571 wounded, while McPherson's losses were similar to McClernand's, 16 killed and 113 wounded. McClernand has been criticized for not getting his advance any closer than two hundred yards to enemy lines, but the critique seems unfair, given his lack of familiarity with terrain. Was it McClernand's fault that Sherman lost so many men, and he did not? At Chickasaw Bayou, Sherman had shown bad judgment in ordering assaults; he did no better May 19. For McClernand to have gone any farther would have put his men directly in the line of fire of the main Confederate line. Despite being rebuffed, Grant made up his mind to try again, and the army attacked three days later on May 22. This attack resulted in a controversy involving McClernand that demonstrated what a key role the friction between him and Grant could play.[11]

McClernand used the intervening time to build up his artillery presence. Battery Maloney, where he would be headquartered during the May 22 assault, was in position about six hundred yards south of Railroad Redoubt, a Confederate stronghold built a few yards south of the Southern Railroad of Mississippi. Not too far away, Battery Keigwin contained some large Parrott rifled guns. The guns knocked some large holes in Railroad Redoubt. McClernand saw that north of the railroad, the 2nd Texas Lunette loomed, and he hoped to swing the right flank of his corps to get the Lunette and Railroad Redoubt. But he did not know what lay north of the Lunette, and he asked McPherson to help cover the flank. Yet, the left of McPherson's line was at least a thousand yards beyond McClernand's right, so there was little chance McPherson could provide cover.[12]

Aside from positioning artillery, McClernand spent the twentieth and twenty-first strengthening his lines. After losing his appeal to Grant for a massed assault, he stretched his line about a mile and a half, with the southern end fish-hooked to protect his dangling left flank. He sent cavalry to his far left to build campfires, and a few skirmishers fired at Rebel lines, all in hopes of convincing the enemy that his line extended farther than it did. He ordered sorties and tried to make the results sound impressive, though Grant thought that the action only positioned Mc-Clernand's lines to be more effective when the grand assault came.[13]

On May 20, another incident occurred that further strained the relationship between McClernand and Grant, and the fault lay totally with Grant. Without informing McClernand, he ordered one of the XIII Corps divisions to remain at the Big Black River bridge to watch for Johnston. McClernand, unaware of Grant's action, directed the division commander, Hovey, to come forward to join in the coming assault. Hovey had to assume that Grant and McClernand had communicated, but Hovey wisely covered his own rear end. He informed Grant of McClernand's order, and Grant reacted furiously, even though he had caused the misunderstanding. Grant's concern over a Johnston threat no doubt played a role in his reaction. Hovey rode on to McClernand's headquarters and explained the situation, and he told McClernand that, on his own, he had left two companies of infantry at the bridge, and he had sent scouts east of the Big Black, and no signs of Johnston's army could be found. Grant felt better and told McClernand to keep one of Hovey's brigades on hand at the front, but the other must return to the river. Army gossip blew the entire incident out of proportion, but most soldiers knew how much McClernand and Grant disliked each other, so they may have concluded that the uproar was intentionally ignited. The truth was that Grant had ignored protocol, whether intentionally or not, only he knew, but none of the blame could be assigned to McClernand.[14]

On May 22, McClernand's forty-five cannon opened fire on Confederate works. Assaults were led by General Eugene Carr against the Railroad Redoubt and the 2nd Texas Lunette. On the left, General Peter Osterhaus sent his troops against Square Fort (later designated Fort Garrott). McClernand could see the battlefield in front of his corps from his position at Battery Mahoney. His visibility was initially good, but the forthcoming smoke and dust of battle marred his ability to tell what was going on all along the line. Iowans breached Railroad Redoubt, and soon a Union battle flag waved in the breeze. A few men entered the Redoubt, but Confederate fire from entrenchments behind the earthworks made occupation impossible. Union brigades hit the 2nd Texas Lunette and portions of Brigadier General William Benton's brigade reached the lunette wall and in the ditch at the outside base of the wall, where a soldier in the 18th Indiana planted a flag pole flying the regiment's colors. Some of McClernand's generals had problems communicating, and he deferred solutions to Carr and Osterhaus, who better knew what was going on than McClernand could tell from his vantage point.[15]

Grant had been watching the entire battle line from a high point, and though he spotted a few Union flags along the line, he also saw troops falling back and concluded the attack had failed. He then received a message from McClernand, the first of three he would send, that the XIII Corps was heavily engaged and needed support on its flanks. McClernand suggested that McPherson could help by increasing the pressure on the right. Whether McClernand knew or did not know that McPherson's corps had done little all day is not known. Grant assumed that McClernand's message was nothing more than the politician's normal braggadocio, and he sent a return message telling McClernand to draw from his own reserves. McClernand only had one brigade not fighting, and that one would not help score a breakthrough. Would Grant have sent so sarcastic a message to McPherson or Sherman if either had sent him such news? The answer is obvious.[16]

Another message reached Grant, and in this one, McClernand stated that his troops had "part possession" of two forts (Railroad Redoubt and the Texas Lunette). This was not entirely true, since the lunette had not been breached. Did McClernand know this was the case? He had after all seen a flag flying at the lunette. The suggestion made later by Grant that McClernand at worst lied or at best misled him was disingenuous. McClernand only reported what he thought to be the case, as he should have. McClernand was excitable, and he was caught up in the fury of the battle, and perhaps he did see more than was there. But how was he to know, to be sure? He only reported what he believed to be the case, and Grant, as the army's commander, would have given McPherson or Sherman support without question. Grant let his hatred of McClernand blind him to his responsibility to support his commanders. He sent word back to McClernand that another division was on the far left and could help out, but that division was much too far away to provide assistance.[17]

To Sherman's credit, when Grant showed him the message, he immediately ordered a renewal of his thus-far failed attack. Sherman despised McClernand as much as Grant, once referring to McClernand as a "dirty dog," but Sherman put the battle first. Grant, doubtless motivated by Sherman's attitude, rode to tell McPherson to launch a diversionary assault as McClernand had suggested. En route, Grant was handed another missive from McClernand that stated his troops had reached Confederate entrenchments at a few points, but they could go no farther without help. He pointed out that the division on the far left at Warrenton could not possibly reach the battlefield in time. McClernand still had one brigade in reserve, but he can hardly be blamed for wanting some troops behind the line in case any part of the XIII Corps line stalled or was forced back. Grant, still convinced that McClernand was grossly exaggerating, told McPherson to send Isaac Quinby's division, which had done little more than observe the fierce fighting on McClernand's right, to help out.[18]

McClernand was delighted and responded that his men were inside two forts, which was still not true since the lunette still remained firm. Obviously, McClernand believed he was right. When Quinby's division began arriving at Battery Maloney, McClernand, noting the hour was growing late at about 4 P.M., decided he could get more men into the fight more quickly by splitting up Quinby's men and spreading them among his commanders. Most would be sent in to help at Railroad Redoubt and the lunette; one brigade was sent to Osterhaus. Some of Quinby's men spotted flags of the 77th Illinois and 22nd Iowa flying at the redoubt, and soon the flag of the 48th Ohio was posted. But all the fighting could not break the Confederate line, which also had been reinforced. Had McClernand shifted some of Osterhaus's troops to reinforce the redoubt and lunette attackers, would that have made a difference? Possibly, but McClernand would have been gambling that his left would not receive a Confederate countercharge; that was not likely, but McClernand must have felt that to shift Osterhaus would be a dangerous gamble. He could ill afford to put most of his corps into the two attacks without, in his mind, making sure the rest were not vulnerable.[19]

Grant blamed McClernand for the increase in casualties that resulted from the latter's continual calls for diversions and reinforcements. Yet, for such a charge to stick, Grant would have to prove that McClernand *intentionally* lied. He could prove no such thing, but he did not care. Grant used the failed assault of May 22 to lambast his old enemy. Dana fired off a letter to Stanton that Grant wanted to fire McClernand "on account of his false dispatch" but that Grant had changed his mind, concluding that it would better on the whole to leave McClernand in his present command until Vicksburg surrendered, "after which he will induce McClernand to ask for a leave of absence." It could be that Grant knew he could not prove McClernand had deliberately sent any "false" messages. Grant may well have realized that he would have had shaky grounds indeed for firing McClernand. Grant would bide his time. He had needed McClernand thus far, though he would have yelled loudly had anyone made such a suggestion. Now the assaults had failed, and the "regular siege" began. McClernand's days were numbered once it became obvious the siege would succeed. All Grant needed was a one slipup. McClernand would oblige.[20]

On May 24, Grant sent Halleck a review of May 22. The message included the following: "The loss on our side was not very heavy at first but receiving repeated dispatches from Gen. McClernand saying that he was hard pressed on his Right & Left and calling for reinforcements, I gave him all of McPherson's Corps but four Brigades [McClernand only received three brigades from Quinby] and caused Sherman to press the enemy on our right which caused us to double our losses for the day. The whole loss for the day will probably reach 1500 killed & wounded. Gen. McClernands dispatches misled me as to the real state of affairs and caused much of this loss. He is entirely unfit for the position of Corps Commander both on the march and on the battle field." He then added the complaint that the XIII Corps caused more headaches than the whole of his department.[21]

Aside from misstating the number of men he sent McClernand, Grant did not tell the story in its entirety. Instead of merely opening fire from his position, Sherman sent men on what amounted to a suicide mission, certainly going well beyond a diversion. Sherman had not done well directing his corps before he saw McClernand's message, and perhaps he felt he could make a better effort this time. In truth, Sherman's additional casualties were much more his own doing than the result of assisting McClernand. As for McPherson, aside from Quinby's losses, the XVII Corps did not suffer notable casualties from aiding McClernand. Grant exaggerated the inadequacies of the XIII Corps. McClernand had performed quite well during the campaign, leading the march down the Louisiana side of the river and more so making the difference at Port Gibson. Grant did not hang around watching after McClernand while he rode with Sherman during the fight at Jackson, and at Champion Hill, Grant chose to stay with McPherson. McClernand had not needed Grant's help when he swept away Confederates at the Big Black River bridge. During the siege, McClernand had done as well as anyone, and he never shared Grant's inflated concerns about Johnston. Whether misleading or not, McClernand's reports clearly showed that in his opinion, his men had accomplished more on May 22 than the other two corps.[22]

Unfortunately for him, his writing these words and others led to his downfall. On May 30, McClernand penned a long congratulatory letter to his corps, and it led to his being relived from command. McClernand's words and what happened to them gave Grant all the ammunition he needed to get rid of McClernand. About the May 22 attack, McClernand commented to his corps:

On the 22nd, in pursuance of the order from the commander of the department, you assaulted the enemy's defenses in front at 10 A.M., and within thirty minutes had made a lodgment and planted your colors upon two of his bastions. This partial success called into exercise the highest heroism, and was only gained by a bloody and protracted struggle; yet it was gained, and was the first and largest success achieved any where along the whole line of our army. For nearly eight hours, under a scorching sun and destructive fire, you firmly held your footing, and only withdrew when the enemy had largely massed their forces and concentrated their attack upon you. How and why the general assault failed, it would be useless now to explain. The Thirteenth Army Corps, acknowledging the good intentions of all, would scorn indulgence in weak regrets and idle criminations. According justice to all, it would only defend itself. If, while the enemy was massing to crush it, assistance was asked for by a diversion at other points, or by re-enforcement, it only asked what in one case Major-General Grant had specifically and peremptorily ordered, namely, simultaneous and persistent attack all along our lines until the enemy's outer works should be carried, and what, in the other, by massing a strong force in time upon a weakened point, would have probably insured success.

McClernand had a habit of issuing such documents, but he had gone too far and should have known how Grant, Sherman, and McPherson would react to such language. Perhaps he did know and did not care. He did not anticipate them finding out about it the way they did, loosening a severe backlash.[23]

McClernand suspected something was wrong when he wrote Grant on June 4. He noted "what appears to be a systematic effort to destroy my usefulness and character as a commander makes it proper that I should address you this note. It is reported, among other things, as I understand, that I attacked on the 22d ultimo without authority; again that I attacked too late; again, that I am responsible for your failure and losses; again, that I am arrested and being sent North; again, that my command is turned over to another officer, and, again, that you have personally assumed command of it." These tidings had originated via landings upriver. None of the gossip at that point in time was true, but some of it portended what would become true. McClernand denied the accusations item by item and concluded, "All these things being known to you, and these false reports being brought to your notice, it remains for you to determine whether truth, justice, and generosity do not call on you for such a declaration as will be conclusive in the matter." Though there is no way to verify the sources of the McClernand stories, they may well have emanated from Grants headquarters, especially from his staff. These may have grown out of Grant's intent, as stated by Dana, to get rid of McClernand after Vicksburg surrendered. The specifics had been seasoned by gossip.[24]

On the evening of June 16, Blair handed Sherman a copy of the Memphis *Evening Bulletin*, a newspaper that contained McClernand's congratulatory message in full. Sherman notified Rawlins. Sherman was plainspoken as usual:

> It gives me no pleasure or satisfaction to notice such a catalogue of nonsense—such an effusion of vain-glory and hypocrisy; nor can I believe General McClernand ever published such an order officially to his corps. I know too well that the brave and intelligent soldiers and officers who compose that corps will not be humbugged by such stuff. If the order be a genuine production and not a forgery, it is manifestly addressed not to an army, but to a constituency in Illinois, far distant from the scene of the events attempted to be described who might innocently be induced to think General McClernand the sagacious leader and bold hero he so complacently paints himself; but it is barely possible the order is a genuine one, and was actually read to the regiments of the Thirteenth Army Corps, in which case a copy must have been sent to your office for the information of the commanding general. I beg to call his attention to the requirements of General Orders, No. 151, of 1862, which actually forbids the publication of all official letters and reports, and requires the name of the writer to be laid before the President of the United States for dismissal.

Sherman admitted that the order was "not technically a letter or report," and though written like an order, it was not, since McClernand's words were not composed as an order.

Reading between the lines, Sherman concluded that McClernand had, in effect, said that McPherson and Sherman had not obeyed Grant's orders. Sherman said McPherson could speak for himself, but that he, Sherman, had sent his corps to attack at three different points at the time Grant's order was to be carried out. Sherman elaborated that McClernand could not know what was going on along the rest of the Union line, and, therefore, he could not make charges and assume anything about McPherson's and Sherman's corps. Sherman further stated that believing McClernand's reports to be true about breakthroughs, he had sent his men back into battle. He neglected to point out that McClernand could have believed everything he had written in his messages to be true. Sherman, in effect, accused McClernand of intentionally lying. This would come to be an oft-repeated refrain. McClernand should have, Sherman continued, "confined himself to facts in the reach of his own observation, and not gone out of the way to charge others for results which he seems not to comprehend."[25]

About the same time, McPherson was handed a copy of the *Missouri Democrat*, which had also published McClernand's "order." He responded directly to Grant. McPherson wrote heatedly, "The whole tenor of the order is so ungenerous, and the insinuations and the criminations against the other corps of your army are so manifestly at variance with the facts, that a sense of duty to my command, as well as the verbal protest of every one of my division and brigade commanders against allowing such an order to go forth to the public unanswered, require that I should call your attention to it." McPherson echoed Sherman; no doubt, the two discussed the issue beforehand: "I cannot help arriving at the conclusion that it was written more to influence public sentiment at the North and impress the public mind with the magnificent strategy, superior tactics, and brilliant deeds of the major-general commanding the Thirteenth Army Corps than to congratulate his troops upon their well-merited successes. There is a vain-gloriousness about the order, an ingenious attempt to write himself down the hero, the master-mind, giving life and direction to military operations in this quarter, inconsistent with the high-toned principles of the soldier. . . . Though born a warrior, as he himself stated, he has evidently forgotten one of the most essential qualities, viz, that elevated, refined sense of honor, which, while guarding his own rights with zealous care, at all times renders justice to others." McPherson refused to take any blame for what happened in McClernand's sector and insisted the assault of the twenty-second had not failed due to any lack of cooperation on the part of his troops but due to the strong works of the enemy.[26]

Grant wasted no time in making the most of this opportunity. On June 17, he sent a brief message to McClernand: "Inclosed I send you what purports to be your congratulatory address to the Thirteenth Army Corps. I would respectfully ask if it is a true copy. If it is not a correct copy, furnish me one by bearer, as required both by regulations and existing orders of the Department." McClernand, aware of what was in the wind, sent a June 18 message to Grant: "The newspaper slip is a correct copy of my congratulatory order, No. 72. I am prepared to maintain its statements. I regret that my adjutant did not send you a copy promptly, as he ought, and I thought he had." McClernand's blaming his adjutant was petty; he should have taken the responsibility, which was rightfully his. Assuming the dates are correct, Grant already knew that McClernand's words were a "true copy." Obviously, he wanted to create a paper trail without thought to chronology.[27]

On June 18, McClernand received a copy of General Orders No. 164, signed by Rawlins and delivered by James Wilson. The contents were brief and to the point: "Maj. Gen. John A. McClernand is hereby relieved from the command of the Thirteenth Army Corps. He will proceed to any point he may select in the State of Illinois, and report by letter to Headquarters of the Army for orders. Maj. Gen. E. O. C. Ord is hereby appointed to the command of the Thirteenth Army Corps, subject to the approval of the President, and will immediately assume charge of the same."[28]

There is no doubt that Wilson relished the opportunity to take the message to McClernand with whom he had a mutual dislike, though Wilson's father had had a good relationship with McClernand. Wilson did not feel the same way, especially during the campaign and siege. Perhaps being around McClernand more than he had ever been before exposed him to a man who had qualities that aggravated him. McClernand did have the ability to offend people, without intent in many cases and without realizing it.

Wilson related in his memoirs about delivering a message to McClernand during the siege; a message from Grant directing McClernand to send more troops to watch the Big Black line of defense at Hall's Ferry, a few miles east of the XIII Corps's position. McClernand exploded in anger, according to Wilson, exclaiming: "I'll be God damned if I'll do it—I am tired of being dictated to—I won't stand it any longer, and you can go back and tell General Grant!" Wilson was astonished and warned McClernand of the sort of trouble he would bring upon himself for disobeying an order, and he would put Wilson in a bad spot if he had to go back and say such a thing to Grant. Wilson then wrote, in which he implicated himself as being insubordinate, that though McClernand outranked him, he told the general, "I will pull you off that horse and beat the boots off of you," rather than be personally insulted. It all sounded very grandiose and pompous, and since Wilson's is the only account of the incident, the validity of it is questionable. He went on to say that McClernand claimed not to be cursing Wilson, that he was a friend to Wilson and his father. McClernand then said, according to Wilson, "I was simply expressing my intense vehemence on the subject matter, sir, and I beg your pardon." Wilson could not wait to get back and report to Grant, who supposedly smiled and said he would use the same expression from then on when he chewed out someone. Wilson also told Grant and Rawlins that he had tired of trying to keep peace, as if that were part of his job description, and he quoted Grant as remarking that he would get rid of McClernand at "the first opportunity."[29]

With this story as background, what happened when Wilson handed the Grant message informing McClernand he had been relieved was predictable. Wilson gave McClernand the message and said that he, Wilson, was to be sure the general read and understood it. After McClernand read the words, he paused, looked at Wilson and commented that he was relieved, then added that they "both were relieved." McClernand well knew that Wilson had enjoyed delivering the message. One can only imagine the looks on both faces as their eyes met.[30]

McClernand responded the same day directly to Grant: "Your order relieving me and assigning Ord to the command of the Thirteenth Army Corps, is received. Having been appointed by the President to the command of that corps, under a definite act of Congress, I might justly challenge your authority in the premises, but forbear to do so at present. I am quite willing that my statement of fact in my congratulatory [order] to the Thirteenth Army Corps, to which you think just exception may be taken, should be made the subject of the investigation, not doubting the result." Obviously, McClernand still did not understand that he had never been the special case he thought himself to be, and he did not know that Grant had been given permission to fire anyone in his department when he thought it necessary.[31]

Dana wrote Stanton that though the issue apparently was McClernand's published comments, the real cause of McClernand's firing "is his repeated disobedience of important orders, his general insubordinate disposition, and his palpable incompetence for the duties of the position." Dana went on to say that if Grant, knowing how Sherman and McPherson felt about McClernand, should be killed or incapacitated, McClernand would assume command by seniority, and the only way to be sure this did not happen was to get rid of McClernand. Dana's words demonstrated that McClernand's order was as much an excuse than a reason for his firing.[32]

Grant continued to make his case against McClernand after the dismissal. He wrote the adjutant general of the army that McClernand's campaign report (not the congratulatory order) "contains so many inaccuracies that to correct it, to make it a fair report to be handed down as historical, would require the rewriting of most of it. It is pretentious and egotistical, as is sufficiently shown by my own and all other reports accompanying." He further wrote that the men of the XIII Corps were generally satisfied seeing McClernand gone. However, there is little evidence to support that assertion. In fact, one soldier in the XIII Corps later wrote that the men were furious when Grant relieved McClernand, and they did not have any confidence in nor respect for Ord. They never regarded him as a true corps commander. One man's opinion is not a majority, but the soldier said what no doubt many men in the corps knew, that Grant and the other corps commanders did not like McClernand, an indication that the men believed personal feelings trumped justice.[33]

Grant wired Halleck the news and added, "I should have relieved him long since for general unfitness for his position." Why had he not, for as Grant pointed out, he had had cause, but he could never bring himself to say the probable reason for keeping McClernand around, that he needed him.

Reading between the lines of a message to Lorenzo Thomas, Grant comes as close as he ever would to admitting as much: "A disposition and earnest desire on my part to do the most I could with the means at my command, without interference with the assignments to command which the President alone was authorized to make, made me tolerate Gen. McClernand long after I thought the good of the service demanded his removal. It was only when the entire Army under my command seemed to demand it, that he was relieved," an exaggerated conclusion to be sure. Whatever attitudes existed, the main point was that Grant in effect said he put off getting rid of McClernand because it would have been difficult to get rid of him earlier. That was not true; he had ample opportunities. That he did not take them says as much, if not more, than what he wrote.[34]

McClernand, of course did not go quietly. He sent a brief message to Lincoln on June 23: "I have been relieved for an omission of my adjutant. Hear me." Lincoln would hear from McClernand at length, but the president was not interested in all the details and refused to convene a court of inquiry. To do so would disrupt operations in the field, but, wrote Edwin Stanton on Lincoln's behalf, "if, hereafter it can be done without prejudice to the service, he will, in view of your anxiety upon the subject, order a court." Lincoln had already received a letter from Yates that noted that McClernand had arrived in Springfield and had been "received by the people here with the greatest demonstrations of respect, all regretting that he is not now in the field." Yates proposed, rather obtusely, that McClernand, with some western troops, be "put in command of Pennsylvania," as such a move "would inspire great hope and confidence in the North west, and perhaps throughout the country." As absurd as Yates's message was, it reminded Lincoln that he must not completely slam the door on McClernand, who still had political connections.[35]

On June 27, McClernand wrote Halleck from Springfield that, pursuant to Grant's orders, he was reporting for further instructions. He noted that Grant had been ignoring his written protests, and he outlined briefly all his corps's accomplishments. "I ask," he said, "in justice, that I may be restored to my command at least until Vicksburg shall have fallen. Only two days before my banishment from the Department of the Tennessee, General Grant had increased my command by the positive addition of one division and by the contingent addition of two others, making it larger that the Fifteenth and Seventeenth Army Corps combined, and therefore cannot consistently object upon the score of distrust of my fidelity or ability." McClernand made a salient point, lost in the furor over his firing.[36]

The McClernand-Grant feud thus came to an end, though the ramifications continued due to McClernand's determination to write his own version of all that happened and due to the later rebuttals and attacks by Grant and his friends. McClernand had truly been outnumbered. Grant, Sherman, McPherson, and Wilson were all West Pointers. So was Ord, and now command meetings at Grant's headquarters would be much more congenial. It is doubtful McClernand had been regularly invited to such conferences. Beyond the West Pointers, Rawlins, Dana, and David Porter strongly disliked McClernand. Thus, he had an impressive coterie aligned against him. Yet, he had not reached out to any of them; in fact, his arrogant persona—and his determination to throw his perceived weight around—had pushed away those who might have been potential friends. His determination to find glory on the battlefield overshadowed his considerable abilities as a combat leader and prejudiced his enemies, who refused to see his soldierly qualities. They focused on his political aura to the point they could not perceive anything else about him. His actions fed that image.

Both McClernand and Grant, when it came to their personal relationship, consistently resorted to hyperbole, neither willing to overlook their personal opinions for the good of the army. Grant ultimately won the clash of personalities, but neither he nor McClernand exhibited gentlemanly qualities, the positive traits of character that put the job at hand above personal feelings. Their story is far too typical of how internal army politics can divert attention from tasks at hand.

Up until he got rid of McClernand, and afterward, Grant never took his mind off siege operations. He could not afford to become too preoccupied with issues other than keeping pressure on the Rebels and taking Vicksburg. His tactical moves were creative and flexible. He never felt comfortable maintaining the status quo; Grant felt that the siege must be active to achieve the final results of surrender. He did not allow the McClernand episode to keep him from acting accordingly.

Major General Ulysses S. Grant, ca. 1863. Ulysses S. Grant Presidential Library, Mississippi State University.

Location of Grant's headquarters along the high ground around the trees. An equestrian statue of Grant is at the left of the photograph. Vicksburg National Military Park.

Major General John A. McClernand, an Illinois politician who was fired in June 1863 from his command of the XIII Corps. National Archives and Records Administration.

Major General E. O. C. Ord, who took John A. McClernand's place after Grant fired the latter. Library of Congress.

Major General James B. McPherson, who commanded the XVII Corps during the campaign. National Archives and Records Administration.

Major General William Tecumseh Sherman, who directed the XV Corps during the campaign. National Archives and Records Administration.

Brigadier General Peter Osterhaus, a German-born division commander. Library of Congress.

Rear Admiral David Dixon Porter, who commanded the Union fleet on the Mississippi River. Library of Congress.

Charles Dana, ca. 1864, War Department envoy, who accompanied Grant during a mission up the Yazoo River toward Satartia. U. S. Grant Presidential Collection, Mississippi State University.

Lieutenant Colonel James H. Wilson, one of Grant's aides. Library of Congress.

Sylvanus Cadwallader, a newspaper reporter whose tall tale about Grant's drinking was published in his memoirs in 1955 and accepted by historians for decades. *San Diego (CA) Union*, September 28, 1908.

John Rawlins, Grant's top aide, who was known to keep a tight rein on Grant's alcohol consumption. Library of Congress.

Major General Henry Wager Halleck, commander of all the Union armies. Library of Congress.

President Abraham Lincoln. Vicksburg National Military Park.

Secretary of War Edwin McMasters Stanton.
Library of Congress.

Colonel Isaac F. Shepard, 3rd Missouri Regiment, who sought justice for black soldiers at Milliken's Bend.
Wilson's Creek National Battlefield.

Confederate General Joseph E.
Johnston. Vicksburg National
Military Park.

Confederate Lieutenant General
John C. Pemberton. Library of Congress.

Ulysses S. Grant, ca. 1864. Ulysses S. Grant Presidential Library, Mississippi State University.

Third Louisiana Redan, along the ridge in background facing east toward Union lines.
Vicksburg National Military Park,

Stockade Redan, facing northeast. Vicksburg National Military Park.

Railroad Redoubt, facing east toward the Union XIII Corps. Vicksburg National Military Park.

Vicksburg at time of surrender, 1863. Sketch by F. B. Schell, pen and ink.
Frank Leslie's Illustrated Civil War, fac. ed. (Jackson: University Press of Mississippi, 1992), 199.

～6～

Closely Hemmed In

On June 8, Grant updated Halleck on siege operations: "Vicksburg is closely invested. I have a spare force of about thirty thousand (30,000) with which to repel anything from the rear. This includes all I have ordered from west Tennessee. Johnston is concentrating a force at Canton, and now has a portion of it west of Black River. My troops have been north as far as Sartartia, and on the ridge back to that point there is no force yet. I will make a waste of all the Country I can between the two Rivers [Big Black and Yazoo]. I am fortifying Haines' Bluff, and will defend the line from here to that point at all hazards."[1]

Grant had issued orders on May 28, telling all his corps generals as well as commanders in charge of detached troops along the Union lines and eastward to picket every road in their rear that provided entrances and exits to Vicksburg. Pickets must "prohibit all persons coming into or going out of our lines without special authority," which usually meant from corps commanders. R. M. Sawyer, assistant adjutant general, distributed General Order No. 44 under Sherman's name on June 9 to underscore Grant's determination to seal Vicksburg. Smugglers, who were Joe Johnston's couriers, would from time to time get small-arms supplies to Pemberton, but many of them were captured. Order 44 states, "To prevent communication between the enemy, now closely invested in Vicksburg, and their friends and adherents without, the following rules must be observed on the north front: A continuous chain of sentinels must extend from the Mississippi River to the main Jackson road." The order elaborated on particulars, but the gist of it was clear: Johnston's infiltration efforts must be stopped. This was not good news for citizens who had rushed into Vicksburg from outlying areas nor for the city residents who had remained despite the threat posed by Grant's inland campaign. They would have trouble getting out now, though some would be given permission to leave. The closer Grant got to victory, however, the less inclined he was to provide passes for citizens. Grant, surely, heard about cave dwellers who sought refuge from artillery and about the damage to homes in town by Union guns and artillery. The remaining residents had made their choice, however, and he intended to capture Vicksburg, no matter the hardships.[2]

Grant's earlier optimism in a May 24 report to Halleck that he did not see how the Confederates could raise the siege had begun deteriorating within days after he wrote it. Ever since, Johnston continued to weigh heavily on Grant's mind, despite the absence of any real threats from the Confederate general. Most reports about Johnston's activities had either been exaggerated or out of context. Johnston's cavalry roamed about, but he certainly would need much more than cavalry to pose a major problem for Grant. Halleck promised him additional reinforcements to handle threats from the Mechanicsburg Corridor. Though the perceived problems Johnston could cause cast a shadow over Grant's thinking, he knew he had to be aware of the remainder of challenges he faced in keeping Pemberton boxed in. He looked to Louisiana across the Mississippi.[3]

Elias Dennis commanded the District of North Eastern Louisiana, the area across from Vicksburg that most concerned Grant. The fight at Milliken's Bend had happened there, and Grant knew he must secure the region. There seemed little chance that Confederates in Louisiana could break the siege, but they could harass Union vessels and clog logistical support. They must be dealt with. Grant sent Joseph Mower's brigade to Dennis, though Grant made clear that Mower would only remain temporarily to help Dennis drive the Confederates far enough way to eliminate threats. If Dennis needed more, Grant promised they would "be promptly sent." He wanted the Rebels pushed beyond the Tensas River and Monroe: "Every vestige of an enemy's camp ought to be shoved back of that point." Dennis must protect supplies but not at the expense of his men. Grant did not order, "not being on the ground myself," Dennis to make certain dispositions, but he suggesting fortifying Milliken's Bend and Lake Providence.[4]

The southern flank of his siege line continued to concern Grant. He still could not afford to assume the Confederates would not try to break through, but as the siege progressed, certainly, Pemberton continued to show no intention of making such a move. Yet, from a tactical point of view, Grant could see Johnston attacking from the northeast, allowing Pemberton to have better chance of escaping. So Grant resolved to close any gaps between McClernand's left and the Mississippi.

He ordered Jacob Lauman, whose division was on the left or south by southwest of McClernand's line, to shift his left brigade, making sure at least one regiment was on the left of Hall's Ferry road, the road that entered Vicksburg from the southeast. Grant warned Lauman that by stretching his front, he left his men vulnerable to being attacked "in detail." The arrival of Lauman's other two brigades could extend farther left, without losing the compactness of the southern flank, at least in Lauman's area.[5]

Grant maintained close contact with David Porter, telling the naval commander to be ready at all times to provide transports, with escorts, to bring the influx of troops from Memphis to Vicksburg. Halleck kept his word; Grant received news that nineteen thousand additional men would soon be on their way downriver. He reminded Porter to do everything possible to protect the troops from Confederate sharpshooters hidden along the banks of the Mississippi. Grant intended to place all the initial wave of reinforcements in positions to protect Haynes's Bluff. Porter determined to keep things moving, and he asked Grant to ensure his corps commanders, especially McClernand (later Ord), took care of the large guns being delivered to their lines. Some of the guns sitting on the shores of the Mississippi weighed so much they were causing cave-ins while waiting to be towed inland to siege-line positions.

Porter had problems maintaining coal supplies for all this fleet. He needed wagons and teams of mules or horses to haul coal onto transports to get it across to the Louisiana side of the river. David Farragut, well downriver in the New Orleans area also wanted coal, and Porter did not have time or the means to supply the ward of his father. (Porter's father had taken Farragut under his wing after Farragut's father died.) Grant responded by issuing orders that all teams and wagons at Young's Point should be turned over to Porter. Porter assured Grant that everything possible was being done to keep the transports close together during the downstream trip. This strategy should speed things up and allow Porter's gunboats to offer more effective firepower against enemy guerrillas. Transports getting scattered upriver caused some delays. Grant understandably grew impatient, knowing the troops he needed were so close, and, yet, time seemed to drag by before they arrived.[6]

On June 11, Grant confirmed to Halleck that long-awaited reinforcements had begun to set foot on Chickasaw Bayou landing. Grant knew these men might have to go into action as soon as they landed. Some Johnston troops had occupied Yazoo City and Canton, and a division of Rebel cavalry roamed in the Mechanicsburg Corridor. Grant counted thirteen thousand additional men that he would have to maintain the Haynes's Bluff defenses, and he could pull an equal number from his siege line should they be required. He notified Halleck that news from Louisiana indicated Rebel Lieutenant General Kirby Smith was moving either to attack Nathaniel Banks at Port Hudson or to attack Vicksburg. Potential enemy threats in northeast Louisiana continued to weigh on Grant's mind.[7]

Halleck was impatient, too. He urged Grant to "fully appreciate the importance of *time* in the reduction of Vicksburg. The large reinforcements sent to you have opened Missouri & Kentucky to rebel raids. The siege should be pushed night & day with all possible despatch."[8]

Grant responded that he had "reliable information from the entire interior of the South." Troops reinforcing Johnston were reportedly on the way in large numbers, and if that proved to be the case, Grant certainly could not control what the enemy was doing. That left him in no position to force the surrender of Vicksburg. He hesitated to dilute the troop strength he had. Beyond that reality, reliable information from within his own district was hard to come by, much less the entirety of the Confederacy. Grant wrote about reports of thousands of troops being sent to reinforce Johnston, including Confederate troops who had been ordered to evacuate Port Hudson. Grant's calculations gave Johnston the potential of thirty thousand men in the short run and thirty-two thousand more west of the Mississippi that could possibly make their way to Johnston. Grant knew large numbers of Rebels could not cross the river west to east with Porter's gunboats controlling the river, but he intended to make Halleck understand that serious threats existed. How much of the news was true did not matter; Grant meant to keep the pressure on for more reinforcements.

In reality, Johnston likely never had more than thirty-one thousand troops, though he insisted to Richmond that he only had twenty-four thousand, the difference giving him greater excuse to do nothing. He also had seventy-six cannon, which surely could have been put to some use. As time passed, Johnston's window of opportunity closed, for the thousands Halleck sent to Grant far surpassed any number Johnston or Richmond could amass.

Grant ended his accounting report with the note that Major General Francis J. Herron's division from Missouri had arrived, and he expected additional troops at any time from Major General Ambrose Everett Burnside's Department of the Ohio. Herron would not be assigned to a corps, which made it easier for Grant to use his troops wherever needed. Despite the overriding concern with Johnston, he sent Herron to flesh out McClernand's line, and he promised McClernand an additional eight thousand men from Burnside on their way to Vicksburg. Grant would not forget the southern flank, especially since he received scattered reports, all false, that Johnston was aiming to cross the Big Black to the south. With Herron joining the southern flank and more men coming, Grant believed by June 12, that "the enemy can be so enclosed as to have all of Herron[']s force free either to act with the extreme left," or elsewhere as events required. Grant left deployment decisions to McClernand's discretion.[9]

On June 15, Grant confirmed to McClernand that eight thousand troops, part of the IX Army Corps (Burnside's troops Major General John Parke commanded), had reached Vicksburg and "will take position on the South side of the city thus making the investment complete." Since making a firm decision on a "regular siege" on May 25, it had taken over three weeks to reach the point of "making the investment complete." This certainly must have seemed like a long time to Grant, but, in fact, considering how carefully Halleck had to act funneling Grant troops from other areas, Halleck had done a remarkable job. Grant felt better, but he warned McClernand that if Johnston attacked the Haynes's Bluff area with large numbers of troops, many men from the south would have to march northeast.

If the situation demanded, Grant would not hesitate to completely uncover his south flank. He instructed McClernand on how reinforcements should impact current deployments, and that McClernand would maintain command of all the new troops as well as his own corps. If Pemberton tried to turn the Union left in an effort to join Johnston, the Rebels must be defeated. Grant admitted this was not likely, for it would give Vicksburg to Union forces. "This is given only as a general plan to be adopted under certain circumstances," Grant wrote. He then appended his message to say that Parke had sent one of his divisions from opposite the Warrenton area on the Louisiana side of the river upstream to cross over into the Yazoo and to Haynes's Bluff. The fear of and false intelligence regarding Johnston's intent and location continued to pull Grant's thinking like a magnet to the northeast. As he shifted troops, however, he assured McClernand that the south flank would continue to have sufficient strength. Only the most extreme emergency would cause

Grant to abandon the security of his left flank. With all the new troops coming in, it is easy to see that McClernand, having more responsibilities, could not imagine being removed from command for any reason.[10]

Grant's strategic thinking gave Johnston credit for military acumen that the latter had not showed. Johnston being a fellow West Pointer dulled Grant's judgment of his opponent's abilities. What if Johnston's presence in Yazoo City and Canton screened a movement north to attack Memphis? Stephen Hurlbut, commanding in Memphis, certainly worried about being attacked, and Grant promised that should it become evident that Johnston had moved north, troops from Vicksburg would be hurriedly sent to Memphis. Grant did not worry about Memphis because it appeared that if reinforcements came from Braxton Bragg to Johnston, there would be an attempt to break the siege at Vicksburg.[11]

No doubt with that thought in mind, Grant consulted with Sherman and stated the obvious. A report from Haynes's Bluff indicated Rebel cavalry gathering near Mechanicsburg and infantry concentrating at Yazoo City. Brigadier General William Sooy Smith's division from West Tennessee had just arrived, and Grant intended to add this force to Haynes's Bluff, which would raise the total number of defenders there to around fourteen thousand. His main reason for contacting Sherman and also McPherson was that he wanted two brigades from Sherman's corps and three from McPherson's corps to be ready at a moment's notice to rush to Haynes's Bluff if needed to fight Johnston. Sherman would be detached from his corps to command the entire force at Haynes's should the reinforcements be needed. Sherman said he would be ready, and he gave a breakdown of the troops he would use. Rawlins notified McPherson of his and Sherman's roles in case of crisis.[12]

Meanwhile, Porter sent Grant positive news about the situation in Louisiana. Alfred Ellet and his marines were en route to attack Richmond, which had been fortified by Rebels. Ellet's assault would force Confederates to evacuate. Most of the town was burned during the fighting or thereafter. Ellet's troops excelled at destruction. Porter intended to use Ellet to police the northwest Louisiana region, hoping in the process to arrest citizens cooperating with Confederates and to confiscate Rebel equipment, especially wagons. The close friendship Grant had established with Porter doubtless eased Grant's mind about potential trouble across the Mississippi. Porter's gunboats could easily intimidate Confederates who operated too close to the river.[13]

Grant shifted his attention back to the Mechanicsburg Corridor when he received a typical gossipy note about Johnston. Cadwallader

Washburn, commanding at Haynes's Bluff, sent two messages to Grant's headquarters. One concerned the activities of a Union spy named Mc-Birney (probably an alias) who had been sent to Yazoo City on June 9. Washburn believed all the news McBirney brought back. Not surprising, Washburn had promised McBirney "pay in proportion to the hazard incurred." McBirney had information about Confederate couriers and other Rebels looking for cattle and horses for Johnston and, more ominously, that two Confederate divisions were in Yazoo City. Washburn wanted to be sure McBirney received just compensation. Washburn also reported that an area citizen, an obvious Union sympathizer but also possibly a Confederate plant, reported some of Johnston's men crossing the Sunflower River north of Vicksburg. Supposedly, large numbers of cattle, hogs, and ample ears of corn were in the Deer Creek area north of the Yazoo, and Johnston was sending detachments to get as much of each as they could. Washburn believed the Rebels would cross upstream in shallow-water locations that Union gunboats could not reach.

The same day, he sent his second message reporting that he was sending 250 cavalry into these areas to drive off Confederates. Meanwhile, pickets captured seven Confederate "deserters," who claimed Johnston was concentrating troops between Big Black River and Sartartia. There is no way to be sure, but Johnston could well have sent out these men to make sure Union commanders received this news, which was false.[14]

Grant had heard so many rambling reports that he sent Washburn a message detailing his reasons for refusing to approve the cavalry foray. Admitting that success would be important, Grant said he feared a small cavalry detachment would constantly be in harm's way, whether from local citizens or Confederates or both. "If captured," he wrote Washburn, "they would certai[n]ly be hung, if not shot when taken." Why Grant made such a foreboding comment is uncertain; perhaps, he wanted to hammer home to Washburn that plans should not be made with a cavalier attitude. Further, Grant dismissed the idea that McBirney's reports indicated preliminary steps for an attack at Haynes's Bluff. If the information was accurate, Johnston likely intended only to get his forces as close as he dared for future operations if the Confederates received reinforcements. Grant sent cavalry to check the river bottoms as far north as Greenville, advising that they should block any Rebel cavalry trying to get into that area. Otherwise, Washburn should be diligent where he was and ask for reinforcements if he needed them. By the middle of June, Grant seemed to finally comprehend that the Johnston threat in the Mechanicsburg

Corridor was not imminent and perhaps never would be. Yet, his worries about Johnston would continue to ebb and flow.[15]

While he orchestrated the siege, Grant took time out to write a letter to his father, Jesse Root Grant. Grant's sister Mary and Jesse had been writing him, but Grant understandably been too busy to reply. Now, with troops in place and feeling more comfortable than he had since the siege began, Grant found a few minutes on June 15 to write a brief note: "All I can say is that I am well. Have the enemy closely hem[m]ed in all around. My position is naturally strong and fortified against an attack from outside. I have been so strongly reinforced that Johnstone will have to come with a mighty host to drive me away—I do not look upon the fall of Vicksburg as in the least doubtful." Grant said he regretted not taking the city on May 22, for if he had, he could have cleared Mississippi of resistance by mid-June, making the state "almost safe enough for a solitary horseman to ride over." As a result of not taking Vicksburg quickly, he had to keep an eye on Johnston, but he admitted wavering on the subject: "The fall of Vicksburg now will only result in the opening of the Miss. River and demoralization of the enemy. I intended more from it [the campaign]. I did my best however and looking back can see no blunder committed." There was some sugar-coating on his words, but his confidence was merited.[16]

Via Rawlins, Grant turned to a problem outside Vicksburg involving cotton trade. In General Orders No. 36, Grant revoked previous orders permitting some trade with Rebel planters that March and April orders coming out of Washington had made moot by revocation. Grant hoped to clarify the situation: "The shipment of goods for sale south of Helena, Arkansas, in this department, by any persons other than sutlers regularly and duly appointed in pursuance of existing law, is positively prohibited." Keeping up with sutler regulations would be up to commanders, who wished to have goods shipped to their troops. Any traders who did not fit the definition of "authorized sutlers" would be required to go to Helena or north of Helena, but they would not be allowed in Vicksburg. All liquor of any kind would not be shipped south of Cairo, Illinois, except that which commissary and medical departments needed. This was another case of Grant having to deal with an issue that was connected to the military but annoying in that it had little to do with capturing Vicksburg.[17]

Julia Grant received welcome news from her husband. On June 9, he said in a letter to her that he had sent several letters to her by courier up until he had captured Jackson. He remembered saying she could start for Vicksburg as soon as she heard the town had surrendered, and he had not written since because he did not expect the task to take so long. To smooth things over, he told her she could start downriver as soon as she wanted, that if the siege had not ended when she arrived, she could stay aboard whatever steamer transported her, and that it could dock at the Chickasaw Bayou landing. At least, he could visit her occasionally. He assured Julia that he and their son Fred, who had ridden along throughout the inland campaign and had stayed for the siege, had "enjoyed most excellent health during the campaign," and Fred was keeping a journal. He intentionally did not mention that Fred had been slightly wounded at the Battle of Big Black River Bridge. He also had found a pony for their young children.

He then turned to the siege and told her there was not much to relate. His army had pushed up close to Rebel fortresses, and he knew they must be captured to end the thing: "The enemy however may make a desperate effort to get a force outside of me to relieve the present garrison. If they do I occupy one of the strongest imaginable positions." Reinforcements were coming from all around the country: "With the whole of them there is but little doubt but that I can hold out against anything likely to be brought against me."[18]

On June 15, Grant sent a second letter, acknowledging it might pass by her if she was coming on downriver. This time, he cautioned her that if she did arrive before Vicksburg surrendered, he would likely have little time to see her: "My duties are such that I can scarsely leave." His headquarters had been established six miles from the landing, and the road usually was choked with supply wagons. Aside from dysentery, he continued in good health, but Fred had been complaining of ailments. Julia's brother Lewis Dent, a plantation lessee upriver, had come downriver to see the Grants, and Fred went with his uncle "to spend a short time." Grant said he had tried to talk Fred into going to Saint Louis, but the young man refused because he was determined to see Vicksburg fall. The siege continued to go well, as his lines pressed continually closer to Confederate entrenchments, and a few shells would remind the citizenry that they should not stop thinking about protecting themselves. Grant knew civilians had dug caves into hills, though obviously he would not see them until he rode into Vicksburg after the surrender. He admitted that Rebel deserters made clear that conditions in the city were terrible, both for the troops and civilians. He had reached the point of not allowing passes for Vicksburgians to leave the city, stating firmly he would not allow "any of them" to come out.

Aside from his family, Grant had to endure the comings and goings of political figures from states his soldiers represented; he paid only cursory attention to these politically motivated intrusions. Illinois Governor Richard Yates became almost a fixture, in part due to his friendship with McClernand and in part because Illinois soldiers formed the largest contingent of men from any Union state, and a good politician could not pass up chances to visit constituents. Samuel Kirkwood, governor of Iowa, also came to Vicksburg. He dared get down into the trenches, where he borrowed a rifle to take a shot at Rebels. He did, and a quick response came, a Confederate bullet smashing into a tree about ten feet above Kirkwood's head. The governor quickly dropped the gun, fell flat on his face, and called out to his Iowa constituents that the enemy bullet had come close. He turned and crawled back from whence he came to escape any further deadly missiles. The soldiers laughed heartily and wondered what kind of wonderful spin Kirkwood would put on his experience. Governor Edward Salomon of Wisconsin visited troops from his state, proclaiming how proud he was of all their accomplishments.

Not all visitors were politicians. Sometimes, groups of women visited camps, though the firing made them nervous. Soldiers were used to it. On one occasion, artillerists loaded their battery of twenty-pound Parrott guns and allowed the women to pull the lanyards. The artillerists seemed unconcerned that the blasts would make the women more nervous. The presence of nonmilitary personnel indicates a rather haphazard attitude toward the siege, and while he felt his siege lines were secure enough to protect such visitors, Grant did not encourage such socializing, but he was realistic; anything good for morale was fine with him.[19]

Although Grant's confidence grew, Johnston never left his thoughts. Grant now believed that whatever the Confederate general had in mind, he could not help Pemberton. Grant, in a message to one of his staff, wrote, "My position is so strong that I feel myself abundantly able to leave it so and go out twenty or thirty miles with force enough to whip two such garrisons. If Johnstone should come here he must do it with a larger Army than the Confederacy have now at any one place. This is what I think but do not say it boastingly nor do I want it repeated or shown."

Grant's last comment is humorous. Grant did not want Halleck hearing that he was bragging about the number of troops he had and how confident the numbers made him. Halleck might decide to send some of them elsewhere. Given the sometimes-contentious relationship he had had with Halleck and how much help Halleck had been in recent months, Grant did not want to risk ruffling the commanding general's feathers, or Stanton's, or Lincoln's for that matter. On June 16, Grant sent word to Halleck that Johnston's troops were known to be at Yazoo City, Benton,

Brownsville, and Clinton, Mississippi, that he was continuing to fortify Haynes's, but he believed he could detach enough men to clean out the Mechanicsburg Corridor. He further said that he rarely lost a man, and the health of his troops was "most excellent."[20]

Grant was not content to starve the Vicksburg Confederate garrison, no matter how much he considered the issue of surrender well in hand. On June 15, he issued instructions to his corps commanders to get ready for systematic firing of artillery all along the siege line. Grant notified Herron that Parke was moving to Haynes's Bluff and that Herron should push his artillery forward to the best positions he could find along the southern ridges. As soon as he was able to deploy a solid front and was able to fire over Rebel entrenchments, Herron should so advise Grant. The cannonade meant preparations would reduce firing initially; once orders came from Grant, the general firing would begin, continuous "for certain periods of time." "It is my intention," Grant wrote, "to shell the town for two hours." The word *town* implies that Grant had in mind shelling Confederates and civilians, when he was referring to the defensive line of Pemberton's army. Grant never intentionally ordered the shelling of civilians, though he certainly knew they were in harm's way, caught between occasional Federal cannon over-shots and Porter's naval guns. Damage to the town and civilians was collateral damage, over which Grant had limited control.[21]

Grant planned even more grief for Vicksburg defenders. On June 16 in a message to Porter, Grant communicated he needed a supply of sulfur, niter, and meal powder (the combination being the recipe for gun powder and the latter being residue left after black powder is sifted through screens into varying sizes). Porter, who had begun firing "incendiary shells" that would "burn a house now and then," responded that he had none, but he knew Chickasaw Bayou landing had ten barrels of powder, because mortar powder was used to attack Confederate works along the river. Grant contacted McClernand also on June 16, the day before Grant asked the XIII Corps commander about the congratulatory order. Grant wanted furnaces built for heating shot, to make them incendiary. He knew that some of McClernand's 24-pounder cannon could be adapted to fire such shells to cause more havoc in Rebel lines. Clearly, Grant intended to up the ante, inaugurating more terror on Pemberton's troops and unfortunate Vicksburg civilians.[22]

While corps artillerists prepared for the systematic bombardment set to begin on June 20, Sherman and Grant aide James Wilson checked the situation at Snyder's Bluff. Sherman found the works still under construction were done well, and he thought two divisions could "hold any force comi[n]g from the North & North East." Sherman also checked what he called the "Skillet Golia[th]," the bottom land, or Skillikalia Bayou valley north by northeast of the Yazoo bluffs, and recommended defensive measures, mainly building "detached forts" and posting Parke's several thousand men to block any Confederate offensives, which were not likely. Grant responded that he could see no way to build the forts quickly other than dividing labor between Sherman's and McPherson's corps. He believed other troops were deployed too far from the bluffs to be of immediate use. Grant instructed, "A heavy detail can be got to do the work by collecting Stragglers and working them constantly under guard, and without reference to the Corps they may belong to." He promised to send staff to check the terrain and asked Sherman to send all the information he had on potential locations.[23]

As Parke took command at Haynes's Bluff, he received a note from Grant. Grant told Parke that no instructions on how he should proceed had been sent, nor did he see any reason to send any, but, as was his custom, the commanding general offered opinions that Parke should consider: push forward the digging in case of any pending Rebel attack; Johnston's army's locations: William Loring, W. H. T. Walker, and John Breckinridge all appeared to be spaced from Clinton to Benton to Yazoo City; and Loring and Walker, the closest to Union defenses along the Yazoo, would be the easiest to attack if Parke went on the offensive.

Parke should keep his cavalry active, for scouting reports indicated that Johnston had four thousand cavalry in the region. Although he had not issued a formal order giving Parke command of the Haynes area, Grant assured Parke that he was isolated from the three other corps and was the senior officer, the de facto commander. Parke replied he had made defensive deployments and was also scouting the area for ground where additional works could be built. He asked that Lieutenant Colonel Orville Babcock, a recent arrival who was an engineer and a new member of Grant's staff, be allowed to remain in the area to scout the terrain. Babcock had already ridden around the area with Wilson, and he would be invaluable in directing construction of entrenchments and other works.[24]

Assured that he had good men, men who knew what they were doing, and feeling he could trust them, Grant turned back to the bombardment. On June 19, he issued general orders regarding the shelling of Rebel works, to begin at 4 A.M. on June 20 and to continue until 10 A.M. He must have decided six hours of constant shelling would be more effective than two, obviously. The shelling must be disciplined; emergency ammunition should be retained: one hundred rounds for each field gun and twenty rounds per siege gun. Rifle pits would be jammed with as many infantry as could squeeze into them. From 6:30 until 10, all troops should be ready to charge if the Rebels showed any signs of "weakness" or should be ready "to repel an attack" by them. Grant made clear that the barrage was not preliminary to an attack, but his corps must be prepared for any eventuality. Corps commanders each had permission (Ord now had command of the XIII) to attack any vulnerable portion of the Rebel line if they could so "without a serious battle." If such an attack was ordered, the commanders must inform each other and Grant's headquarters about actions taken and whether they needed assistance. The booming of artillery was all that happened, and the resulting damage, which was little, to Confederate defensive works gave Union troops no tactical advantage. Porter sent Grant word that he was disappointed he could not participate, but he was bogged down with logistical problems.[25]

Charles Dana wrote that the two hundred or so cannon that opened fire on Vicksburg that morning elicited no response from the Confederates. No enemy soldiers could be seen, and musketry fire from the Rebels "amounted to nothing." Artillerists could tell they had damaged buildings, but no one could say which buildings. Dana said that if "mills, foundry, or storehouses," targets Grant surely wished to be hit, suffered any damage, hits could not be verified. Dana concluded, as did Grant and his generals, that the bombardment did not ensure "success by assault."[26]

While planning the cannonade, Grant was distracted on several occasions. It seemed that he could not focus on the siege and taking Vicksburg without all sorts of diversions. The first one was really his fault. He had received a long letter dated June 2 from Sherman, and he had understandably set it aside. Sherman wanted Grant to approach Lincoln regarding the use of the draft "to fill up our old regiments." News reports indicated that one hundred thousand men would be assigned to these regiments, and two hundred thousand more would be organized into new units.

Sherman elaborated at length on his views:

I do not believe that Mr. Lincoln, or any man, would, at this critical period of our history, repeat the fatal mistakes of last year. Taking this army as a fair sample of the whole, what is the case? The regiments do not average 300 men, nor did they exceed that strength last fall. When the new regiments joined us in November and December, their rolls contained about 900 names, whereas now their ranks are even thinner than the older organizations. All who deal with troops in fact instead of theory know that the knowledge of the little details of camp life is absolutely necessary to keep men alive. New regiments, for want of this knowledge, have measles, mumps, diarrhea, and the whole catalogue of infantile diseases; whereas the same number of men, distributed among the older regiments would learn from the sergeants and corporals and privates the art of taking care of themselves, which would actually save their lives and preserve their health against the host of diseases that invariably attack the new regiments.

Certainly, these problems played a prominent role in all Civil War campaigns, but they especially were a tragic part of the entirety of the Vicksburg campaign, and the siege in hot, humid Mississippi compounded them at Vicksburg. Sherman added that mixing new recruits with experienced regiments would aid in learning drill techniques, caring for their rifles, marching, and other skills that would take a long time to learn if the entire regiment was made up of new recruits. He knew that Lincoln certainly wanted "to support and sustain the army, and that he desires to know the wishes and opinions of the officers who serve in the woods instead of in the 'salon.'" Sherman asked Grant if official Washington would listen to him, if he carried enough weight to get Lincoln's attention. If Lincoln did not listen, Sherman wrote, the war would be extended for many years, and "the old regiments would die of natural exhaustion." Sherman believed taking care of this matter in the proper way would be more important to the Union cause that capturing "Vicksburg and Richmond."[27]

On June 19, Grant wrote Lincoln, enclosing Sherman's letter. Grant underscored Sherman's position by telling Lincoln, "[O]ur old regiments, all that remains of them, are veterans equaling regulars in discipline, and far superior to them in the material of which they are composed." A new recruit, mixed in with these veterans, "would become an old soldier, from the very contact, before he was aware of it." Officers, equipment, transportation, and other essentials were already available and would not cost the government anything but "pay and allowances." A regiment made up of new recruits would cost much more. "Officers and men have to go through months of schooling, and, from ignorance of how to cook and provide for themselves, the ranks become depleted one-third before valuable services can be expected," Grant contended. He concluded with a comment that a politician, especially a president, could grasp: "Taken in an economic point of view, one drafted man in an old regiment is worth three in a new one."[28]

Grant did not get a response until after Vicksburg fell. On July 14, a message from Halleck arrived: "The course you recommend was determined on by the War Dept some time ago, and will be carried out as soon as the draft is made." Halleck went on to scold Grant for corresponding directly with the president. Such communications, Halleck wrote, must be made through "proper military channels," in effect, directly to him. That would speed things up, and "that course would be in compliance with Army Regulations and the usages of service." This was typical Halleck, and Grant, indeed, should have sent his inquiry to both Lincoln and Halleck. The exchange did not necessarily underscore personal tension between Grant and Halleck, but Grant could not ignore the implication, nor could he react angrily, for Halleck had seen to it that the Union forces at Vicksburg had increased many-fold. But Grant must have wondered how much more he had to do than capture Vicksburg to be treated a little more respectfully. The irony was that within a few months, Grant would be Halleck's boss. The entire affair demonstrated that both Sherman and Grant were looking ahead, trying to make sure the army was organized in the most efficient manner possible. The timing was questionable, Vicksburg being still in Confederate hands when Grant forwarded the correspondence, but the points were well taken.[29]

Grant did some dressing down of his own when he received a telegram from the War Department requesting a copy of one of his general orders. The inquiry did not come directly from Halleck, but Halleck instigated it. Grant responded, "I herewith enclose a file of the General Orders issued by me this year, and also beg to state that in each case the orders were mailed to the Adjutant General of the Army, immediately after their publication. A complete file of my General Orders for 1863 will this day be sent to the War Department." Grant must have wanted to tell Halleck, "Just in case your staff has lost others."[30]

A comical message came to Grant before the cannonade began. McClernand's replacement, E. O. C. Ord, sent word that a freed slave, in talking to one of the officers at Warrenton, said he had overheard his former owner saying that Johnston was on an island in Hinds County, Mississippi. Hinds County has no islands, but that was not all. The freedman said Johnston had 150,000 men ready to attack Warrenton, presumably from this island. The Mississippi River, about fifteen miles to the west of Hinds County, has islands but not one that could accommodate that many men. Grant, who knew Ord well, patiently responded (one can only imagine how he would have responded to such a message from McClernand, who would never have pestered Grant with such a wild tale) that the island referred to was probably the island where Jefferson Davis's pre-war home was and that "no such rumor of a large force being there can be true." Ord could send his cavalry to scout, but he should know Hinds County was east of the Big Black River, Grant said. Ord had not proven himself to be an able commander. He rejoined the army after recovering from a serious wound during the Corinth campaign, and he got the job because he was conveniently available, and Grant knew him. Additionally, he was a West Pointer, and his roommate there had been Sherman. Grant must have winced after wasting time reading such a ridiculous message. In his memoirs, Grant makes no mention of Ord when he writes about firing McClernand.[31]

Grant received another tale of gossip, almost but not quite as absurd as the one Ord forwarded. When two pickets, one Union and one Confederate, decided on a personal ceasefire, the Confederate told his counterpart some interesting "facts" about the situation in Vicksburg. The grand Union cannonade had produced casualties but had done little damage to structures and roads. Confederate commanders had expected an assault, and when it did not come, Pemberton's officers surveyed their troops to see if they would participate in an attack on Union lines. This would be a rather strange way to run an army, but the Confederate insisted that the very question almost led to mutiny. The men received quick assurance that they should continue their duties and would have enough rations to last at least another week. Then came the most interesting, and dubious, turn in the conversation. According to the Rebel picket, during the next seven days, the Confederates "would have 2,000 boats finished, and they could make their escape by the river." The boats were being built from wood Confederates collected "tearing down houses to get the material out of which to build boats." Grant passed the information to Porter, along with an assurance that a strong picket line with cannon masked behind levees would be deployed along the riverfront. Porter should arrange to illuminate the river should the grand attempted exodus take place. Mower would be in touch with Porter about the best means to thwart the escape.[32]

Porter responded that he had been prepared for some time for such an eventuality. He pointed out that he had cannon and sharpshooters, the latter marines from Ellet's ram flotilla. The remainder of Ellet's riflemen was positioned across the river near the failed canal, and one battery was with them. As for his gunboats, Porter signaled they would be ready, but a shortage of coal remained a problem. Porter reminded Grant that orders to collect carts to transport coal had not been carried out. Otherwise, "[a] system of signals has been established all along the levee—and . . .

with the Gun boats which are ordered to rush on regardless of everything and swamp the boats with their wheels[.]" Porter added two of the best side-wheeler transports were being made ready, each containing about two hundred infantry, to help destroy the enemy boats as they attempted to cross or go down the river. Porter passed on information that a Rebel deserter had said the Confederates had "many skiffs and every man is making a paddle." If the Rebels tried to go upstream "in the eddy," Porter had three gunboats each at Milliken's Bend and Young's Point. Sixty barrels of tar would be ready for lighting up the river if necessary.[33]

That Grant and Porter gave credence to the escape story is remarkable. How the Confederates would be able to escape in large numbers in only two thousand boats seemed not to be considered. Pemberton had around thirty thousand men, though the severely wounded and sick would reduce that number, so escape by boat would require leaving many more men behind if only two thousand boats were built. Would the boats be big enough to carry artillery? That was not likely, so no matter which direction the Rebels went, they would in effect be on a forlorn-hope mission. Union infantry and artillery plus gunboats would have a turkey shoot.

Yet, when Union forces did enter the city after the surrender, Grant wrote that they found a number of boats. He did not say how many, but they proved there was some truth to the story and indicated Rebel desperation. No Confederate accounts of such a large boat-building project have survived, and, surely, such a major construction undertaking would have caught the attention of Pemberton's soldiers and required extensive labor among those fit to do such work. Perhaps a few deserters and townspeople had tried to find a means of escape and had settled on boats. Maybe a few of them had tried it, but if so, none of Porter's sailors had noticed, nor had Union troops on the north or south flanks of the siege lines. Such a plan would have been astonishingly unrealistic, not to mention ridiculous. Grant and Porter must have assumed that Pemberton's army had reached a point of desperation that would lead its leaders to try anything.

The boat rumor never materialized, but then Grant embraced another bit of unreliable intelligence. On June 22, he signaled Porter, "There is every indication of Jo Johnstone making an attack within the next forty eight hours. I have given all the necessary orders to meet him some twenty-five miles out, Sherman commanding. As Johnstone undoubtedly communicates with the garrison in Vicksburg, and the troops West of the Miss, there is probably an understanding by which there may be a simultaneous attack upon Youngs Point, our lines here and by Johnstone on the outside." Grant sent orders to Elias Dennis to be on the alert, and other

Union bases on the Louisiana side of the river would be warned. Grant concluded, "My hands will be very full here in case of an attack. I will direct Gen. Dennis therefore to consult with you in all matters relating to defences on the West side of the river." Grant also sent word to Herron to be ready to move to reinforce troops along the Haynes's Bluff line. He reiterated his concern, "An attack from Johnston within forty-eight hours is not improbable."[34]

Other urgent messages emphasizing the pending Johnston attack went to Ord, McPherson, and Parke. Ord, Grant said, must send the remainder of his division to Peter Osterhaus to help the latter handle a potential Confederate cavalry attack, expected to take place along the Big Black River at Bridgeport, north of the Big Black bridge and Southern Railroad of Mississippi. If Osterhaus should be forced to withdraw, he must burn the bridge and find Sherman in the Bear Creek area. Ord should send out a strong line of pickets to warn of any threat to his rear by Rebel cavalry. Grant also sent directly to Osterhaus a message warning of Loring's suspected presence in the area south of Vernon.

Osterhaus must have wondered what all the fuss was about. He sent word to Grant on the twenty-second about a "pretty smart Contraband" who had showed up at headquarters. The man, who had come from Mobile, Alabama, passed through Jackson on June 9. From there, he went to Raymond and reached Union lines on the road through Edwards Station. While in Jackson, he observed an estimated twenty-five hundred Confederate troops, but the only signs of military activity between Jackson and the Big Black were scattered Rebel patrols. The only hint of Confederate aggression had been a cavalry attack on an Iowa cavalry regiment at Bridgeport on the west side of the Big Black a few miles north of Edwards. This seemed little more than an aberration, because all remained quiet on the Jackson Road. The Rebels at Bridgeport had recrossed the Big Black. In effect, Osterhaus had received no reports of a major Johnston offensive anywhere.[35]

The Iowans' fight with Rebels near Bear Creek and Bridgeport did not seem to concern Osterhaus or Sherman, but it unsettled Grant and apparently fueled the fear of an imminent attack. The Iowans had been flanked, and the victorious Confederates captured thirty-three men. Grant assumed the little battle could mean Johnston was advancing. However, it soon became clear that the Confederates had retreated back across the Big Black, and Johnston still was nowhere in sight. The Iowans had been embarrassed and lost a few men, but that was the extent of damage to Sherman's Big Black line.[36]

Grant's needlessly urgent preparations to meet perceived threats continued. Parke must advance four of his brigades, with cavalry in the van, as close to the Big Black as possible. The men must travel light, moving as quickly as possible to stop the reported presence of Loring around Bear Creek. Parke obeyed and promised to meet with Sherman. Parke also sent word that he had heard of the Iowa cavalry fight but that Rebels had not crossed the Big Black in force. McPherson received orders to have John McArthur's division ready to rush to the Mechanicsburg Corridor lines if Sherman sent for them. Meanwhile, rapt attention had to be paid to the besieged Confederate army, should Pemberton order an attack in concert with Johnston. Grant's lines tightened, and he knew that several Rebel couriers had been captured. Why he thought Johnston and Pemberton could coordinate an operation can only be attributed to his ongoing preoccupation with Johnston.[37]

What besides Bear Creek had prompted this sudden rush of activity that made Grant so sure an attack was coming within forty-eight hours? It was mainly due to misreading Johnston's intent by Grant, his officers, and scouts. Grant clung to the belief that the most logical threat from Johnston would come via the Mechanicsburg Corridor. He had believed it since the siege began, and in mid-June, he remained convinced of it. When scouting news indicated Johnston had withdrawn all his troops east of the Big Black, Grant felt better, but by June 20, he decided he had all along been focusing north and northeast when he should have been looking east.

Cadwallader Washburn reported that some of Johnston's troops had crossed the Big Black, but they had crossed from west to east, retreating rather than advancing. Grant was not aware of that fact, and he concluded that Johnston had decided to forget the corridor and focus now on crossings farther south along the Big Black. However, Johnston's own scouting reports had convinced him, and he needed little convincing, that he could not fight his way across the river and through the ever-stronger Union works. Before June 22, Johnston had indeed decided not to attack anywhere. Johnston sent word to Pemberton that he (Johnston) did not have enough men to do anything. There had never been much hope that he would, except among the beleaguered troops trapped in Vicksburg.

Grant did not know of Johnston's decision to call the whole thing off. He believed, quite logically, that since no attack seemed to be imminent from the corridor, Johnston must have decided to attack from east to west directly. Johnston had, indeed, entertained that notion but only very briefly. Yet, Grant could not assume anything; he received reports of Rebel cavalry continuing to operate along the east bank of the Big Black. Supporting this notion was intelligence agent Charles Bell, who sent word that Johnston had withdrawn his troops from the corridor and started moving three divisions south from Vernon. This news inspired the forty-eight-hour timeline. That theory, false though it turned out to be, led Grant to send Sherman with a heavy force to block any crossing of the Big Black by Rebels from the east. The panicky orders had been for naught, but Johnston's decision to do nothing combined with Grant's decision to do everything to stop him signaled the final phase of the siege.[38]

~7~

BIG BLACK, BLACK POWDER, BRUSH FIRES

GRANT NOTIFIED SHERMAN on June 22 that the enemy was crossing the Big Black, and it appeared Johnston intended to attack along Bear Creek. He told Sherman that Parke had already begun marching four brigades and cavalry to meet the threat. Parke's assignment would be to hold the Rebels as close to Big Black River as possible "until their position is clearly defined when we can draw all our forces from Snyders Bluff and the forces previously indicated here to their support. [Brigadier General James] Tuttle[']s Division should be marched out within supporting distance of Parke at once. You will go and command the entire force." Sherman had the option to handle logistics as he pleased, and he could draw troops from Snyder's Bluff and the three brigades from McPherson's corps. Sherman could do all these things without checking with Grant. Grant, in effect, gave Sherman an independent command, required by the supposed emergency. Grant promised additional troops from the Union left flank if needed.[1]

Grant's renewed panicky demeanor led to a June 23 message to General Herron: "Heavy firing is reported on our left. Is it in your front? What are the indications?" Before receiving Grant's inquiry, Herron had sent word that, if allowed, he could force his way into the Rebel siege lines. The next day, Herron sent two messages to Grant, one of which read, "Nothing of special importance has occurred on my front since yesterday." His sharpshooters were leading an advance against enemy siege lines and should be dug in by nightfall within four hundred yards of the main Rebel front. There had been a brief skirmish, but Herron had few casualties: one killed, one wounded.[2]

Before he received Herron's note, Grant sent a message to McPherson that Ord had heard shooting on his left. Perhaps Confederates had sent a patrol. Could McPherson detail forces if needed? McPherson likewise had heard what sounded like heavy fighting on his left and assumed it must be Ord's corps. Grant quickly sent Ord word not to fire unless "you see something to fire at." Ord responded that he was hearing heavy firing on his left, "as if a Sally," (usually implied troops rushing out, firing and falling back); Ord sent word to his left-wing commanders to support each other in case of a full-scale attack. Ord also said he needed heavy artillery. The shooting turned out to be a Confederate sortie that amounted to practically nothing. Grant's words indicated he continued in an up and down pattern of emotions. Johnston's lack of action only occasionally modified Grant's reactions.[3]

Grant contacted Sherman about getting word to Herron and Andrew Jackson Smith to be ready, and Sherman could pull two additional brigades from his own corps without endangering the siege line. Grant stated firmly, "Should Johnston come, we want to whip him if the Siege has to be raised to do it. Use all the forces indicated above as you deem most advantageous, and should more be required, call on me and they will be furnished to the last man here and at Young's Point." Grant had obviously had enough of being concerned about what Johnston would do. If only he had known he was losing sleep over nothing.[4]

Sherman wrote one of his typically long messages to Grant detailing his troop deployments, including what roads they were on and how he would be communicating with Parke. The time on his letter was 11 A.M., June 23, and he wrote he intended to go to the Big Black that afternoon: "I hear nothing of Johnson at all, no traces of him or signs of his approach. The Country is ill adapted to Large masses." The terrain made it difficult for even a regiment to form a solid front. Sherman thought the only way to attack Johnston was to wait for him to cross the Big Black. If he did, Sherman assured Grant, the Confederates would be beaten back. Osterhaus would block all roads leading directly from the Big Black into Vicksburg. Sherman mentioned the Iowa cavalry skirmish with Rebels, but he, obviously, did not think it a harbinger of things to come.

Some local citizens seemed to think all Sherman's troops had come out to find the Confederates who attacked the Iowans. Sherman promised Grant, "I will send you positive inteligence tonight if Johnson be comi[n]g or not this side of Black River. On the best evidence now procurable he is not coming this way or at this time." Sherman added that he assumed he was not to cross the river looking for Johnston unless he had defeated him in battle. Rawlins reminded Osterhaus to block all roads across the Big Black south of the railroad. Surely Johnston must be planning to cross somewhere. Yet, Cadwallader Washburn echoed Sherman's report: "I have Just returned from the front[;] all is quiet."[5]

At this point, Grant was sidetracked, and, perhaps, it was a good thing to have his attention diverted from Johnston. Grant contacted Porter about a Confederate named Hiram Bledsoe who had traveled from Yazoo City to a spot on the Mississippi above Greenville. Reports indicated Bledsoe led 150 cavalry and a light artillery battery. Grant had sent his cavalry to Sherman's new front along the Big Black, so Grant could spare none to check on Bledsoe. Could Porter assist by sending the marine brigade to disperse Bledsoe's detachment? Perhaps the marines could land at Greenville and attack the Rebels from the rear. Apparently, Grant feared Bledsoe's horsemen would fire at Union transports. A note from Washburn indicated that such attacks had increased in recent days: "Our transports are being so much annoyed by river batteries, and they have become so bold about it, it seems to me that they ought to be cleaned out."[6]

Porter replied the marines were currently en route to Delhi, Louisiana, scouting for information on Confederate activity in north Louisiana. They would not return for a couple of days. Therefore, Porter warned, it would take too much time to get the brigade ready for a separate expedition to Greenville. Porter said he had a couple of gunboats on the river at Greenville, and he would send a convoy if Grant wanted. Intelligence reports indicated that Confederates were setting up twelve pieces of artillery in an area across the river from Greenville. Porter had already sent one additional gunboat upstream with another to follow, and he reiterated the marines could not help. This operation seemed yet another Grant overreaction to a report about so few Rebel cavalry.[7]

Grant followed Porter's advice, and Porter seemed to take the reports much too seriously, because rumors were notoriously inaccurate. He had enough gunboats to run off Confederates anywhere close to river. The news proved to be bogus, just like the tidings that constantly swirled about Johnston. If Confederates indeed got close enough to the river to fire at vessels, Porter's guns could easily have pounded them, causing many enemy casualties or a high-speed retreat. Why Grant chose to micromanage the situation is odd. He sent a force of infantry and artillery, commanded by Lieutenant Colonel Samuel Nasmith and detached from Snyder's Bluff and Sherman's XV Corps, temporarily under the command of Frederick Steele while Sherman was at the Big Black. Nasmith reported to Grant on July 1, "Not being able to find or hear of any enemy on this side of the river, I am satisfied, from information received from reliable sources, that there has been no enemy near Greenville, on the Mississippi shore, for nearly four weeks."

On June 26, Porter added another facet to the grand waste of time when he wrote Grant that there had been a big scare at Milliken's Bend. Word had spread that Confederate Major General Sterling Price was approaching "with a large Army!!" Porter sent gunboats to help save the day. "When day broke," Porter humorously wrote, "the big army had vamo[o]sed into thin air, and nothing was heard of them." Since Price was in Arkansas at the time, that was not surprising. The rumor mill, likely turned in part by Confederate scouts and sympathizers for their own amusement, had gotten the rapt attention of Grant and Porter and led to many troops and boats being shifted here and there for no reason. Porter did not take the Price story seriously, but Washburn's spreading of unfounded information had become common.[8]

Getting back to reality, Grant wired Henry Halleck on June 27. Johnston had postponed the expected attack, and reports indicated he would not make a move until he received ten thousand reinforcements currently en route from Braxton Bragg's army in Tennessee. These additional Rebels would likely arrive within a week. Grant asked for no additional troops. He told Halleck, "I feel strong enough against this increase & do not despair of having Vicksburg before they arrive." However, Grant often seemed determined to personally cast shadows on his optimism: "This latter however I may be disappointed in. I may have to abandon protection to the leased plantations from here to Lake Providence to resist a threat from Kirby Smith's troops. The location of these leased plantations was most unfortunate & against my judgment. I wanted them put north of White River [in Arkansas]."[9]

While he continued dealing with a rather warped chessboard of war, Grant saw fruition come to an operation that had been in progress practically since the failed May 22 attack. Grant wanted to blow holes in the Confederate lines, not with artillery but with black powder set off in tunnels dug under key defensive positions. Union engineers directed several approaches, all named after officers, to Confederate works. On the far right, Brigadier General John Thayer's was especially challenging due to a very high bluff in his front. Three approaches on Thayer's left consisted of Hugh Ewing's, Ralph Buckland's, and Joseph J. Lightburn's, all brigadier generals in Sherman's corps. The remaining approaches that followed the

Union line around to Grant's left flank were those of Giles Smith, Thomas Ransom, John Logan, A. J. Smith, Eugene Carr, James Slack, Jacob Lauman, and Frances Herron. The most significant proved to be Logan's.

Logan's approach, called by his soldiers "Logan's Canal," targeted the 3rd Louisiana Redan. McPherson's engineering acumen led him to conclude that breaking through the redan could, hopefully, force Confederates to give up their outer ring of defenses. Union troops could outflank Rebel works on both sides of the redan if it could be breached. The main path to the redan was a mostly flat ridge along which the Jackson road entered Vicksburg. The redan had been built on the north side of the road, and from the front of the redan, relatively open space spanned an area about five hundred yards to the east, towards McPherson's corps or, more precisely, toward John Logan's division. The terrain in places favored approach trenches, but overall, it gave Confederate defenders unobstructed fields of fire. The location of the redan high on a ridge was daunting indeed. Little wonder that Union soldiers called it Fort Hill, though the actual work named Fort Hill anchored the left of the Confederate line. Viewed from Union lines, however, it is easy to see why the soldiers referred to the redan as Fort Hill. Its position on a high ridge made it, indeed, look like an impregnable fort.[10]

McPherson's chief engineer, Captain Andrew Hickenlooper, directed operations and wrote a detailed, postwar account. Grant's headquarters were not too far away, so there is no doubt he kept in touch with progress there. If McPherson thought the 3rd Louisiana works were the key, Grant had no problem giving support. Hickenlooper noted that due to the redan's strength and its formidable position and heavy armament, it became the chief target of the XVII Corps. Logan's division deployed in front of the redan, so if the redan was to be taken, Logan's troops had to do the job, which initially required much digging that dragged on for several weeks. The main labor fell to Brigadier General Mortimer Leggett's brigade consisting of the 30th Illinois and the 20th, 68th, and 78th Ohio Regiments.

The initial work included construction of the usual approach necessities: sap-rollers, gabions, and fascines, and 150 men (down from 300 who initially began digging) worked in day/night rotating shifts. The digging began 150 feet southeast of the Shirley house, the "white house," as it was called. The men in blue were surprised that the Confederates had not destroyed the place, which provided cover from Rebel firing. Logan's approach followed the zigzag pattern and west of the Shirley home; McPherson's artillerists set up a naval battery (guns supplied by

Porter and dubbed Battery McPherson) east of the house and Battery Hickenlooper two hundred yards or so west of the structure. Artillerists aimed the guns directly at the 3rd Louisiana Redan and provided essential cover-fire for soldiers digging the trenches.

During the burial truce, Hickenlooper took advantage of the ceasefire by walking over the terrain between the Shirley home and the redan. Soaking up details in his memory, he knew by the time the ceasefire ended what directions the digging would take. Once the detachments resumed their work, they learned quickly never to stick their heads above ground. The artillery could not protect them from Confederate sharpshooters, who proved their accuracy by putting bullets through caps raised on sticks by the digging parties. The Federals were amused but also reminded of how lethal enemy fire could be if any one of them momentarily forgot the danger and raised his head too high. The digging and firing continued, and occasionally, Confederates managed to set the sap rollers on fire as they were pushed ahead to protect the diggers. Though aggravating, such incidents did not slow Logan's men, for another roller would quickly be brought forward. Hickenlooper wrote he was confused how the Rebels were setting the fires, until after the surrender, when one explained that "cotton saturated with turpentine and placed in the hollow of a minie-ball had been fired at the saps," thus having a fireball effect.

One technique Union artillerymen used as the sap approaches got closer to the redan was the invention of the "Coehorn mortars," which were makeshift mortar guns made by hollowing out sections of gum trees, the sections being bound with iron bands. Like regular mortars, these guns could lob shells over Confederate earthworks, and unlike regular mortars, they were light enough to be moved around easily (the concept of a mobile mortar had been invented in the late 1600s by a Dutch officer named Coehorn). On June 22, the trench reached the base of the front of the redan. Already, orders had been issued for all men who had coal-mining experience to report to Hickenlooper. He chose thirty-six "of the strongest and most experienced" and divided them into two groups, each working a shift on the usual day/night rotation.

The men dug a gallery (a hole) four feet wide by five feet deep "at right angles to the face of the parapet of the fort." The main gallery underneath the ground reached forty-five feet toward the redan, and a smaller parallel one went down fifteen feet. Other shafts branched off the main gallery. Due to typical red-clay soil on that part of the siege lines, no braces had to be built to hold the dirt in place. By the morning of June 25, the miners began putting the black powder in place, eight hundred pounds of it at the end of the main gallery and seven hundred pounds into each remaining shaft for a total of twenty-two hundred pounds. Two strands of fuses from each load of powder Porter supplied were laid behind the powder and stretched to a safe distance. Timbers and earth covered the fuse paths to prevent the explosion backfiring into Union lines.

Confederates in the redan, all too aware of what was going on, dug countermines but to no avail. They also lit fuses of small cannonballs and tossed them over the wall as hand grenades. The miners who carried the powder into the shafts were thus at risk, but none were shot as they ran the gauntlet.[11]

Grant waited impatiently, finally receiving word that the operation of placing the explosives would be completed by 3 P.M., June 25. His many rides along the siege line kept him in touch with the progress of the Logan approach, and he, no doubt, felt elated that at last, success seemed to be at hand. Of course, how well it worked remained to be seen. On June 25, he sent messages to Herron and Ord that the explosives would be detonated at three o'clock. Herron should have his infantry ready, and as soon as the sound of the explosion reached their ears, all artillery in position to hit the redan should open fire for fifteen to twenty minutes. If Herron noticed any Confederates in his front moving to reinforce the redan area, he should make enough noise to indicate his intent to attack. The Confederates must not be allowed to shift troops toward the explosion.[12]

A similar message went to Ord; Grant emphasized to Ord that McPherson would be in charge of the assault to take the "main fort," demonstrating what a key spot the redan was in Grant's mind as well as McPherson's and Hickenlooper's. Ord must be ready, too, to pose a threat to any Confederates shifting from his front to their left. Ord's artillery would join in the barrage following the explosion. McPherson reiterated the time of the explosion in separate messages to Ord and Grant.[13]

Union soldiers knew what was about to happen. As 3 P.M. approached, an almost haunting silence covered the battlefield. The Confederates knew the Yankees were up to something, and the ones in the redan knew more than they wanted to think about. The wise moved back from the main work. One Union soldier wrote, "I remember seeing birds flyover us and noted the unusual quiet. The dust lay thick and when stirred up hung in a thin cloud over us." Most Confederates in and around the redan retreated into a traverse, a defensive work behind the redan. Only a few men from one regiment, the 43rd Mississippi, remained within the redan works, frantically digging another countermine. One can easily imagine Grant pacing and checking the time as three o'clock came and went. Union soldiers up and down the line must have looked at each other wondering what had gone wrong. Had the alert all been for nothing?[14]

At last, a half hour late, the earth in front of the redan rose like a giant waterspout. A Union soldier recalled the moment as "a dead heavy roll," followed by shouting, screaming, and a large, black cloud rising, a mixture of dirt and black-powder residue. He estimated the volcanic-like effect arose perhaps forty feet in the air, and suddenly, the front of the redan wall caved in, dirt pouring down onto the base of the wall. Grant's cannoneers heard and immediately began firing, and McPherson's infantry rushed forward, yelling at the top of their lungs. They ran into Confederate fire from all around the damaged redan. The Rebels arose from the safety of the traverse and poured volley after volley into the assaulting Union troops.

Dirt softened by the explosion created hazardous footing for Federals, and some found themselves trapped inside a crater where part of the redan once stood. Not all the redan wall had been blown away, and Confederates used it as a shield while firing into the crater. Logan became distraught as he watched his men being cut down. Rebels resorted to sending a mass of ignited rolling cannonballs into Union ranks. Some of Logan's men managed to pick a few up and throw them back before they exploded. The fighting raged through the afternoon and into the night as Logan rotated attacking troops, who, as they raced back and forth, tried to avoid dead comrades. Grant had hoped his men could occupy a Confederate entrenchment on the north side of the redan, which would put them in place to pour flanking fire into the defenders and perhaps create a breakthrough. Hickenlooper was told to get at least two cannon inside the crater, but the heavy fighting made that impossible.[15]

Grant received an anxious inquiry from Ord: "How is McPherson doing holding his own. Shall I hold men ready to move that way[.] If so, how many." Grant assured Ord that McPherson had "secured" the crater created by the blast, and it was big enough "to shelter two Regiments." The Rebels had tried to drive the troops off, and Grant thought Logan had lost around thirty killed and wounded. The plan remained to get two pieces of artillery to the crater before sunrise and to dig rifle pits on the left to protect the gunners. "If we can hold the position until morning it evidently will give us possession of a long line of rifle pits to the right, and a fair way of advancing to enfilade to the left," Grant said, adding in a separate note that Ord should keep a division "sleeping under arms" for the remainder of the night and to have them prepared to move at any time. They would likely be needed at first light: "All should be vigilant."

Grant may have expected Pemberton to place more troops at the redan to shore up the line, but the Confederates were too thinly scattered
along the siege line to take the risk. During the night, Grant finally ordered Logan to pull back from the crater. Logan had lost 34 killed and
209 wounded, far more than Grant's estimate during the early fighting;
Confederate casualties totaled 21 killed and 73 wounded. The one-sided
nature of the fighting was obvious. McPherson refused to be thwarted.
He ordered Hickenlooper to get to work on another mining operation on
the right side of the crater.[16]

Grant advised Halleck of the situation on June 26: "Yesterday a mine
was sprung under the enemy's work, most commanding the fort, pro-
ducing a crater sufficient to hold two regiments of infantry." Logan's men
had occupied the crater immediately, and Grant believed they still held it,
which, depending upon where he was when he wrote, likely in his tent, he
thought to be the case. He admitted no batteries had been placed inside
the crater, but he said, "Expect to succeed." He added that Johnston had
moved east of the Big Black: "His movements are mysterious and may be
intended to cover a movement from his rear into East or West Tennessee
or upon Banks—I have Gen. Sherman out near his front on the big black,
with a large force watching him. I will use every effort to learn any move
Johnston may make, and send troops from here to counteract any change
he may make, if I can." Grant still did not see that the only mystery about
Johnston was why he bothered hanging around when he did not intend
to do anything. Likely to keep Jeff Davis from firing him.[17]

The day of the explosion, Grant sent Sherman two messages. Whatever
happened with the explosion, Grant refused to be mesmerized by it. Johnston was still out there somewhere, and Grant determined to keep close
contact with Sherman. Sherman advised on June 24 that Johnston was
still nowhere to be found. Also, Sherman heard that Banks had captured
Port Hudson. Grant replied that nothing had changed at Port Hudson
as far as he knew; the Confederate garrison there was holding out, and
Banks had been thrown back twice. An erroneous message that stated
Port Hudson had surrendered to Banks came from Herron, who was
misinformed. A Rebel deserter reported that Johnston was not south of
the Southern railroad that led to Jackson.[18]

Grant wrote more extensively to Sherman in a follow-up message.
Another Rebel deserter, originally from Indiana, advised that his Texas
cavalry regiment had never gotten closer than Mechanicsburg and was
now on the east side of Big Black. His brigade was at Bolton, a small town
east of Edwards. He confirmed that Johnston had no forces south of the

railroad. According to this man, Johnston had established his headquarters somewhere between Brownsville, northeast of the Big Black, and Canton. The word among Confederates with Johnston was they numbered around thirty-five thousand, only about three thousand more than Johnston actually had. As reports on numbers usually went, this deserter was fairly accurate. Johnston thought Grant had ninety thousand, but he believed that Pemberton could keep them occupied long enough for him to attack Grant's rear. If Johnston truly believed that, he was disingenuous and delusional.

A Rebel courier had also been captured, and he was carrying mail, some of it private letters from Major General Martin Luther Smith to his wife and one letter from Colonel William Withers, an officer of the 1st Mississippi Light Artillery. Smith's words were telling; he believed Vicksburg would fall very shortly, and he looked forward to going north as a prisoner, where he expected to be exchanged. Smith had had enough and wanted to be with his family. Other letters spoke of the excessively high prices for food, and some expressed the continuing hope that Johnston would still save them. Grant wrote rather sarcastically, "Their principle faith seems to be in Providence & Jo Johnston." Sherman had not yet heard about the mining operation, and Grant briefed him, adding, "I think it advisable to keep your troops out until Jo Johnston evinces a design to move in some other direction." Road obstructions should remain in place, and, wanting Sherman to feel free to act, Grant told him if he discovered a change in Johnston's plans, "move to counteract it."[19]

While keeping his eyes on messages and reports regarding siege operations, Grant could never escape housekeeping activities, and he maintained contact with Julia. He longed to be with her, but he would never subject her to danger. Letters were his lifeline, though he had little time to write.

On June 26, he wired Major Thomas Hendrickson, commandant of the Alton, Illinois, military prison about an April 5 message he had written to Colonel William Hoffman about the imprisonment of some of Grant's men on court-martial offenses. When Grant received his copy of the message is not clear, but he obviously did not consider it a top priority, though he now took time to comment. He asked Hendrickson to send him a list of all the enlisted men who were locked up, plus details about what companies and regiments they belonged to. Grant intended to have inquiries made of the charges against the men, and, if they proved to be solid cases, he wanted them transferred to a military prison in Memphis, Tennessee. Grant's main concern was that these soldiers had been subjected to army legal processes without any details being forwarded to him, and he wanted to be sure all regulations had been followed. The number of men under question apparently was only sixty-nine, but they were his men, and if Grant could get them transferred to Memphis, he would have more control over the outcome of their cases. Grant had been through enough administrative entanglements that he did not like being left out of the loop when his department was involved.[20]

Grant also attended to mail problems. On June 29, he sent a blunt wire to Absalom Markland, agent for the post-office department, in response to the agent's message that detailed change in the method of mail distribution for the Department of the Tennessee from Memphis to Cairo. Grant responded, "The mails for this department are carried by Government [men] through their own agents, I believe, as far as Memphis. From that point they are distributed by agents detailed by me." All the mail for his department had to come to Memphis, no matter where it had been sorted and, in Grant's opinion, "should be gotten to that point with as little delay as possible." Distribution of mail at Cairo not only would likely slow delivery but it also would likewise not speed it up. "I have, therefore," he wrote, "to request that no change be made in the present satisfactory postal arrangement." Grant's duties at times transformed him into a bureaucrat trying to control departmental affairs, which closely resembled a government. Whatever his frustration, he was gaining experience that benefited him in the future.[21]

On June 29, Grant wrote Julia a brief message, assuring her that he anticipated the fall of Vicksburg within the week. He wrote of Johnston that the Confederate was still hanging around the east side of the Big Black "and will attack before you receive this or never." Grant assumed that Johnston had many men who were needed elsewhere by the Confederacy, so he had to fight. He cannot back out without giving battle or losing prestige." Grant would be proven right up to a point but not a sharp one. He felt so certain that Vicksburg would be surrendered very shortly that he wanted Julia to come downriver with the kids. They could find a place for the children to begin school and a place to live. At least, he and Julia could spend some time together while he remained in the Vicksburg area. After the capture of Vicksburg, Grant had no idea where he might be sent, but he knew it would take time to finalize the surrender, and he did not want Johnston to fade into the east without be challenged. Grant noted that his son Fred had returned from visiting his uncle and that he seemed a bit ill. After the surrender, Grant suggested sending him north, all the way to Minnesota, where milder weather might improve his health.[22]

Grant, meanwhile, waited in vain for Johnston to show signs of life, and he turned his attention to north Mississippi and Louisiana. He endorsed and encouraged Stephen Hurlbut's suggestion to concentrate available troops at significant bridges. Memphis and Corinth should receive special attention. Hurlbut wrote that Confederates apparently had massed as many as ten thousand men and fourteen pieces of artillery to attack the Memphis and Charleston railroad or for other, unknown reasons. Skirmishing had broken out in several places, and Union troops had destroyed some bridges and crops that might benefit Rebels. Hurlbut also wanted to strike blows along the Mobile and Ohio Railroad. He had tired of William Rosecrans's pleas for men because he did not have enough to hold his own line. Hurlbut believed Rosecrans's persistence was only an effort to have a written record in case of disaster, which Hurlbut thought very unlikely. Also, word had been received that several thousand of Price's men were prowling near the Helena area. Hurlbut feared, too, that the talked-about abandonment of Fort Pillow on the Mississippi above Memphis would encourage Rebel attempts to close the river in the Memphis area.

Such fears were silly and never materialized. Hurlbut believed that Grant's capture of Vicksburg would send Johnston to either join Bragg in Tennessee or encourage him to move north or east to the Tombigbee River, in effect leading to the abandonment of the state of Mississippi by the Rebels. He speculated that Price might strike Helena or go as far south as Lake Providence (perhaps Hurlbut was the source of the Price–Lake Providence false alarm). Hurlbut sounded as if he was under siege, and Grant must have taken his worried message with several grains of salt, though, as in the case of so many other reports, he could not afford to ignore Hurlbut entirely.

Grant believed that any troops from Bragg's Tennessee force that might threaten Hurlbut could be a cover for Bragg to send more men to Johnston. Grant mentioned to Hurlbut he had received a report Johnston anticipated being reinforced with ten thousand troops. Still believing that Johnston had to do something, Grant told Hurlbut, "There is scarsely a shadow of a doubt but I will be attacked by next Wednesday or Thursday [by Johnston] unless Vicksburg should fall in the mean time. It will be impossible for me to send troops from here in the mean time." Grant assured Hurlbut that if he (Grant) received reputable reports that Johnston had decided to move away from the Vicksburg area, "I will send all my surplus force to counteract his movement whether it be to East or West Tennessee. Should more troops become absolutely necessary for the maintainance of your position, before I can send them, telegraph directly to the Gen. in Chief [Halleck] for them." Grant had no intention of allowing Rebel cavalry and rumor deter him from forcing Pemberton to surrender and blocking Johnston from crossing the Big Black.[23]

In Louisiana, things were happening, but they did not amount to nearly as much as Union reports made them sound. Some of John Walker's troops attacked a Federal outpost at a place called the Mounds, five miles west of Goodrich Landing, northwest of Vicksburg on the Mississippi. Though the Rebels allegedly captured a few Arkansas African troops, the attack was notable mostly for the many dwellings Walker's men burned. Throughout Northeast Louisiana, Walker scattered several thousand troops, but he was never able to use them effectively. Some of these men had been sent from Arkansas by Price, which accounted for his name continually coming up in Union correspondence. Captain Embury Osband sent word on June 30 that the Rebels, six thousand of them with eight pieces of artillery, had attacked Lake Providence, another false report.

On the twenty-seventh, Grant warned Elias Dennis that Edmund Kirby Smith, a Confederate general in Louisiana who was more focused on Port Hudson than Vicksburg, might bring troops to the river across from Vicksburg to aid Pemberton's army in its imaginary escape. Dennis should deploy a strong line from Lake Providence to Young's Point to prevent this, but he should not expect help from Grant: "With Johnston in my rear, I cannot detach troops for this purpose." If necessary, planters should be alerted. The unlikely emergency never occurred.[24]

Sherman turned Grant's attention away from the numerous brush fires of administrative details that persisted. Sherman sent a lengthy message to Rawlins on June 27. He had grown tired of waiting for Johnston, and rather than waiting for Grant's approval, he set in motion a policy intended to strengthen his position on the Big Black. Had he known Johnston's mindset, he would not have wasted his time, but he knew that whatever he decided, Grant would support him.

In his message, Sherman indicated he had intended to come to see Grant on the twenty-sixth, but Sherman believed it was more important for him to acquaint himself further with the terrain his troops had to negotiate. He found the ridge-laced ground "so broken and complicated" that he felt he had to take a close, personal look at the geography all the way up and down his battle line. He could see that the Big Black had many easy crossings, undoubtedly inviting to the Confederates. Sherman extended his lines extensively to cover them all and still maintain a solid front between them. Rebel cavalry could be seen on occasion, eyeing various crossings.

Sherman had an epiphany at the Messinger family home, which sat near one of the crossings: "The family consisting of many women, whose husbands and brothers were evidently serving an easy purpose of keeping up communications, so I moved them all by force, leaving a fine house filled with elegant furniture and costly paintings to the chances of war." Also, several war-widowed women and the Hill family living on Birdsong Road from Birdsong Ferry, a few miles north of Edwards on the Big Black, had been relocated within Union lines. "These may appeal to the tender heart of our commanding general, but he will not reverse my decision when he knows a family accessible to the enemy—keen scouts—can collect and impart more information than the most expert spies. Our volunteer pickets and patrols reveal names and facts in their innocence which, if repeated by these women, give the key to our points."

Sherman elaborated further on the landscape: "Innumerable roads and cross-roads intersect the country, which cannot be obstructed, but which, running on narrow ridges, with narrow corn-fields, admit of easy defense. It is only by familiarity with the country, its ugly ravines, its open, narrow ridges all coming to a common spur, that a comparatively small force can hold in check a large one." Sherman surmised that whatever crossing Johnston chose, it would take days to get his men and logistical support across the Big Black, and, once across, he would be moving almost blindly, and he could not tell where Union troops might be lying in wait. Roads were already blocked and would further slow the Confederates. If that proved to be the tactical scenario, Sherman could mass his troops and attack or wait and let Johnston try to attack. If, however, Johnston tried crossing at several places, Sherman would divide his forces and use them as required. If he was forced back, Sherman had already chosen ground where he would fight it out.

Sherman decided, unless Grant wanted otherwise, that he himself needed to stay on the Big Black line. Sherman asked Grant to review General Orders No. 49, which specified the duties and expectations of troops on the Big Black line. If Grant saw any need for changes, Sherman made clear he would make them without question. He added there had not been "a sound, syllable, or sign to indicate a purpose of crossing Big Black River toward us, but I still enjoin on all that our enemy is too wary to give us notice a minute too soon." After all, Johnston had many reasons to attack, and he would not let the word leak out as to when.

If Sherman and Grant could have seen Johnston's July 3 message to Pemberton, they would have changed their minds quickly as to how dangerous Johnston was. "I hope to attack the enemy in your front about the

7th, and your co-operation will be necessary." What cooperation? Johnston would create a diversion, and Pemberton must cut his way out. He could tell where Johnston attacked by listening for sounds of battle. Johnston also made an absurd proposal that Pemberton cross the Mississippi and join forces with Kirby Smith. Maybe Johnston thought the idea of building boats was not so far-fetched. His words were condescending and an insult to Pemberton's intelligence. It did not matter; Pemberton never received the message, and, certainly, he would have been just as well off if Johnston and his so-called Army of Relief had been sent to reinforce Bragg.[25]

Grant responded as Sherman no doubt expected: "The dispositions you have made are excellent." Grant thought it would be "impossible" for Johnston to cross the Big Black north of the railroad "without being discovered and your troops ready for him." The only concern Grant had was that Johnston might move south of the railroad where Sherman's defensive position was not so potent. Yet, "[a] move of this kind certainly could not be intended for anything more than a diversion to relieve the Vicksburg Garrison." Grant did not believe Johnston would try to bring logistical support, mainly supply wagons, on any kind of operation that required his crossing the river.

Ord's cavalry was assigned to scout southern approaches, and Rebel riders in that vicinity seemed disinclined to cross the Big Black. One Ord scout found no sign of the Confederates south of the railroad east of the river. Grant did not think deserters would be much help now, for what they knew could be old information. Johnston could have changed his plans many times. Grant concluded, "You need not fear General, my tender heart getting the better of me, so far as to send the secession ladies back to your front. On the contrary I rather think it advisable to send out every living being from your lines, and arrest all persons found within, and who are not connected with the army."

Sherman's proposal and Grant's reaction did not indicate cruelty to citizens but military expediency. If Johnston attacked, they would be in harm's way, and if no attack came, at least these people could not participate in intelligence activities, which could cause them considerable trouble with Federal officials. The tender-hearted general retained his compassion, but his patience, like Sherman's, had reached its limits. An example came on June 30 when a brief flag of truce had gone up as a request from within Vicksburg by a man and woman who wished to leave the city, claiming they were British citizens. Grant said no. Feeling the town was on the verge of falling, Grant did not want to open gates to those who wished to flee. Such a policy would surely exacerbate military operations.[26]

While Sherman and Grant took a hard-line stance against Confederate civilians near the Big Black, McPherson's new mining operation against the 3rd Louisiana Redan neared completion. The miners had worked quickly and planted two tons of powder beneath the Rebel stronghold. They had heard Confederates digging countermines, and this knowledge spurred the Union miners to complete their task more quickly.

On July 1, McPherson sent Grant a message: "The mine on Logan[']s front is ready & the enemy appear to be digging in towards it[.] Shall I explode it & what disposition do you desire me to make of my troops anything more than having the rifle pits filled with sharpshooters[?]" Grant responded immediately: "Explode the mine, as soon as ready. Notify Ord the hour, so that he may be ready to make a demonstration, should the enemy attempt to move towards you." Grant thought sharpshooters in rifle pits would be sufficient preparation. McPherson should take whatever advantages the explosion offered, whether moving up artillery or advancing his sharpshooters quickly. McPherson shot back a reply that the mine would be detonated at 3 P.M. that day.[27]

McPherson set the time after sending an 11 A.M. message to John Logan: "The mine in your front will be exploded as soon as the proper disposition of the troops can be made." He cautioned Logan that this time, the explosion would not trigger an assault but rather signal troops in the trenches, the sharpshooters, to be ready to take advantage of any opportunities. The men should also be ready as before to repel any enemy counterattacks.[28]

The explosion this time happened on time and did considerably more damage than the initial blast. The left side of the front portion of the redan as well as its right ripped apart, and Confederates had to dig additional works behind the destroyed terreplein. Black men used by Confederates to dig the countermines were all killed except for one, who became legendary. The blast lifted the survivor several feet in the air, and he landed, practically unhurt, within Union lines. Logan's soldiers found the whole event amusing, and one asked the black man how high he reckoned he went. The answer would be oft-quoted, then and through the ages: "Dunno, massa, but t'ink about t'ree mile." Some of the soldiers charged others, who had not witnessed the event, a small fee just to come by and take a look at the miracle man.

In addition to killing the black counterminers, the blast buried a number of Confederate soldiers. Others quickly retreated, found their guns, or a gun, and ran to the crest to meet the expected Yankee assault, which did not come. Firing broke out with Union artillery pounding the area, mortars wreaking havoc among Missouri Rebels. Small arms fire from both sides continued for hours, lasting until July 3. The second mine did not produce the bloodshed of the first, but the negative impact on Confederate morale was considerable. Chief Confederate engineer Major Samuel Lockett recalled that the redan, in effect, was destroyed, and he assisted in desperate measures to build up shields of canvas and dirt to get "something between us and the deadly hail of shot and shell and minie-balls." The explosion's impact and Union fire accounted for nearly one hundred casualties. Pemberton realized, as did his troops on his left flank, his line had almost been breached and likely soon would be.[29]

McPherson reported the aftermath to Grant: "The mine was successfully Exploded today damaging the enemy's works considerably & killing & wounding a number of their men. Six men were blown out on our side. . . . four of them killed one mortally wounded & one a negro slightly hurt[;] the siege guns[,] a portion of Logan & Ransoms arty opened on them with good effect as well as Ransoms Sharp shooters[.] Ransom who was in a position to see the inside of the works says the rebels must have lost a good many men." McPherson had been told that large numbers of Confederates had withdrawn through bottom land toward the Union extreme right flank to get out of range of the thirty-pounder Parrott rifled cannon.

McPherson believed the Rebels had been taken by surprise, and that was probably true regarding the timing. Certainly, they had expected another Union mining operation, for they could hear the work going on. Grant wanted to know if Logan could, after darkness fell, take possession of all the terrain cleared of Rebels and maintain the position without risking too many casualties. McPherson did not answer directly but sent a brief message to Grant that he would come over to confer with the commanding general. McPherson may have feared a Confederate counterattack once the presence of his troops at the redan was discovered.[30]

No doubt elated at the seeming success of the second mining operation, Grant had no time to celebrate. He had to turn his attention to his left flank, where E. O. C. Ord seemed to be confused and addled; Grant quickly realized Ord's messages amounted to little more than a commander's bewilderment at what was going on.

On July 1, Ord wanted to know what to do about a Rebel citizen who had surrendered, who had a sick wife expected to die, and who was destitute and had no servants. The man has "behaved well & is anxious to give his parole & be with his wife[;] can I parole him as I should do if it was left with me[?]" Grant responded that Ord could use his own judgment. He then ordered the general to deploy his troops at potentially threatened places along the Big Black; Herron sent word that enemy troops were crossing at Hankinson's Ferry. Grant for once did not flinch. A few Confederate cavalry hanging around the Big Black were no great threat; they never had been.[31]

Ord sent word about two captured Confederate prisoners who had a small black boy with them. Illinois cavalry had caught them trying to cross the Big Black in a canoe. The men had letters in their possession, which Ord sent along to Rawlins for Grant to examine. The information mainly referred to the lack of rations in Vicksburg. The letters meant nothing to Grant. Since the siege began, deserters had wandered into Union lines complaining about lack of food. Grant wanted Ord to focus on the alleged Confederate activity along the Big Black.[32]

Grant pointedly asked Ord, "Have you any information besides what I sent you? If it is really true that the enemy have 2000 troops at Hankersons ferry they should be met. I will telegraph Gen. Herron to ascertain more fully." Grant contacted Herron to make sure the news was reliable. If Herron thought so, he should send word to Ord for a brigade to stop the Rebels. Herron responded, "I do not place any confidence in the report of the infantry being at Hankinson's Ferry, but think it probably a scout of their cavalry crossed. I have telegraphed fully to General Ord." Sherman had already reported there was no sign of Johnston south of the railroad, so Herron was obviously right.[33]

Ord continued to press Grant for instructions. Should he send a brigade to the ferry? He had heard nothing other than the information Herron sent, which did not instruct him to detach any men. Ord had decided that if the Rebels were doing anything, it was probably a feint. Grant at one point replied, "A cavalry picket to give notice if crossing is attempted will be sufficient. Only move troops after it is known there is a force to oppose." Shortly afterward, Ord sent word that he had reports the enemy had crossed west of the Big Black in the Hankinson's Ferry area. Ord sent Brigadier General Michael K. Lawler's brigade to cover the terrain between Warrenton and the ferry. He then received a message from Major James G. Wilson that his Illinois cavalry regiment had clashed with Rebel horsemen at Hankinson's and had lost several men. Also, during the cavalry fight, about two hundred Confederate infantry had joined in. Grant responded that it might be a good idea to redeploy Ord's troops to cover a wider area. Scouts should be sent, and by tomorrow, "We can tell better then what to do." Lawler reported no problems other than trees blocking roads, and other reports indicated that a small Confederate detachment had done nothing more that conduct a hit-and-run attack.

Grant did his best to settle Ord's nerves: "Sherman has had a Scout out to Bolton. He can discern no indication of troops having passed South. Johnston must be watched at all points however. Big Bayou should be obstructed as high up as possible, except where we use the crossing." Ord received word from Osterhaus on July 1 that one of his patrols had encountered about fifty Rebels on the Edwards road and driven them off. Grant sent word to Sherman that the Rebels had been reported on the east side of the Big Black and that Ord had sent Lawler to check. He told Sherman that Johnston might be trying to find a way to get south of the city, to force Sherman to shift troops in that direction.

Grant followed up with a less-dire message to Sherman. Citizen reports to the south indicated twelve thousand of Johnston's army had passed south of Baldwin's Ferry. Grant admitted he did not believe the news, but he had to be sure. Had Sherman heard anything about Johnston's location? Sherman replied he had found things "absolutely silent along Black River." A scout had been sent out and could find no sign that Johnston's army or wagons had crossed south of the railroad. Troops could be sent to beef up Union presence between Hankinson's Ferry and Warrenton. However, Sherman concluded, "I think Johnstone may feint to the south but do not think he will risk chances in the pocket of of [sic] Black River." Sherman agreed that he must be vigilant, but he believed his scouts would get any urgent information to him quickly. Reports, Sherman advised, placed Johnston in all directions, but none had been accurate.[34]

On July 3, Grant finally received the news he had been hoping for. Pemberton wanted to talk. Grant had endured fighting the enemy, erroneous and nonsensical reports and correspondence, unnecessary fears of a Confederate army in his rear, nervous lieutenants, an antagonistic lieutenant, problems of racial bigotry, and emergencies that mostly were not. With Rawlins available to help him keep up with the administrative circus of his department, Grant had managed to hold things together until the end finally came into sight. His natural tenacity had served him well, not always heroically but well. In war, winning is the bottom line, and Grant was about to accomplish that goal.

~8~

SURRENDER, CLUTTER, IMPACT

THE JULY 3 MESSAGE from John Pemberton to Grant was concise and to the point. "I have the honor to propose to you an armistice . . . with a view to arranging terms for the capitulation of Vicksburg—To this end if agreeable to you, I will appoint three commissioners, to meet a like number to be named by yourself, at such place and hour to day as you may find convenient—I make this proposition to save the further effusion of blood which must otherwise be shed to a frightful extent, feeling myself fully able to maintain my position for a yet indefinite period." Pemberton added that General John Bowen, who had known Grant in prewar Saint Louis, would deliver the message.[1]

Grant acknowledged receipt of Pemberton's note and replied, "The useless effusion of blood you proposed stopping by this course can be ended at any time you may choose, by an unconditional surrender of the city and garrison. Men who have shown so much endurance and courage as those now in Vicksburg, will always challenge the respect of an adversary, and I can assure you will be treated with all the respect due to prisoners of war." Grant refused to agree to the use of commissioners "because I have no terms other than those indicated above." Grant took the same stand as he had at Fort Donelson. Unconditional surrender had worked then; now it did not.[2]

The exchange seemed simple and straightforward, but Grant would learn soon enough of caveats. With a truce in effect, Bowen, anxious to relieve the suffering of his men, manipulated the situation, and it almost torpedoed the negotiations. After the initial exchange of messages, Bowen contacted Grant to see if the latter would be amenable to meeting with Pemberton at 3 P.M. Grant, assuming that Bowen spoke for Pemberton, said he would talk with Pemberton. Bowen also told Pemberton that Grant wanted to talk personally at 3 P.M. Bowen lied in order to bring the two to a face-to-face meeting, hoping for a breakthrough. Thus, Pemberton, one of his aides, and Bowen rode to meet Grant. Pemberton had received Grant's reply to the initial message, but he had not prepared a written response. Pemberton assumed Grant wanted to elaborate. When Pemberton learned from Grant that he had not proposed the meeting, the Confederate general grew angry, and when Grant made clear that his unconditional surrender edict was firm, Pemberton became livid. He assured Grant that the Confederate army would keep fighting and that Grant would suffer additional casualties before he entered Vicksburg.[3]

What happened next is not clear because there are conflicting accounts. Adam Badeau, who worked closely with Grant on his memoirs and was Grant's military secretary during the 1864–65 Virginia campaign but not in Vicksburg, penned what amounted to Grant's version. Badeau wrote that Bowen suggested the two commanding generals move aside so their representatives could discuss the matter. Badeau doubtless reflects Grant's recollection. Pemberton denied that Bowen made any such proposal, and he said that Grant was the one who suggested the two of them walk away while their contingents negotiated. Grant then, according to Pemberton, chose McPherson and A. J. Smith to speak for him, and Pemberton chose Bowen and Pemberton aide Louis Montgomery. These four men consulted while Grant and Pemberton made small talk. These talks resulted in Grant conferring with his commanders and staff, resulting in what Grant called the closest thing to a "council of war" he ever held. Pemberton had previously met with his generals, who assured him that breaking out of the siege to the south was not an option, and that meeting precipitated his first contact with Grant. Now Pemberton awaited an anticipated follow-up proposal from Grant, this time with no confusion about who wanted to meet with whom.[4]

While Grant pondered his next move, he sent messages to all his corps commanders and to the unattached Francis Herron that any Rebel deserters coming into Union lines would be treated as prisoners. He also ordered Herron to cease fire until he heard otherwise from him, because the surrender of Vicksburg was being negotiated. Herron could fire only if he heard guns on the Union right firing the evening of July 3 or the next morning. Rawlins sent a follow-up note that vigilance must be maintained in case any Confederates tried to sneak past Union lines. Rawlins further wrote that Grant would be offering paroles, and prisoners would be allowed to return to their homes. Grant thought it permissible for Union pickets to pass the information along to Confederate counterparts. Ord kept up his usual chatter throughout the day, notifying Grant that his men could hear the enemy working on trenches. Grant responded that he expected his soldiers to do the same. Ord reported that an "Irish deserter" had come in claiming there was no flour left in Vicksburg, very little bacon, and a continuing reduction in bean rations. Also, Ord wanted to know if it was okay for engineers to take advantage of a ceasefire to survey enemy lines.

Ord then sent what has to rank as one of the most humorous, unwieldy messages of the entire war: "In reply to your intimation that if Genl Pemberton wished an interview he would show a white flag at some specified point[,] Genl Bowen stated to Genl Smith that he knew Genl Pemberton would be glad to meet Genl Grant & Genl Bowen on the return of Genl Smith from you appointed the point where the Jackson & Vicksburg Road crosses the rebel trenches as the place where the white flag would be raised at three (3) oclock P M–This point is in front of Gen McPhersons—The rebel time is forty eight (48) minutes faster than mine I will send you my time[.]" If that was not enough to lighten the atmosphere at Grant's headquarters, Ord followed up with: "Shall I notify my men of the enemys offer it will renew their energy after the momentary relaxation by indicating the hold we have on the enemy[.]" Grant replied, "Certainly let them know it[.]" He made no effort to respond to that message's obtuse predecessor, which is unfortunate. Perhaps, Ord would have elaborated on the time discrepancy. Whose watches were wrong and why? Was he conceding the Confederates could move faster than his troops? Did he mean the Confederates had some kind of ruse in mind? Whatever he meant, no one but Ord cared.[5]

Grant finally put into writing his new proposal to Pemberton, based on the conversations that had taken place between the lines at a point north of McPherson's corps. The crux of the terms involved the paroles of Pemberton and his army: "As soon as rolls can be made out and paroles signed by officers and men you will be allowed to march out of our lines the officers taking with them their side arms and clothing, and the Field, Staff & Cavalry officers one horse each. The rank & file will be allowed all their clothing but no other property." If Pemberton agreed, then Grant would send one division into Vicksburg on July 4 for guard duty.[6]

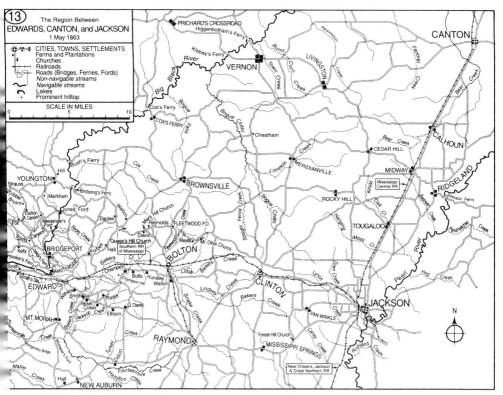

The Edwards-Canton-Jackson area in Grant's rear, May 1, 1863. Map 13, Warren E. Grabau, *Ninety-Eight Days* (Knoxville: University of Tennessee Press, 2000).

Beyond the basics, acceptance of the terms meant "any amount of rations you may deem necessary can be taken from the stores you now have, and also the necessary cooking utensils for preparing them. Thirty wagons also, counting two horse or mule teams as one, will be allowed to transport such articles as cannot be carried along. The same conditions will be allowed to all sick and wounded officers and soldiers as fast as they become able to travel." Paroles for sick and wounded would have to be signed. The offer to allow Pemberton's men to take whatever they needed from the food they had may have sounded hollow, but, contrary to the tales of no food left, many Confederate supplies were available. These included 38,668 pounds of bacon, 5,000 bushels of peas, 51,241 pounds of rice, 82,234 pounds of sugar, 721 rations of flour, and 428,000 pounds of salt. The figures indicate the extremes to which Pemberton and his officers had gone to make supplies last as long as possible. Grant, surely, was surprised to see the relative abundance and delighted to offer the Confederates the option of taking with them whatever they needed from their own storehouses.

There remained issues to be worked out before the thing could be finished. Pemberton responded that he "[i]n the main" found Grant's terms acceptable. However, "in justice both to the honor and spirit of my troops manifested in the defense of Vicksburg," Pemberton wanted the agreement amended to include the evacuation of Confederate lines at 10 A.M. on July 4 and to surrender Vicksburg and the army by allowing his men to march out of their works with their colors and guns, "stacking them in front of my present lines." Once that was done, Grant would order his men to occupy the defensive works. Pemberton further wanted his officers to have the right to keep their "side arms, and personal property," which Grant had already stipulated, plus he wanted Grant to guarantee citizens' rights and property would be "respected."[7]

The negotiations continued into July 4. Grant made a strong effort to bring the surrender to a conclusion. Both Pemberton and Grant had tense moments, each waiting for the other to reply to the latest proposal. Grant's reaction to Pemberton's latest assured the Confederate general that the amendments cited were not necessarily unreasonable but could not be acceded to in full, a much more positive response than outright rejection. The parole process would be slow, so Pemberton's army could not march out until it had been completed. Each soldier had to sign a parole, and with several thousand men involved, that obviously "will necessarily take some time."[8]

Grant refused to make a firm commitment to protecting citizens and private property: "While I do not propose to cause them any undue annoyance or loss, I cannot consent to leave myself under any restraint by stipulations." Confederate officers could, as previously stated, keep their sidearms and personal property plus one horse each. Grant had no problem with each Rebel brigade marching to the front lines and stacking arms at 10 A.M., but he again reminded Pemberton they must return until the parole process had been completed. If he had not heard from Pemberton by 9 A.M. on the fourth, Grant wrote, "I shall regard them as having been rejected and shall act accordingly." If Pemberton should agree, he must order white flags to be hoisted along his lines to keep Grant's soldiers, who might not be aware of the surrender, from firing into Confederate lines.[9]

Grant waited, and at last he received a reply from Pemberton: "I have the honor to acknowledge the receipt of your communication of this date; and in reply to say that the terms proposed by you are accepted." At last the siege was over; Grant had won his greatest achievement up to that time. Pemberton later argued that he waited until the fourth because he believed he could get better terms that date. Perhaps, but his reasoning sounded more like an after-the-fact rationale than a before-the-fact plan. Grant believed that Pemberton knew he could not long maintain his defense of Vicksburg if Grant ordered an attack on July 4.

While he exchanged notes with Pemberton, Grant corresponded with David Porter and Sherman to keep them apprised of negotiations. He asked Porter to cease all fire from the gunboats unless otherwise informed or unless he heard the land batteries start shooting. Grant promised he would "fire a national salute into the city at daybreak [July 4] if they do not surrender," and he sent word to Herron, McPherson, and Ord to be ready to fire the salute. He, of course, delayed further orders because negotiations had not ceased by daybreak. He sent Porter more than one such message to make sure the news had been received. Grant confessed to Porter that paroles and allowing Rebel officers to keep their side-arms did not suit him, "but all my officers think the advantage gained by having our forces and transports for immediate purposes [elsewhere] more than counterbalance the effect of sending them north."

Grant knew that many of his troops indeed were needed in other areas of the war, and Halleck was anxious to send them there. He may have been opposed in principle, but he knew in reality his officers were right. Porter agreed. After receiving confirmation of the surrender, he congratulated Grant on capturing Vicksburg "on any honorable terms." Porter noted, "You would find it a troublesome job to transport so many men and I think that you will be left so free to act it will counterbalance any little concession you may seem to make to the garrison."[10]

On July 3, Grant notified Sherman of Pemberton's initial contact and responded to a Sherman message of the same date that reported all quiet on the Big Black front, plus defensive works to block Johnston were progressing nicely. Grant responded with a substantial understatement: "I judge, Johnston is not coming to Vicksburg," but Sherman should remain vigilant, not that Sherman had seen any signs of Johnston. Though Grant at that point did not know the ultimate course the surrender negotiations would take, he told Sherman bluntly, "When we go in [to take possession of Vicksburg], I want you to drive Johnston from the Mississippi Central Rail Road,—destroy bridges as far as Grenada with your Cavalry, and do the enemy all the harm possible—You can make your own arrangements and have all the Troops of my Command, except one Corps—McPhersons—say,—I must have some Troops to send to Banks to use against Port Hudson."[11]

The same day, Sherman contacted Grant to remind him to announce the surrender as soon as possible so the hunt for Johnston could begin. He planned moving on Canton or Jackson, whichever Grant wanted. Sherman wanted to go after Johnston with his own XV Corps, Ord's XVII Corps, and John Parke's IX Corps in reserve. Sherman was certain Grant would take Vicksburg, making the holiday the best since 1776. "Of course," Sherman cautioned, "we must not rest idle. . . . dont let us brag too soon." Messages continued back and forth hour after hour. Grant believed Pemberton would surrender the evening of July 3 or the next morning. Sherman should proceed with preparations to march east, destroy the Mississippi Central/New Orleans, Jackson, and Great Northern Railroad (the name changed at Canton) north of Jackson. Sherman's corps would move east; he sent orders to Parke. Sherman passed along the amounts of rations that would be needed. He intended to concentrate at Bolton and move east from that point. He assumed Pemberton had notified Johnston of the surrender. Pemberton had not been in touch with Johnston since negotiations with Grant had begun, but Johnston was aware of Pemberton's intent for he had turned down Pemberton's request to negotiate with Grant himself. Johnston did not want to stain himself by participating in the surrender, even though he had done nothing to prevent it.[12]

Responding to Sherman's wish to be immediately informed about the surrender and what directions he should go when he moved east, Grant briefly updated the situation. He made clear that though he had ideas about the pursuit of Johnston, Sherman could do what he felt best: "I have directed Steele and Ord to be in readiness to move . . . the moment Vicksburg is surrendered." He made clear to Sherman that he not only wanted Johnston driven away but also "broken up as effectually as possible." Grant did not instruct Sherman on how or where to go, but he suggested a simultaneous campaign against Canton and Jackson. If Johnston was still around, Grant reasoned, surely, he would be in one place or the other or both.[13]

The July 3 correspondence deluge continued. Sherman sent Rawlins a lengthy letter acknowledging receipt of two Grant messages. Sherman mentioned he had heard some firing in Vicksburg that confused him under the circumstances. Sherman asked Parke to check on this, and Grant sent word to Parke and Sherman: "Flag of truce only covered the bearer of dispatches. Firing was continued by the balance of the line." The shooting must have occurred during the early exchange of messages between Grant and Pemberton because Grant had shortly afterward ordered a ceasefire. Grant's messages to Sherman obviously had been delayed, to the point Sherman had trouble keeping up with events in Vicksburg as they unfolded. Sherman passed along information sent by Colonel Clark Wright of the 6th Missouri cavalry that Confederate picket activity along the Big Black had increased, and loud commands heard from the east side of the river indicated Johnston's advance was nigh. Sherman noted he did not consider Wright's reports reliable, though he did think that Johnston would likely attack. Peter Osterhaus said there was little Rebel activity east of his position on the Big Black.

Despite factors to the contrary, Sherman and Grant continued to believe Johnston might, or would, go on the offensive. Neither could believe Johnston would make no effort at all. Sherman added that once the surrender of Vicksburg became official, he needed to move against Johnston. He went on to outline the current disposition of his troops and propose routes for the reinforcements to take when they came to join him He believed his force should go to Jackson and as far as Meridian to destroy the railroad. Then he could concentrate at Jackson and go north to hit the Mississippi Central. Any troops not needed for that foray could return to Vicksburg and be sent to Nathaniel Banks at Port Hudson. Sherman personally did not think Banks needed help. The place was already tightly besieged and would certainly fall once Grant occupied Vicksburg. Troops would also be available for Banks once Sherman defeated or scattered Johnston's force.

Finally, Sherman noted his logistical needs and his desire to have James Wilson's maps to complement the ones he already had. Before implementing his plans, he would await Grant's approval. He obviously had not received Grant's message that Sherman could determine his own course. On July 4, Grant notified Sherman that a Pemberton response to Grant's latest proposition was expected very soon. If Pemberton continued to resist, Grant felt sure the Confederate army would force their general to accept the terms. Notifications and orders had already been sent to set in motion the concentration of troops coming to join Sherman. He promised to inform Sherman "the moment Pembertons answer arrives." Grant did just that.[14]

Sherman responded gleefully, "The telegraph has just announced to me that Vicksburg is ours. . . . I can hardly contain myself. Surely will I not punish any soldier for being 'unco happy' this most glorious anniversary of the birth of a nation. . . . Did I not know the honesty, modesty, and purity of your nature, I would be tempted to follow the examples of my standard enemies of the press in indulging in wanton flattery; but as a man and soldier, and ardent friend of yours, I warn you against the incense of flattery that will fill our land from one extreme to the other. Be natural and yourself, and this glittering flattery will be as the passing breeze of the sea on a warm summer day. To me the delicacy with which you have treated a brave but deluded enemy is more eloquent than the most gorgeous oratory of an [Edward] Everett." Sherman's praise continued, but his words spoke volumes of the depth of his friendship with Grant. That friendship and the innate trust it implied would become more and more evident during the future course of the war.[15]

While Union soldiers celebrated, Grant issued Special Orders No. 180 on July 4, which addressed a clutter of administrative details that must be attended to postsurrender. First, after the surrender announcement, General Herron sent one brigade to occupy Rebel fortifications and deployed guards to block any citizen or Confederate soldier from coming into or leaving Vicksburg. Grant doubtless focused on main roads, for there was no way to prevent Pemberton's soldiers from finding escape routes as long as they did so alone or in very small groups. Citizens intending to return to Vicksburg via steamboat needed permission to disembark.

The plans to exercise some kind of control quickly became problems. Ord reported to Grant on the fourth that no guards had shown up along the Confederate lines of defense. Union soldiers were busying themselves raiding stores and homes, and Confederates were simply walking east out of town. Grant reported the problems to McPherson and pointed out that Ord could not take care of such things since he and his corps would be joining Sherman's expedition. McPherson seemed more concerned with which troops would be marching into Vicksburg to ceremonially take possession of the town.[16]

Grant led the ceremonial procession into Vicksburg and down to the riverfront to congratulate Porter and his navy. For the first time, he saw the caves so many citizens had been forced to live in. He toured some of the caves, noting the number of rooms cut out inside: "Some of these were carpeted and furnished with considerable elaboration." He found the security of the caves remarkable, for they had stood firm against the constant barrage of navy shells. He was obviously impressed with citizens' ingenuity.[17]

Union soldiers partied, but they were ordered not to fire rifles and cannon. Grant felt the Confederates deserved a measure of respect for what they had endured. Likely the strains of the song *The Battle Cry of Freedom* rang out from the voices of thousands of Grant's soldiers. It had become the favorite song of his men throughout the campaign. He, doubtless, did nothing to stop such singing, but when he heard cannon fire from his right flank, he grew angry at Steele, who commanded there in the absence of Sherman. Grant's son Fred wrote that Grant commented that Steele "ought to know better than to allow any triumphing over our conquered countrymen." Steele was not directly at fault, but he found the battery that was and immediately stopped the gunfire.[18]

Meanwhile, John Logan received the assignment of temporary commander of Vicksburg, and he was ordered to lead his division into the Confederate defenses and establish a camp. He deployed sentries in the same manner as Herron. An additional duty fell to one regiment to "preserve order and to prevent pillaging and other destruction of property." Five companies were assigned to guard all Confederate property captured and to oversee the work of the black men as might be assembled and needed for work in the quartermaster department. Others were organized into groups to police the town "and all the grounds within the entrenchments." It would be up to Herron and Logan to stop the Confederates from leaving town and, as Logan's order indicated, bring order to the downtown area.

Finally, chief engineer Captain Cyrus Comstock supervised the "destruction of the outside approaches made to the enemy's works." McPherson supplied workers from his corps, and black males provided additional labor. All large artillery pieces would be moved from offensive to defensive positions. Division engineers or division quartermasters had to collect mining tools. Fortunately, many Union soldiers assigned to destroy the trenches and other defensive positions did so half-heartedly; the survival of a number of these works provides a clearer picture of what happened during the siege than history might otherwise have provided.

Grant's immediate task was to clean up Vicksburg as much as possible, to control movements of prisoners and civilians, to have a provost marshal assigned to prevent his troops and others from plundering businesses and homes, and to transform siege works into Union defense positions. He could not afford to assume that Confederates would not be sent to try to recapture the city. Without a navy and hampered by manpower shortages, the Confederate War Department seemingly had no chance of taking Vicksburg back, but in Grant's view, as with Johnston, he had no intention of being lax or presumptuous.[19]

Aside from seeing to a semblance of order in Vicksburg, Grant's headquarters received requests from regiments to inscribe their varying banners with names of battles fought during the campaign. James Wilson suggested a board of officers be set up to deal with details. Rawlins, Sherman, Hurlbut, and other officers got involved in the discussions. Grant stayed out of the way; he had a town to reconstruct and Sherman's pursuit of Johnston to think about. He left this less-significant issue to his staff and other officers.[20]

On July 3, Grant had received a message from steamboat superintendent George Graham requesting celebratory activities on boats on the river for the Fourth of July. Included would be firing of cannon and reading of the Declaration of Independence. Grant simply endorsed the message, "Yes." On the Fourth, Rawlins received a message from Graham asking for a copy of the Declaration and another asking for "glad tidings[,] something that I can depend upon for fourth of July." Rawlins responded, "Vicksburg will probably be surrendered at 10 oclock today. the terms have not yet been fully settled, will be by nine oclock, will send you word. Dont go off half cocked." Grant left this issue in Rawlins's hands while he focused on getting messages upriver to Memphis via Charles Dana. But with all else going on, Dana missed the first boat going north. Porter did not wait to get word of the surrender to Secretary of the Navy Gideon Welles, who received it a day before Grant's news reached Henry Halleck. The situation typified the chaos that sometimes frustrated Grant's headquarters. Orderly correspondence was impossible.[21]

In his note to Halleck via Dana, Grant defended his parole decision: "The only terms allowed is their parole as prisoners of war[.] This I regarded as of great advantage to us at this juncture. It saves probably several days in the capture term—leaves troops and transports ready for immediate service. Gen Sherman with a large force will face immediately on Johnstone and drive him from the state." Grant promised Halleck he would send troops to Ambrose Burnside and Banks. Halleck's July 8 reply must have surprised Grant: "I fear your paroling the garrison at Vicksburg without actual delivery to a proper agent as required by the 14th article of the cartel may be construed into an absolute release & that these men will be immediately placed in the ranks of the enemy. Such has been the case elsewhere. If these prisoners have not been allowed to depart, you will retain them till further orders." Two days later Halleck sent another wire: "On a full examination of the question, it is decided that you as the commander of an Army was authorized to agree upon the parole and release of the garrison of Vicksburgh with the Genl [Pemberton] commanding the place."

Grant's reaction was not recorded at the time, but he doubtless felt relieved, and the thought probably ran through his mind—"same old Halleck." Grant was a professional military man, however, and he would have followed orders, but in doing so, the reinforcements he had pledged to others would have been delayed getting to their destinations. Perhaps, that truth led to Halleck's quick retreat. In any event, Grant did comment in his memoirs that Halleck did not know at the time he sent Grant the first message that the Confederate prisoners had already been turned over to the Confederate commissioner on the exchange of prisoners. Grant kept quiet, especially after receiving the second message.[22]

Following his July 4 announcement, Grant wrote Halleck a summation of fruits of the surrender. Grant guessed that more than thirty thousand Confederates had surrendered, and his men had counted 170 pieces of artillery. Much ammunition had been found, and large amounts of food had been located: flour, bacon, sugar, and thirty thousand small arms, which seemed to be in good shape. This news, doubtless, had a positive impact on Halleck, though whether it figured in his about-face regarding paroles is not known.[23]

Grant had other correspondence to attend to. He sent word to Banks about the surrender and explained that troops had been deployed to cover the line from Haynes's Bluff to the Big Black. Sherman had left to search for Johnston. Sherman's campaign, bound to succeed given his manpower advantages and Johnston's temerity, would keep Johnston from trying to reinforce Port Hudson. Despite his victory, Grant did not offer immediate reinforcements to Banks. He noted the paroling of Pemberton's army and observed, "It leaves the transports and troops free for immediate use. At the present juncture of affairs in the East, and on the river above here, this may prove of vast importance." Grant mentioned further to Banks that Porter seemed to think Banks was on the verge of success, and Grant wrote optimistically, as he had in the past, that he hoped his message found Banks in possession of Port Hudson. Banks responded with words of congratulations and told Grant that Port Hudson should capitulate in less than a week. He was right. Major General Franklin Gardner, Confederate commander, surrendered on July 9.[24]

When Porter heard the news, he offered use of his vessels to get messages to Banks and also noted that some Rebels were still moving around on the Louisiana side of the river. Porter on his own initiative sent gunboats at every opportunity to chase the Confederates away, but he thought Grant might want to send infantry. Grant did nothing more than send word to Elias Dennis to use artillery to protect Lake Providence. The capture of Vicksburg and Banks's ultimate capture of Port Hudson opened the Mississippi to Union traffic (though Confederate sniping continued) and pushed the Trans-Mississippi Theater into the backwater of the war compared to securing Vicksburg and ridding Mississippi of Joe Johnston. Porter and Grant met again on July 6 at the Mississippi River shore to exchange congratulations.[25]

Grant spent part of the fourth sending marching instructions to Ord, who had tried unsuccessfully to correspond directly with Sherman. Grant instructed Ord as Sherman had suggested. He assured Sherman that Ord would begin moving the night of the fourth, though he would likely get only one division into motion, due to the lateness of the day. In a separate message, Grant told Sherman that both Ord and Steele (still commanding Sherman's corps) would begin marching east the evening of the fourth. Grant approved leaving the IX Corps in reserve until Sherman determined he no longer needed that corps; at that point, he should send it back to Vicksburg so Grant could get it underway to Burnside. Sherman need not expect campaign instructions from Grant: "[D]rive Johnston out in your own way."[26]

On July 6, Sherman informed Grant that all his troops had arrived, though many were not in good condition, some affected "by Vicksburg 4th July," a clear reference to too much celebrating after Pemberton surrendered, which the continuing oppressive heat and clouds of dust exacerbated. The Big Black had risen about four feet unexpectedly, making some fords impassable for the moment. Sherman intended his army to cross the afternoon of the sixth, assuming the river went back down, and he determined to be in Clinton by July 8. As his army moved east, Sherman found evidence of Johnston's retreat. He believed Johnston had been readying to cross the Big Black on the fourth or fifth, but, according to reports Johnston had heard on July 3, Pemberton had initiated the surrender proceedings. Sherman found abandoned Confederate camps at Bolton. He believed Johnston had withdrawn east along the railroad, and that would prove to be the case.[27]

While Sherman continued his quest, Grant had to address postsiege issues regarding freed slaves. He outlined his policy to McPherson, who would be responsible for implementing details. The policy applied to "negroes captured in Vicksburg." For the immediate future, no males would be allowed to enlist in black units, later to be designated U.S. Colored Troops. Able-bodied black men should continue cleaning up the city, unloading incoming freight on riverboats, and working on preparation of fortifications that the occupying forces could use. A question that bedeviled McPherson was the issue of Pemberton's officers taking their black servants with them when they left Vicksburg. Grant told McPherson that he had pointedly refused that request. However, following the surrender, Confederate officers approached Grant with a follow-up question. What did he intend to do "about servants who were anxious to accompany their masters, remarking that many of them had been raised with their servants and it was like severing families to part them."

Grant responded that he would not institute "compulsory measures" to keep servants in Vicksburg. His main concern was that all blacks be aware they were now free. If they understood that and still wanted to go with their former owners, fine. He believed those individuals might benefit the Union cause by reporting to former fellow slaves that "the Yankees set them all free." Grant assured McPherson that he should not be overly concerned about enemy officers complaining that their servants had been "enticed" to stay. This could easily be a phony excuse to get their former slaves returned. Grant noted that his policy not to force servants to stay who wanted to leave with their former owners "is no reason the strength of the garrison should be used in preserving a neutrality between our men and the negroes that would enable the Confederate officers to carry off their negroes by force."

Regarding two other issues raised by McPherson, Grant ordered that no more than one day's rations should be given to Pemberton's soldiers when they marched out of the city, and he believed that giving them one thousand horses seemed beyond the terms of capitulation. Grant's generosity had its limits, especially when it seemed the Confederates were trying make the best of the surrender beyond the original parameters Grant's and Pemberton's negotiations set down.[28]

On July 6, Grant, busy as he was, followed military protocol by mailing a very long report covering the Vicksburg campaign from the march down the Louisiana side of the Mississippi to the siege and Confederate surrender to Assistant Adjutant General John C. Kelton. Rawlins copyedited Grant's draft. The length of the report indicates that Grant had to have begun work on it prior to the surrender. At some point later in July, he signed the final version. Rawlins personally delivered the report to the War Department. James Wilson claimed in his biography of Rawlins that Rawlins's polishing and editorial work was mostly responsible for the neat content of the final copy. This was an exaggeration, typical of Wilson building up Rawlins at Grant's expense. Grant always left editorial duties to Rawlins, but Grant composed his own reports.[29]

Grant must have relished writing a letter to his father about the surrender. The two had had tense moments in the past, so Grant could be forgiven for personal satisfaction in announcing his great triumph. He reviewed the particulars of the surrender and the aftermath of captured prisoners and ordnance. He also included a proud comment on his army: "The weather now is excessively warm and the roads intolerable dusty. It can not be expected under these circumstances that the health of this command can keep up as it has done. My troops were not allowed one hours idle time after the surrender but were at once started after other game."[30]

Grant turned again to clarify policy to McPherson regarding black servants and surrendered Confederates. Grant's orders had an obtuseness that understandably confused McPherson in his efforts to obey the rules as written. A classic example regarded Grant's comments that he would not prevent a former slave from leaving with a former master if the former slave so desired to leave. His comment grew out of a particular case and was not intended to be broadly interpreted. Grant explained that on that occasion, "the officer said he had a family and children and could not get along without a nurse. Further that the nurse had been raised in the family and was like one of them and would take it as hard to be seperated as would an actual member of the family." If McPherson saw "any indication that a suspicious number of blacks are going to accompany the troops out then all should be turned back except such as are voluntarily accompanying families, not more than one to each family." In effect, he did not intend the word *voluntary* to be defined by Confederates.[31]

When McPherson passed the particulars of the clarified rules on to Pemberton, the latter was not happy. McPherson pointed out that some Confederate officers had intimidated their servants into going with them, that some Vicksburg citizens had urged black men and women to leave with the army, and that others had been brought into Vicksburg to work on fortifications and, therefore, owed no allegiance to Pemberton's officers. Pemberton countered that the many should not be condemned by the "misconduct" of a few, that whatever citizens did should not impact the policy toward his army. He accepted the responsibility for those black men who worked on the fortifications, implying that such situations should not be used to deny these laborers' right to leave if they wanted to go. Pemberton received no response; the matter was settled as far as Grant was concerned.[32]

Parole procedures also became contentious. Grant wrote McPherson twice on July 8 on that subject, one message duplicating in part the other. Grant was obviously annoyed by the differing interpretations of the process by the Confederates and himself. He restated to McPherson the overriding policy: "[N]o prisoners will be allowed to leave our lines until all are paroled who will accept." Further, those who declined paroles would be put on river steamers and held there until they changed their minds. If that did not work, they would be sent north to prisons. Once the parole process was complete, all parolees would be "required to leave our lines." Those who hesitated would be escorted out by guards. Anyone trying to muddy the waters should know that Pemberton's acceptance of surrender terms bound Rebel officials to "acknowledge the entire garrison of Vicksburg on the morning of the 4th inst. prisoners of war. The only object in issuing paroles to the officers and men, is that they may feel the Same obligation that Southern authorities will in this matter."

The whole purpose of the written rolls naming names was to give Washington authorities evidence that would facilitate negotiations for exchanges of prisoners. Grant urged McPherson in another note that troops who had signed paroles were to be moved east out of Vicksburg. Grant then sent word to Bolton that Union officers there should soon expect to see the Confederates, who would begin marching out on July 9. He was too optimistic; they did not begin leaving until July 11.[33]

Grant agreed to Pemberton's request to leave Major General Martin Luther Smith behind to facilitate paroling of Rebel sick and wounded and, in some cases, to allow furloughs. Grant promised that Smith would be treated well and given assistance. Communications between Pemberton and Smith, after the former left the city with his army, would be allowed, and Grant promised all messages would be delivered to Smith and from Smith to Pemberton, using flags of truce to avoid any misunderstandings about the process.[34]

On July 9, Grant sent word to Francis Herron to prepare to move his division downriver to Port Hudson by the eleventh. Grant, at that point unaware of the fall of Port Hudson but expecting the place's capitulation at any time, wanted Herron to return when the Rebel garrison surrendered. The next day, Grant sent word to Banks that Herron would be coming with his division's infantry. Grant acknowledged Banks might have captured Port Hudson before Herron arrived, but he thought Banks might want to go after Richard Taylor's forces in Louisiana, and Herron's division would come in handy for such a campaign. Obviously, Grant changed his mind about allowing Herron to stay at Port Hudson after the surrender. Banks eventually did go after Taylor, but not until 1864, resulting in the disastrous, for Banks, Red River campaign. Grant advised Banks that new reports indicated Sherman was within ten miles of Jackson. Other than the continuing desire to destroy Kirby Smith's Trans-Mississippi forces, Grant wrote, "I have but little idea of what is next to be done with our Western forces. Hope to have instructions from Washington soon, however."[35]

Grant heard about a resounding Confederate defeat upriver at Helena, Arkansas, ironically on July 4. Helena, still an important Union staging area, had been stripped of most Union forces to reinforce Grant.

Confederate Lieutenant General Theophilus Holmes, commander of the District of Arkansas, decided to attack the Union post, both to help relieve Grant's hold at Vicksburg and to destroy Helena as a threat to eastern Arkansas. Holmes's plan came to nothing. Major General Benjamin Prentiss, commanding Union troops at Helena, fought well, but Holmes's gross incompetence in managing the battle contributed more to the Confederate defeat than Union resistance.[36]

Grant passed along the good tidings to Banks, and he added that on July 5, he had heard from Washington that Major General George Gordon Meade had beaten General Robert E. Lee in Pennsylvania (Gettysburg). He closed his letter by pointing out that Herron and his men had left their baggage at Vicksburg, and he trusted Banks would send them back upriver as soon as feasible, another illustration that Grant sent Herron downstream for show. He could tell Halleck he had sent help to Banks while letting Banks know that Herron was a temporary gift. Perhaps, he initially had in mind Herron helping Banks to secure Port Hudson. If so, he shelved that idea quickly. Grant wanted Herron back, and he wanted Benjamin Grierson and his cavalry, Grant's cavalry force being smaller than he felt he needed.[37]

On July 11, Grant finally received the long-anticipated news of Banks's victory. The surrender came on July 8, though Gardner did not formally surrender until the next day. Banks told Grant he would like to keep Grierson and his cavalry for two more weeks and then would send them to Vicksburg. Banks now envisioned going to Texas to build up a Federal presence there. He asked Grant for ten thousand to twelve thousand men if they could be spared. Banks acknowledged Grant's desire to send troops east, but Banks wanted to be sure trustworthy western soldiers did not leave.[38]

Grant congratulated Banks, noting the "removal of the last obstacle to the free navigation of the Mississippi. This will prove a death blow to Copper headism in the Northwest besides proving to demoralize the enemy. Like arming the negros it will act as a two edged sword cutting both ways." He brought Banks up to date on recent activities: Soldiers had been sent to Natchez to grab five thousand cattle moved from across the river and intended for Pemberton's army. He also recalled Herron before the latter could do anything for Banks; he wanted Herron to bring his troops back to Vicksburg and then up the Yazoo River to Yazoo City. Herron was to make sure the enemy navy yard there was completely destroyed; Porter would provide support. Grant acted due to a report that Johnston had sent a large number of former slaves to Yazoo City to fortify the town.

The same report, supposedly written by Johnston, contained news that Johnston had defeated part of Sherman's army and captured three of his brigades. (On July 12, Jacob Lauman's division had been pounded in an ill-advised attack, which led to Lauman being removed from command, but Johnston's troops had not captured any Union brigades.) Grant said he would send a corps to Banks "if I am not called on to do some duty requiring them." Further, until Sherman met and defeated Johnston, Grant refused to commit any troops to Banks.[39]

Grant finally heard from Sherman on July 9, but the news was no more than a progress report. The van of Sherman's army had reached Clinton and moved east toward Jackson. No fighting had yet occurred. Grant informed Sherman of the fall of Port Hudson in a July 11 message and noted that he had heard nothing from Sherman for two days. He passed along information about Yazoo City and wondered if Johnston was receiving reinforcements. He concluded, "Hoping to hear of your giving Johnston a good threshing, and driving him beyond Pearl River, with the loss of his artillery, transportation and munitions of war."[40]

Sherman responded July 11 that his army had arrived at Jackson's outskirts. He asked for an additional division to guard his supply and communications lines between Champion Hill and Clinton, and he requested a supply depot be established at Big Black bridge. The next day, he wrote Grant that his artillery had opened fire on the city and was being deployed in a semicircle from north of Jackson to the southern reaches, the Union line being on the west side of the town. He requested more rifled artillery and ammunition. Sherman added, "I fear the weather is too hot for me to march to Grenada." He proposed that troops along the Memphis to Corinth corridor move south and wreck bridges and railroads. Such would free him to focus on Johnston and to destroy the rail line from Jackson to Canton. Could not Grierson be sent to him? Unfortunately for Sherman, Grierson would be delayed leaving Port Hudson until July 18, by which time Sherman had defeated Johnston and chased the Confederates away from Jackson. Grant sent Grierson on to Memphis for future operations in west Tennessee. He did join Sherman in the latter's expedition against Meridian in 1864.

Sherman offered all sorts of advice on what Grant should do next, ignoring the fact that Grant could do nothing until he received orders. Such was typical of Sherman; he always had opinions and was anxious to share them. He advised Grant on how the remainder of his old corps should be handled. Grant continued to hear from Sherman on a consistent basis about the situation at Jackson. At one point, he observed,

"Johnston evidently intends to make a strong fight at Jackson, behind his parapet."[41]

Grant wrote a lengthy July 13 note to Sherman. He expressed his thoughts on the situation at Jackson, thoughts that covered a broad spectrum. Grant had tired and grown frustrated as what amounted to a siege played out with Sherman trying to pressure Johnston into abandoning the capital city. Grant reiterated Sherman's mission: to break up Johnston's force, driving it from the rear of the army at Vicksburg and to destroy all he could of railroads and railroad cars and any supplies that might be helpful to the Rebels. Sherman should return to Vicksburg as soon as all these goals had been achieved. He left to Sherman how far cavalry should be sent north or east. Did Sherman think Johnston continued to receive reinforcements? If he was not, perhaps he had decided to hold Sherman in place while the railroad going east to Meridian was being stabilized, providing an opportunity for the Confederates to move as many railroad cars out of harm's way as possible. In a worst-case scenario, if Johnston indeed had received or was receiving troops, could Sherman pull back to the Big Black without any problems?

Grant did not believe Sherman should send infantry farther east than their current position, unless a Johnston retreat offered possibilities. If Sherman thought he did not have the manpower to drive Johnston away and if his staying where he was proved dangerous, he should return to Vicksburg. Meanwhile, Grant continued to reinforce Sherman. Finally, he reported that an intercepted Confederate letter in the east indicated that Jefferson Davis had been unable to send Johnston all the troops the latter wanted. Grant believed Confederate concern for the eastern front meant that Johnston could not expect more help.

Obviously, Grant had put the surrender of Vicksburg behind him and focused his anxiety on Sherman's expedition. Grant's words indicated he believed Johnston might prove to be a tough opponent while doubting he would receive additional help from the Confederate government. Grant's words revealed the same roller coaster of emotions he had shown throughout the siege regarding Johnston's threat to the Union rear, which had come to nothing. Grant could not express total optimism until Sherman had scattered Johnston and his troops. That was the only news that would relieve his worries.[42]

The next day, Sherman responded he had enough troops. He, likewise, did not believe Johnston would get more men, and in any event, Sherman had enough artillery to make it difficult for Johnston to stay where he was much longer. Cavalry had already made much progress tearing up the railroads running north and south out of Jackson. Sherman then proceeded to write a long epistle about the campaign he had conducted thus far.[43]

On July 14, Sherman received a short note from Grant asking if Johnston had been reinforced to the point that more men should be sent from Vicksburg. Grant, on the one hand, believed Johnston would not get reinforcements, but, on the other hand, had he? Grant's obsession with Johnston clung to him tenaciously. Obviously, delivery of messages was being delayed. Grant wrote, "If it becomes absolutely necessary I will send everything but one Brigade and the Convelescents from here." Sherman responded that evening in a very patient tone to Grant's almost hysterical offer: "All is well with us. I think I have enough. Johnstone is still in Jackson & our skirmishers are engaged all around the lines & but little execution done by either party. Our lines of investment are well covered by rifle trenches. We are now firing every five minutes from four different Batteries day & night & as soon as the ammunition train is up will increase the fire."

Union artillery shot and shell had enough range from Sherman's lines to reach the Pearl River on the east side of Jackson and into and beyond the rear of Johnston's lines. If Johnston had been getting more men, he had not shown it by his actions. A ceasefire had been called to bury the dead resulting from the July 12 action, a repeat of the situation early in the Vicksburg siege. The truce indicated that Rebels intended to stay for a while or they could be buying time. Sherman wondered if the truce bought time for Johnston to plan an escape. Confederates had not conducted any sorties and had stayed in place while Sherman extended his lines on both flanks. False news that Union armies had occupied Richmond, Virginia, increased Sherman's optimism. He sent newspapers through the lines so Johnston could read more about it. Once Johnston gave up the fight, "[i]f he moves across Pearl River & makes good speed I will let him go." Sherman had no desire to chase Johnston down, wearing out Union troops already exhausted from heat and battle. Surely, the Confederates were, likewise, worn and would have no desire to fight once they left Jackson.[44]

Grant continued to see the Union glass at Jackson half empty. Herron, who had reached Yazoo City, received a somewhat-cryptic note from Grant. Herron could stay where he was as long as Porter thought his presence necessary to protect both the town and Porter's men while they salvaged a gunboat, the USS *DeKalb*, blown up by a mine on July 13 (with Herron on board) and sunk in the Yazoo. Once Porter released him, Herron should return to Vicksburg, his men bringing all supplies they wanted from Yazoo City and destroying the rest. Herron could also bring cotton and "all the negro men you can" and, of course, any prisoners.

Grant made clear he did not want Herron in Yazoo City too long "because it may become necessary for me to send all the forces that can be possibly spared to Jackson."

On July 15, Grant sent Herron an urgent message that a reported four thousand enemy cavalry had gone north of Jackson with the likely goal of attacking Sherman's supply line. Herron must move as many of his men as could be spared from Yazoo City eastward to block this enemy cavalry column. Johnston had indeed sent cavalry in search of Sherman's wagon trains, but their success was minimal, and they were forced to retreat to Jackson.[45]

Grant decided he should again update Halleck, and on July 15, he sent the general in chief news of Sherman's successful investment of Jackson, attacks on the railroads, Herron's capture of Rebels and armaments at Yazoo City, the sinking of the *DeKalb*, the sending of troops to intercept enemy cattle at Natchez, and the assistance provided to Banks. He asked if he should send the IX Corps back to Burnside once Sherman drove Johnston out of Jackson. Grant covered his anxiety well; he knew Washington wanted positive news. At the same time, he asked Halleck about sending troops back to Burnside, Grant wrote Major General John Schofield in Saint Louis that he did not know how much longer he would need troops sent from that area. Schofield wanted to campaign in Arkansas, but Grant would in no way make a commitment to give up men as long as Sherman besieged Johnston.[46]

Events at Jackson continued to grate on Grant's nerves. Some paroled Confederate officers came to see him to get permission to buy food for their families on the east side of Jackson. They told Grant they understood that Sherman would have the town by the next day, July 16, and they did not want to travel too far east to get what they needed. The conversations led Grant to wonder if Johnston's cavalry was meant as a diversion to allow Johnston to abandon Jackson, and by destroying some of Sherman's supplies, Johnston might be hoping to slow Sherman's pursuit. Grant worried that Herron could not get his detachment to block the enemy cavalry in time to protect the wagons. If Johnston had indeed sent most or all of cavalry on this expedition, Sherman should consider sending some of his troops east to destroy any supplies left unprotected by Rebel cavalry.[47]

Sherman was well aware of all that was going on and had taken steps to meet threats to his supply line. He knew about Herron, and he sent a brigade west to protect the wagons. He sent word to Grant that if Johnston indeed intended to retreat, he hoped to be aware of it quickly. As far as he knew, Johnston's big guns had not been moved. He added,

"[T]he wooded nature of the outskirts covers the interior of the city also the campfires & Burning Railroad ties have so filled the air with smoke that we see but little." He sent word to pickets to be especially watchful for any major movement of Johnston's troops. Sherman hesitated to make a move east until he knew his wagon train was safe. Meanwhile, word came to Sherman's headquarters that much destruction of railroad equipment, including locomotives, had been carried out at Canton.[48]

At last on July 17, Grant received news that he had been longing for. Sherman sent a telegram at 8 P.M.: "Genl. Johnston evacuated Jackson last night. I will occupy with one Division of Steele & hasten the enemy on his way, but in mean time the weather is too hot for a vigorus pursuit. Rail Road north & south is very absolutely annihilated." In a second message the same day, Sherman reported, "I have just made the circuit of Jackson[.] we are in full possession & Johns[t]on is retreating east with thirty thousand men who will perish from heat thirst & disappointment." A few hundred of Johnston's men surrendered, and heavy Confederate artillery had been left behind. Sherman had accomplished his mission, and he stuck to his decision to let the Rebels go: "I do not pursue because of the intense heat, & dust & fatigue of the men but I will perfect the work of destruction & await orders[.]"[49]

Grant, though happy, did not like the idea of Johnston retreating unhindered. He cautioned Sherman to save railcars but, as much as possible, to destroy the railroad running east as he had the north and south tracks. Grant believed that even a slight pursuit would force Johnston to leave his supply wagons and cause large numbers of Confederates to desert. Grant still had no desire for Sherman's infantry to march after Johnston, but he thought cavalry would be effective. Grant suggested leaving the rail cars alone based on the assumption that Jackson would be occupied "for the present." He continued leaving final decisions to Sherman, taking care not to order anything. In a separate message, he elaborated, "Continue the pursuit as long as you have reasonable hopes of favorable results, but do not wear your men out. When you stop the pursuit return by easy marches to the vicinity of this place[.]"

Sherman responded that nearly all his cavalry was still wrecking railroads north and south of Jackson, Sherman making sure that Grant understood it would take time to recall these riders, and he believed they were being more productive where they were. Sherman stated plainly he did not think occupying Jackson for any length of time would be worth the trouble. With all his sick and wounded, and most every man "determined on furloughs," he doubted he could maintain more than a shell of his corps.

Simply maintaining a presence along the Big Black for sorties when necessary would be sufficient to prevent future trouble from Confederates.[50]

Vicksburg had fallen, and Sherman's victory secured the capture of the city. Grant, however, was not done in Vicksburg. While Sherman's campaign against Jackson had been in progress, Grant continued to deal with other issues. He chose McPherson to command the city of Vicksburg, and the citizens responded very favorably to the fair-minded general. He wrestled with restoring the town's shattered economy, and he set up a program to feed people in need. Long lines developed every day at various distribution points as desperate people waited to be fed. McPherson took care of this and other issues and in the process became very popular with the town's citizens, who appreciated his compassion, fairness, and devotion to easing the human condition. Grant had chosen well. Grant asked Porter to help with monitoring riverboat passengers traveling from Vicksburg to New Orleans to make sure they were "proper," that is, not Confederate sympathizers or officials who might cause problems or who needed to be retained for any other reasons. Porter had special concerns about spies and about guerrillas who continued to shoot at riverboats.[51]

Grant heard and read requests from civilians who wanted to go beyond Union lines to property east of Vicksburg and to have their travel and property protected. Grant usually granted the requests to travel, but he refused to provide escorts once the citizens passed Union lines. He had issued orders to all Union troops not to ransack homes and property, but he knew he could not control soldiers bent on disobeying those orders. He intervened to protect his formerly slaveholding friends in Natchez, Henry Duncan and his father, Stephen Duncan, who were strong Unionists. Grant became incensed when the Duncans' former slaves, freed by the Duncans, were forcibly carried away by those recruiting for black regiments. The Duncans had apparently contracted with the freedmen to continue working. Grant asked Dennis to investigate the incidents and to make sure the Duncans received reparations. He wanted those who participated in taking the freedmen from the Duncans arrested, and "all officers among them" sent to Grant's headquarters.[52]

Grant successfully intervened to have the medical director of his department, surgeon John Mills, restored to his position, after Mills had been, in effect, forcibly retired by Washington bureaucrats. While waiting for a response, Grant sent Mills's temporary replacement, surgeon John Moore, a complaint from Confederate General Martin Luther Smith that Rebel sick and wounded whom Pemberton had necessarily left behind as prisoners had not been receiving proper medicines and food. Grant ordered Moore to investigate: "[E]very thing necessary for the health and comfort of those confined in hospital" must be supplied."[53]

Women from as far as eight miles east of Vicksburg came to see Grant about having guards at their home. According to these women, guards had been assigned to almost all homes in the countryside but not theirs. They complained to Grant that "negroes are armed and wors than the straggling soldiers." Grant asked McPherson to order his cavalry to patrol as much of the outlying areas as possible and gather all the guards and see to it that they returned to their regiments. All armed black men should also be retrieved and assigned work details inside Vicksburg. Grant added, with humor that he perhaps did not intend, "It is highly probable that most of the guards are self constituted guards. In that case they should be punished same as stragglers."[54]

Regarding the handling of wounded and sick prisoners, Grant decided to act on General Smith's request to move by boat to Mobile, Alabama, and Alexandria, Louisiana, all who could not tolerate land transportation. To send these men to Mobile, Grant sent a staff member to Banks's headquarters at Port Hudson to facilitate river transports. Banks's staff arranged for the boats to go to New Orleans and from there to Mobile. Grant added that he still could not send troops due to Sherman's situation at the time. Banks had complained about Confederate activity in Mobile but admitted that he did not feel threatened.[55]

So it went. Grant had captured Vicksburg and no longer had to worry about Jackson or Johnston. He had been congratulated by Abraham Lincoln, who wrote that Grant's crossing the Mississippi was the move Lincoln had earlier thought would work. Whether Lincoln was wise after the fact or truly anticipated the key to success ahead of time, only the president knew. Lincoln went on to confess that he had thought Grant wrong in not proceeding south to join Banks after the Battle of Port Gibson. He also feared Grant wrong in taking the initial path taken in the early stages of the inland campaign. "I now wish to make the personal acknowledgment that you were right, and I was wrong." However, Lincoln would not go along with Grant's, and Sherman's, wish to campaign against Mobile. For the moment, Lincoln felt the French threat to Mexico made concentration of Union troops in west Texas necessary. Therefore, Grant could not take as large a force as he likely would need to attack Mobile. Indeed, Grant was losing men: John Parke took the IX Corps back to Burnside; Grant also had to send five thousand men to Schofield from Vicksburg plus another eight thousand from Helena and west Tennessee, and he sent the XIII Corps to Banks.[56]

Grant stayed in Vicksburg for many weeks, setting up headquarters in the William Lum home. Julia and Fred came to Vicksburg, and the Grants and Mrs. Lum became very good friends. Julia met one woman who praised Grant's generosity in getting food to civilians. The woman found it ironic that the defenders of Vicksburg had done so much to keep Grant and his army out of the town, and now they welcomed his benevolence. Unfortunately, by the end of 1863, the Lum home was razed to make room for additional earthworks. Grant continued to languish with endless administrative details, and he and Julia occasionally took boat rides on the Mississippi. Grant travelled as far south as New Orleans and as far north as Cairo, Illinois. He kept abreast of campaigning in Arkansas and Louisiana, sideshows to be sure, but his responsibility nonetheless. At last, he finally had an opportunity to get back into war, but in ways he never anticipated.[57]

William Rosecrans had been defeated at the Battle of Chickamauga in northwest Georgia on September 19–21 and had retreated into Chattanooga, allowing himself to be besieged by Bragg. Grant received orders from Halleck on October 17, dated the previous day, to proceed to Louisville, Kentucky, where he would receive further instructions. Edwin Stanton, Secretary of War, surprised Grant by meeting with him personally at Louisville. Grant would take over in Chattanooga, chase Bragg away, and, ultimately, go to the eastern theater where he would assume command of all the armies.[58]

What had U. S. Grant learned directing and administering the siege of Vicksburg? What lessons and experiences would benefit him as he moved forward, eventually becoming commander of all Union armies?

The May 19 and 22 failed assaults taught him that overconfidence could be costly to the men he commanded. Yet, he also saw that to keep his army effective during siege operations required keeping them active. Part of that activity was military necessity; the digging of trenches and creation of defensive works along his siege lines meant that his soldiers must become used to shovels whether they liked it or not—and few did. Yet, the unsuccessful assaults made them realize they must both defend themselves and stay on the offensive. Grant's attitude that his noose around the Confederates must continually be tightened filtered down through the ranks. He understood, both instinctively and realistically, that the siege must be proactive in order to force the enemy to surrender. The general policy of continued aggression went with him to Chattanooga and Virginia.

His obsession with Joseph E. Johnston seemed to impact Grant in a positive way as he moved forward in the war. Sherman once said of Grant, "Grant did not care a damn about what the enemy did. He focused instead on what he intended to do."[59] He learned it the hard way during the Vicksburg siege, and that philosophy would serve him well at Chattanooga and especially in Virginia. His concerns about Johnston ebbed and flowed, but he spent many hours wrestling with fears of an attack by Johnston. In terms of normal military strategy, his views were well founded. Grant would not have sat on the sidelines if he was expected to help Union forces trapped in a siege. He made the mistake of thinking that Johnston held the same views. He did not know Johnston's background of service in the Confederacy: Johnston's feud with Jefferson Davis, his unhappiness at being given command of the western theater, his anti-administration views of what should be done about Vicksburg. So, being unaware of Johnston's baggage, Grant's worries based on his assumption that Johnston would practice basic military strategic principles were justified. Johnston's inaction, ultimately, contributed to Grant changing his attitude toward concerns about what the enemy might do. He never again wrung his hands over concerns about enemy armies. In Chattanooga, he took the battle to the Confederates and eventually drove them away, sealing Chattanooga for the Union. He made clear in Virginia that the Army of the Potomac must stop wondering what Lee was doing and focus instead on what it would do to Lee. His experience with Johnston was a lesson he never forgot.

Except for the John McClernand affair, Grant demonstrated administrative skills in dealing with subordinates. Grant allowed deep-seated personal feelings to mar his relationship with McClernand, though, certainly, the fault was not his alone. He already had warm interactions with Sherman and McPherson, and though McClernand's replacement, E. O. C. Ord, proved too erratic at times, Grant made good use of him. Other generals gave Grant little trouble; most acted professionally regardless of whether their backgrounds were West Point or not.

Grant's Midwestern background made it easy for him to develop a good rapport with his army; in Virginia, he would face a challenge in that area, but once the Army of the Potomac realized it was being led by a fighter rather than just another retreater, the soldiers there embraced him. Grant led by being who he was; there were few pretentions about him. His style served him well. When he did get angry, his demeanor was usually justified. At Vicksburg, with an army in place for many weeks, he had an opportunity to hone the skills of managing a large force and for the most part keeping them content.

One trait he developed was avoiding micromanagement of his generals. He made clear his plans and expected results. Certainly, he freely gave his personal opinions on how operations could be carried out, but for the most part, he hesitated to give orders that might hamstring his officers. He knew what he wanted, but he could not be in many different places to observe conditions, such as terrain, creeks, roads, and undergrowth. So he left the detail work to his officers, especially those he trusted to get the job done. This policy worked well for him.

He developed managerial skills beyond maintaining good military relationships in the Vicksburg area. Certainly, he managed to satisfy Halleck, Stanton (with the help of Dana), and Lincoln, though he had no direct contact with Lincoln until after Vicksburg surrendered. The support he received proved their faith in him. Managing to keep Washington satisfied would be of great benefit when he moved on to Virginia and would serve as the foundation for skills he would need as a politician.

With the assistance of Rawlins, Grant managed to deftly resolve most all issues that confronted him. He dealt with many administrative aggravations, which served him well in Chattanooga and especially in Virginia. Some issues that came up were important; others were sometimes minor and/or ridiculous. The whole of it all gave Grant an opportunity to experience the complexities of overseeing a military department and making it function, and he proved to be more than competent in dealing with the big picture and intricacies.

As for military matters, his most significant duties, he proved adept at handling difficult tactical issues. His siege lines, his efforts to defend the Big Black River crossings, his outreach to the Louisiana side of the Mississippi, and his ability to read commanders and know whom he could count on to take care of things (excepting McClernand) demonstrated that he had the kind of feel for command that is an absolute necessity for any successful commander. At times, shifting troops proved to be remarkably complex, but he managed to carry on without risking his siege lines and other trouble spots, real or imagined.

The Vicksburg siege laid the foundation for the confident, competent commander who ultimately left the western theater to go east, assume command of all Union forces, and lead eastern Union forces to victory over Lee. He left his friend Sherman behind to finish off the west. Grant emerged from the siege not only a victor but also a man whose experiences made him ready for new and greater challenges. He fulfilled the duties of great responsibilities awaiting him in Virginia as he had met and overcome the imposing task of besieging and capturing Vicksburg.

BIBLIOGRAPHIC NOTES

NOTES

INDEX

BIBLIOGRAPHIC NOTES

The Papers of Ulysses S. Grant, a thirty-two volume collection of significant Grant papers, has been enhanced by the inclusion of additional correspondence that expands the parameters of Grant's life. This newly included correspondence is especially important because the wording comes directly from originals. The published papers have been digitized and are now available to the world at http://library.msstate.edu/usgrantassociation. Volumes 8 and 9 are applicable to the Vicksburg siege. Because documentary publishing is of necessity a selective process, the Grant website is all the more valuable because it includes a finding aid to over sixty-six thousand pieces of correspondence not included in the published volumes.

The old standbys *The War of the Rebellion: A Compilation of the Official Records of the Union and Confederate Armies* (*OR*) and *Official Records of the Union and Confederate Navies in the War of the Rebellion* (*ORN*) are still vital to any study of the Civil War. The pertinent volume from the army records for the current volume is volume 24, parts (volumes) 1–3, but it is not as neatly arranged for Grant information as the published Grant papers, and papers have been edited to correct grammar. Still, the *OR* volumes are vital, along with volume 25 of the navy records, to the study of the siege.

The Ulysses S. Grant Presidential Library at Mississippi State University contains the largest number of Grant documents known to exist. The Ulysses S. Grant Association has maintained and makes possible this collection. True, many of the papers are photocopies, but their being together in one location makes the documents available in a way no other repository can match. In addition to the copies related to the Vicksburg campaign are microfilmed copies of Grant materials in the Library of Congress and the National Archives. A large group of subject files augments the collection. For example, included are copies of James Wilson's papers (originals in the Library of Congress), especially important for a study of the siege. Wilson's papers include correspondence with Charles Dana and Sylvanus Cadwallader. A separate Cadwallader collection is in the Library of Congress. Copies of this correspondence are also in the Grant presidential collection. The collection also has a microfilm copy of National Archives Record Group 393, Department of the Army of the Tennessee records, necessary to an understanding of the Vicksburg campaign and siege.

The Vicksburg National Park Archives, too often ignored by historians, are a treasure trove of campaign studies, regimental records, and the experiences of common soldiers as related through thousands of letters, diaries, memoirs, and other writings. The breadth and depth of any aspect of the Vicksburg campaign cannot be fully understood or appreciated without examining these files. The printed guide available at the park greatly facilitates the use of these records. Also valuable are manuscript sources in the Old Courthouse Museum in Vicksburg. The courthouse withstood the siege and is today a fascinating museum as well as a primary-source repository.

Primary sources in states represented by the Union army are significant for understanding the Vicksburg campaign and siege. These sites include but are not limited to university libraries, state historical archives and societies, and state libraries. The Illinois State Historical Library, now a part of the Abraham Lincoln Presidential Library, contains hundreds of documents that Illinois participants in the Vicksburg campaign wrote. These documents are especially important because Illinois had more soldiers participating in Vicksburg operations, including the siege, than any other state. Other significant primary-source collections are in the Indiana Historical Society and the Indiana State Library, both located in Indianapolis, the United States Army Military History Institute, Carlisle Barracks in Pennsylvania, the Perkins Library at Duke University, and the University of North Carolina Southern Historical Collection in the Wilson Library at Chapel Hill.

Vital in any study of Grant is *Memoirs of Ulysses S. Grant*, 2 vols. (New York: Charles L. Webster, 1885), especially volume 2 for the Vicksburg campaign. There have been many subsequent editions. Also very helpful are William Tecumseh Sherman's memoirs. For this study, the author used William T. Sherman, *Memoirs of William T. Sherman*, 2 vols. (New York: Great Commander Series, 1994), a reprint of the original 1875 edition. Sherman's memoirs, like Grant's, have been republished in several editions.

The many biographies of Grant, frankly, elaborate very little on his siege experiences. None paints those forty-seven days with a detailed brush. The best biography to date is Jean Edward Smith's *Grant* (New York: Simon and Schuster, 2001). Brooks Simpson's biography of Grant,

Ulysses S. Grant: Triumph over Adversity, 1822–1865 (Boston: Houghton Mifflin, 2000), promises to be a landmark study. Simpson's investigation of the Yazoo drinking story is but one example of his tenacity as a researcher.

Useful Vicksburg campaign studies are Warren Grabau, *Ninety-Eight Days: A Geographer's View of the Vicksburg Campaign* (Knoxville: University of Tennessee Press, 2000); Edwin C. Bearss, *The Campaign for Vicksburg*, vol. 3 of 3 vols. (Dayton, OH: Morningside, 1985–66); and Michael B. Ballard, *Vicksburg: The Campaign That Opened the Mississippi* (Chapel Hill: University of North Carolina Press, 2004).

In addition to Smith's and Simpson's biographies of Grant, others are helpful in fleshing out the siege milieu. Invaluable to the current volume is Richard L. Kiper's *Major General John A. McClernand: Politician in Uniform* (Kent, OH: Kent State University Press, 1999). Other helpful works are John F. Marszalek, *Sherman: A Soldier's Passion for Order* (New York: Free Press, 1995); Michael B. Ballard, *Pemberton: A Biography* (Jackson: University Press of Mississippi, 1991); and Craig I. Symonds, *Joseph E. Johnston: A Civil War Biography* (New York: Norton, 1992).

A study that explores an often overlooked aspect of the Civil War is William B. Feis, *Grant's Secret Service: The Intelligence War from Belmont to Appomattox* (Lincoln: University of Nebraska Press, 2002). Feis provides an excellent look at the milieu of spy activities throughout Grant's Civil War years.

NOTES

Abbreviations

OR   *The War of the Rebellion: A Compilation of the Official Records of the Union and Confederate Armies*, 128 vols. (Washington, DC: GPO, 1880–1901). All citations refer to series 1. Following *OR* are volume number, (part number), and page number(s).

ORN   *Official Records of the Union and Confederate Navies in the War of the Rebellion*, 35 vols. (Washington, DC: GPO, 1894–1927). All citations refer to series 1. Following *ORN* are volume number and page number(s).

PUSG   John Y. Simon, ed., *The Papers of Ulysses S. Grant*, 31 vols. to date (Carbondale: Southern Illinois University Press, 1967–). Most volumes are available at http://digital.library.msstate.edu/collections/index.php?CISOROOT= /usgrant.

USGPL   Ulysses S. Grant Presidential Library, Ulysses S. Grant Association, Mississippi State University, Jackson

VCS   Vicksburg Campaign Series, Vicksburg National Military Park Archives, Vicksburg, Mississippi

1. Long Road to Vicksburg

1. *OR*, 24(3), 317; Grant to Porter, May 22, 1863, Grant to Halleck, May 22, 1863, *PUSG*, 8:249, 250.

2. The foregoing overview is largely taken from Michael B. Ballard, *U. S. Grant: The Making of a General, 1861–1863* (Lanham, MD: Rowman and Littlefield, 2005), 1–150, and Michael B. Ballard, *Vicksburg: The Campaign That Opened the Mississippi* (Chapel Hill: University of North Carolina Press, 2004), especially 319–413.

3. James Harrison Wilson, *Under the Old Flag*, 2 vols. (New York: Appleton, 1912), 1:197; Sherman to Ellen Sherman, April 23, 1863, in William T. Sherman, *Sherman's Civil War: Selected Correspondence of William T. Sherman, 1860–1865*, ed. Brooks D. Simpson and Jean V. Berlin (Chapel Hill: University of North Carolina Press, 1999), 455; Ballard, *Vicksburg*, 202.

4. Ulysses S. Grant, *Memoirs of U. S. Grant*, 2 vols. (New York: Webster, 1885), 1:529.

5. Ibid., 530–31; S[amuel]. Black, *A Soldier's Recollections of the Civil War* (Minco, OK: Minco Minstrel, 1911–12), 51.

6. *OR*, 24(3), 333–34.

7. Samuel Fletcher and D. H. Fletcher, *A History of Company A, Second Illinois Cavalry*, (1912?), *Internet Archive*, http://archive.org/details/historyofcompanyooflet.

8. "Excerpts from the Diary of Henry Seaman," *Civil War Times Illustrated*, copy in 13th Illinois file, Regimental Files Sub-Series, VCS.

9. Edwin C. Bearss, *The Campaign for Vicksburg*, 3 vols. (Dayton, OH: Morningside, 1985–86), 3:862–71.

2. A Regular Siege and Paranoia

1. Grant, *Memoirs*, 1:528.

2. *OR*, 24(3), 343.

3. Grant to Halleck, May 24, 1863, *PUSG*, 8:261.

4. Ibid.

5. *OR*, 24(3), 348; Grant, *Memoir*, 1:535.

6. Grant to John C. Kelton, [July 6, 1863], *PUSG*, 8:504; Edwin C. Bearss, "The Vicksburg Centennial Commemorative Association presents Siege of Vicksburg Centennial, June 30–July 4, 1963," VCS; D. H. Mahan, *A Treatise on Field Fortifications* (New York: Wiley, 1861), 146–54.

7. Howard C. Westwood, "The Vicksburg/Port Hudson Gap—The Pincers Never Pinched," *Military Affairs*, October 1982, n.p., 10–11, VCS.

8. John M. Godown to Fannie, June 22, 1863, Godown Papers, Indiana State Library, Indianapolis; Christopher Duffy, *Siege Warfare: The Fortress in the Early Modern World, 1494–1660* (New York: Routledge, 1979), 211–12.

9. Ballard, *Vicksburg*, 360.

10. Wells Leggett to mother, June 6, 1863, Mortimer D. Leggett file, and Young to mother, May 28, 1863, Gilbert Young Letters, Journals, Diaries, and Letters Sub-Series, VCS; Frank Swigart, "Vicksburg Campaign," *National Tribune*, August 9, 1888; James C. Vanderbilt to mother, June 24, 1863, Vanderbilt Papers, Indiana State Library, Indianapolis; Grant, *Memoirs*, 1:530.

11. Wilson, *Under the Old Flag*, 1:211–3; Charles Dana, *Recollections of the Civil War* (New York: Appleton, 1898), 78–79; Adam Badeau, *Military History of General U. S. Grant*, 3 vols. (New York: Appleton, 1885), 1:338.

12. Orville Babcock, diary, June 21, 1863, USGPL; Committee of the Regiment, *The 55th Illinois, 1861–1865* (1887; repr., Huntington, WV: Blue Acorn, 1993), 249; James Flint Merrill "Reminiscences, 7th Rhode Island Infantry," n.p., n.d., Journals, Diaries, and Letters Sub-Series, VCS; Anthony Burton, diary, 5th Ohio Independent Artillery, June 17, 1863, Journals, Diaries, and Letters Sub-Series, VCS; Gilbert W. Young to mother, May 28, 1863, Gilbert W. Young letters, Journals, Diaries, and Letters Sub-Series, VCS; Ebenezer Werkheiser to sister, August 29, 1863, Werkheiser letters, Journals, Diaries, and Letters Sub-Series, VCS; J[ohn] J[ackson] Kellogg, *The Vicksburg Campaign and Reminiscences, from Milliken's Bend to July 4, 1863* (Washington, IA: Evening Journal, 1913), 59–60, Journals, Diaries, and Letters Sub-Series, VCS; Chaplin N. M. Baker, *National Tribune*, June 26, 1902, photocopy, 116th Illinois file, Regimental Files Sub-Series, VCS.

13. "Memoirs of Captain Kellogg," 59–60.

14. *OR*, 24(1), 343, 338; Grant to Jacob Lauman, May 23 and 28, 1863, *PUSG*, 8:259, 282; Dana, *Recollections*, 79–80; Hamlin Garland, *Ulysses S. Grant: His Life and Character* (New York: Macmillan, 1920), 232.

15. Grant to McClernand, May 24, 1863, *PUSG*, 8:204–5.

16. *OR*, 24(3), 346–47.

17. Grant to Halleck, May 25, 1863, Grant to Stephen Hurlbut, May 24, 1863, Grant to Prentiss, May 25, 1863, John Rawlins to Hurlbut, 1863, *PUSG*, 8:267, 272–73, 297.

18. William B. Feis, *Grant's Secret Service: The Intelligence War from Belmont to Appomattox* (Lincoln: University of Nebraska Press, 2002), 166–70.

19. Dora Miller, diary, May 28, 1863, files, Old Courthouse Museum, Vicksburg; Belzer Grebe, memoir, 19, Journals, Diaries, and Letters Sub-Series, VCS; *OR*, 24(3), 457, 402, 24(1), 281; Ballard, *Vicksburg*, 337, 381–82; Michael B. Ballard, *Pemberton: A Biography* (Jackson: University Press of Mississippi, 1991), 179–80.

20. Grant to Porter, May 24, 1863, Porter to Grant, May 25, 1863, Grant to Porter, May 27, 1863, *PUSG*, 8:263–64, 285; *ORN*, 25:38.

21. Porter to Grant, May 23, 1863, *PUSG*, 8:258.

22. Stephen Lyford to Grant, May 25, 1863, Grant to McClernand, May 28, 1863, Grant to Porter, May 29, 1863, Alfred Ellet to Grant, May 30, 1863, *PUSG*, 8:276, 281, 284–85.

23. *OR*, 24(3), 347.

24. Badeau, *Military History*, 1:329; Ballard, *Vicksburg*, 349.

25. Ballard, *Vicksburg*, 349–50. The social interaction continued through the ensuing weeks, though some bitter feelings developed. An example was the shooting of Douglas the camel, a mascot of the 43rd Mississippi. The exact date he was killed by a Union sniper is not known, but the story goes that several members of the 43rd made sure the sniper was killed. Douglas was a remnant of the camel experiment begun during the years Jefferson Davis was U.S. Secretary of War. He imported camels to be used in dry areas of the western territories. The experiment did not pan out, and camels became scattered across the country. Douglas had survived the battle at Corinth in October 1862, but he wound up buried somewhere in Vicksburg. Whether Union soldiers knew about Douglas is not known, but he is not mentioned in any letters and diaries read by the author. Terrence Winschel, "The Camel at Vicksburg," VCS; J. W. Cook, "Old Douglas—The Camel Burden Bearer," *Confederate Veteran* 11, no. 11, 1903, 494.

26. *OR*, 24(3), 349–50.

27. *OR*, 24(1), 90.

28. Dana, *Recollections*, 81–82.

29. *OR*, 24(3), 359.

30. Ibid., 359–60.

31. Ibid., 367.

32. Ibid., 352; Order 141 issued under Rawlins's signature for Grant, May 26, *PUSG*, 8:288.

33. Grant to Porter, May 29, 1863, Grant to Blair, May 29, 1863 (two messages), Blair to Grant, May 28, 29, 1863, *USGPL*, 8:285–86, 287–90.

34. Grant to Sherman, May 25, 1863, Grant to Johnson, May 25, 26, 1863, Grant to Osterhaus, May 29, 1863, Osterhaus to Grant, May 29, *PUSG*, 8:275, 280, 291–92.

35. Grant to Hurlbut, May 31, 1863, *PUSG*, 8:297–98.

36. Ibid.; William T. Sherman, *Memoirs of William T. Sherman*, 2 vols. (New York: Webster, 1875; New York: Great Commanders Series, 1994), 1:246. Citations refer to the Great Commanders edition.

37. *OR*, 24(3), 354–55; Blair to Grant, May 29, 1863, *PUSG*, 8:290.

38. Grant to Blair, May 29, 1863, Blair to Grant, May 29, 1863, *PUSG*, 8:287–88; William E. Parrish, *Frank Blair: Lincoln's Conservative* (Columbia: University of Missouri Press, 1998), 171.
39. Grant to Blair, May 29, 1863, Blair to Grant, May 29, 1863, *PUSG*, 8:289.
40. Blair to Grant, May 31, 1863, *PUSG*, 8:290.
41. Committee of the Regiment, *Story of the Fifty-Fifth Regiment*, 248; Ballard, *Vicksburg*, 390.
42. *OR*, 24(3), 374, 380.
43. Ibid., 375, 379.
44. Grant to Kimball, June 3, 1863, Kimball to Rawlins, June 4, 1863, Grant to Kimball, June 4, 1863, Grant to Jonathan Richmond, June 4, 1863, Grant to Porter, June 4, 1863, Grant to Kimball, June 5, 1863, *PUSG*, 8:309–10, 315–16; *OR*, 24(3), 384.
45. Kimball to Rawlins, June 5, 1863, *PUSG*, 8:316–17.
46. Grant to Kimball, June 5, 1863, (two messages), Kimball to Rawlins, June 5, 1863, ibid.
47. Kimball to Rawlins, June 6, 1863, Grant to McClernand (same message to McPherson and Sherman), June 6, 1863, *PUSG*, 8:321.

3. River of Lies

1. *OR*, 24(3), 397, 24(1), 94; Dana, *Recollections*, 82–83.
2. Dana, *Recollections*, 83.
3. Ibid.
4. Ibid., 83–84.
5. *New York Sun*, January 28, 1887.
6. James Wilson Diary, June 7, 1863, copy, USGPL, original in Library of Congress, citations refer to the copy; Simpson, introduction to Benjamin P. Thomas, ed., *Three Years with Grant: As Recalled by War Correspondent Sylvanus Cadwallader* (1955; repr., New York: Bison Books, 1996), xiii (citations refer to the 1955 edition). For information on Wilson's draft, see Brooks Simpson, *Ulysses S. Grant: Triumph over Adversity, 1822–1865* (Boston: Houghton Mifflin Harcourt, 2000), 208.
7. Ronald L. Fingerson, "A William Tecumseh Sherman Letter," *Books at Iowa* 3 (November 1965), Special Collections and University Archives, *University of Iowa Libraries*, http://www.lib.uiowa.edu/spec-coll/bai/fingerson2.htm. The original Sherman letter is in the University of Iowa Library's Special Collections Department.
8. Thomas, *Three Years with Grant*, viii–xi; Emmet Crosier, *Yankee Reporters, 1861–1865* (New York: Oxford University Press, 1956), 320; J. Cutler Andrews, *The North Reports the Civil War* (Pittsburg, PA: Pittsburg University Press, 1955), 66.
    Sylvanus Cadwallader (November 17, 1825–September 23, 1908) was an Ohio native who got into the newspaper business early in life in Wisconsin and moved to Chicago and later New York. His later years were spent in the west. He was married twice; his first wife died after five years of marriage, and his second, Mary Isabella Paul, died in 1903 after twenty-eight years of marriage to him. Cadwallader spent his last years in San Diego, California, and both he and his second wife are buried there in Mount Hope Cemetery. Jane Kenaly, archivist, San Diego History Center Library (also "Cadwallader, Sylvanus, biographical

information," Subject Files, USGPL).

9. Thomas, *Three Years with Grant*, xiii, xiv.

10. *OR*, 24(3), 372; Stewart Bennett and Barbara Tillery, eds., *The Struggle for the Life of the Republic: A Civil War Narrative by Brevet Major Charles Dana Miller, 76th Ohio Volunteer Infantry* (Kent, OH: Kent State University Press, 2004), 106.

11. Thomas, *Three Years with Grant*, 102–11.

12. Rawlins to Grant, June 6, 1863, *PUSG*, 8:322–23; James Harrison Wilson, *The Life of John Rawlins: Lawyer, Assistant Adjutant-General, Chief of Staff, Major General of Volunteers, and Secretary of War* (New York: Neale, 1916), 128–30. Earlier in the war, Rawlins had dismissed out of hand a charge of drunkenness against Grant by William Bross, editor of the *Chicago Tribune*. Bross printed his accusation that Grant was drunk while discussing a truce with Rebels, the exact time not given and based on an anonymous letter. The letter was more an attack against Julia than her husband, citing her as a "secesh" wife, due to her Missouri slaveholding family. Rawlins dismissed the accusation by saying that the assertion was totally malice and likely was rooted in the anger of contractors who overcharged their services, charges Grant refused to pay. Rawlins had enough confidence about Grant's innocence that he wrote no letter at the time. In fact, he wrote Elihu Washburne that though Grant had occasionally drunk champagne, he had never gotten drunk on any occasion. Roy P. Basler, ed., *The Collected Works of Abraham Lincoln, Supplement, 1832–1865* (1953; repr., Westport, CT: Greenwood Press, 1974), 118; Bruce Catton, *Grant Takes Command* (New York: Little, Brown, 1968–69), 95–97.

13. Wilson, *Under the Old Flag*, 1:210.

14. Grant, *Memoirs*, 1:256.

15. Cadwallader to Wilson, February 18, 1887, Wilson Papers, Library of Congress, copies in Wilson subject file, USGPL.

16. John Y. Simon, manuscript [untitled], John Rawlins subject file, USGPL.

17. Cadwallader to Wilson, February 25, 1897, Wilson to Cadwallader, September 8, 1904, Wilson Papers.

18. Wilson, *Life of John Rawlins*, 18. See also Cadwallader to Wilson, August 31, 1904, and Wilson to Cadwallader, September 8, 1904, Wilson Papers. According to these letters, Rawlins had instructed his wife to give his papers after his death to Wilson. She gave them to a former Grant staffer, William Hillyer, whose son later told Wilson that in his father's papers, he had found some Rawlins papers and had given them to Grant. Wilson thought Grant likely gave them to his son Fred, but the papers never surfaced. Hence, Wilson and Cadwallader believed Grant or his son destroyed them.

19. Wilson to Cadwallader, October 12, 1904, Cadwallader to Wilson, October 27, 1904, February 7, 1905, and Wilson to Cadwallader, February 15, 1905, Wilson Papers.

20. Wilson to Cadwallader, December 8, 1898, ibid.

21. Dana to Wilson, January 18, 1890, ibid.; *ORN*, 25:58; *OR*, 24(3), 378.

22. Wilson to Cadwallader, January 20, 1890, Wilson Papers.

23. Bruce Catton, "Reading, Writing, and History," *American Heritage*, http://www. americanheritage.com/content/reading-writing-and-history-3, originally published in *American Heritage* 7, no. 5 (1956).

24. Bruce Catton, introduction to John Y. Simon, ed., *The Personal Memoirs of Julia Dent Grant* [Mrs. Ulysses S. Grant] (New York: Putnam's Sons, 1975), 4–5, 114; Catton, *Grant Takes Command*, 66–67.
25. Shelby Foote, *The Civil War: A Narrative*, 3 volumes (New York: Random, 1958–74), 2:417–21.
26. Samuel Carter III, *The Final Fortress: The Campaign for Vicksburg, 1862–1863* (New York: St. Martin's Press, 1980), 245–47.
27. William McFeely, *Grant: A Biography* (New York: Norton, 1981), 132–35.
28. Simpson, *Ulysses S. Grant*, 207–8.
29. Simpson, introduction to Thomas, *Three Years with Grant*, x–xv. The Garland story is on page xiii.
30. Brian J. Murphy, "Truth behind U. S. Grant's Yazoo River Bender," *Weider History Group*, 2012, http://www.historynet.com/truth-behind-us-grants-yazoo-river-bender.htm, originally published in *America's Civil War*, online, June 12, 2006.
31. Jean Edward Smith, *Grant* (New York: Simon and Schuster, 2001), 231, 662n152; J. L. Ringwalt, *Anecdotes of Ulysses S. Grant* (Philadelphia: Lippincott, 1886), 96–97.
32. Winston Groom, *Vicksburg, 1863* (New York: Vintage, 2010), 372–77.

4. Rampant Racism

1. Noah Andre Trudeau, *Like Men of War: Black Troops in the Civil War, 1862–1865* (Boston: Castle Books, 1998), 47–49.
2. Warren Grabau, *Ninety-Eight Days: A Geographer's View of the Vicksburg Campaign* (Knoxville: University of Tennessee Press, 2000), 399; *OR*, 24(2), 141; Ballard, *Vicksburg*, 391; Sullivan to Grant, June 3, 1863, *PUSG*, 8:329.
3. *OR*, 24(3), 220; Ballard, *Vicksburg*, 419–20.
4. Ballard, *Vicksburg*, 70, 106, 108, 161–62, 286.
5. *OR*, 24(2), 447; Grabau, *Ninety-Eight Days*, 390, 392.
6. *OR*, 24(2), 447–48, 470.
7. *OR*, 24(2), 446–49, 469, 453, 24(1) 95; Dana, *Recollections*, 86; Joseph Lester to father and sister, June 21, 1863, 6th Wisconsin file, Journals, Diaries, and Letters Sub-Series, VCS.
8. *OR*, 24(3), 443–44; 24(1), 86; Aaron C. Butler to family, June 14, 1863, Aaron E. Butler Papers, Wisconsin Historical Society, Madison; Grant to Taylor, June 22, 1863, Porter to Grant, June 7, 1863, Grant to Taylor, July 4, 1863, *PUSG*, 8:400–401, 327, 468.
9. Ezra J. Warner, *Generals in Blue: the Lives of the Union Commanders* (Baton Rouge: Louisiana State University Press, 1964), 435–36.
10. Isaac F. Shepard, Court of Inquiry Papers, TS, Wyles MS 74, Isaac F. Shepard Papers, Department of Special Collections, Davidson Library, University of California, Santa Barbara, 3–4. The author is indebted to David H. Slay for providing a copy of the transcript. See also Special Order 143, Record Group 393, Department of the Tennessee, National Archives, Washington, DC.
11. Shepard, Court of Inquiry Papers, 4–5.
12. Ibid., 7–10, 13.
13. Ibid., 16–20.

14. Ibid., part 2; see also General Orders 107, June 14, 1863, and General Orders 108, June 17, 1863, Record Group 393, Department of the Tennessee, National Archives.
15. Shepard, Court of Inquiry Papers, 82–84, III, IV; J. C. Vanderbilt to Mother, June 24, 1863, James C. Vanderbilt Papers, Indiana State Library, Indianapolis.
16. Thomas to Grant, June 26, 1863, *PUSG*, 9:25.
17. Grant to Thomas, July 11, 1863, *PUSG*, 9:23–24.
18. Thomas to Stanton, October 5, 1863, Grant endorsement of Thomas letter to Stanton, October 9, 1863, *PUSG*, 9:26–7.
19. Shepard, Court of Inquiry Papers, 36.
20. Ibid., 37, 42.
21. Ibid., 49–50.
22. Ibid., 14, 17–19, 37–38, 40, 44, 51, 55–56.
23. Grant to Dennis, June 11, 15, 1863, *PUSG*, 8:354, 375.
24. Shepard, Court of Inquiry Papers, 84; *OR*, 24(3), 571.
25. Noralee Frankel, *Freedom's Women: Black Women and Families in Civil War Mississippi* (Bloomington: Indiana University Press, 1999), 35–36; Eaton to Grant, July 23, 1863, Grant to Nasmith, June 25, 1863), *PUSG*, 8:342–43, 426; Lincoln to Grant, August 9, 1863, *PUSG*, 9:197.
26. Rawlins, Special Orders No. 157, June 11, 1863, *PUSG*, 8:318.
27. Rawlins, Special Orders No. 157, June 11, 1863, Cadwallader to Grant, June 11, 1863, McClernand to Grant, June 8, 1863, Rawlins to McClernand, June 11, 1863, *PUSG*, 8:318, 398, 322; *OR*, 24(3), 397; Special Orders No. 40, May 25, 1863, Department of the Tennessee, Record Group 393, National Archives.
28. Gilbert Pierce to Rawlins, June 13, 1863, Osterhaus to Rawlins, June 12, 1863, McClernand to Rawlins, June 15, 1863, *PUSG*, 8:334, 340, 370.
29. McClernand to Rawlins, 1863, *PUSG*, 8:550.
30. S. Cuthburson and J. W. Coleman, "The Siege and Defense of Vicksburg," report, 13, VCS; *Supplement to the Official Records of the Union and Confederate Armies*, 100 vols. (Wilmington, NC: Broadfoot, 1999), 24:397, 413; William Taylor to Jane, June 16, 1863, 100th Pennsylvania file, Regimental Files Sub-Series, VCS; Ballard, *Vicksburg*, 400, 419; Frankel, *Freedom's Women*, 39–40.
31. Bennie J. McRae Jr., research. and comp., "Organization of United States Colored Troops by State/s," *LWF Communications*, 2009, http://www.lwfaam.net/cw/org_usct.htm, accessed November 4, 2012. Information on Mississippi and Louisiana Colored Troops is found on this website's links.
32. Rawlins, endorsement, June 24, 1863, Shepard to Rawlins, July 3, 1863, June 24, 1863, *PUSG*, 8:565–66.

5. Congressman and Coterie

1. Helen Todd, *A Man Named Grant* (Boston: Houghton Mifflin, 1940), 30; Ballard, *U. S. Grant*, 11–27.
2. Todd, *Man Named Grant*, 30; Richard L. Kiper, *Major General John Alexander McClernand: Politician in Uniform* (Kent, OH: Kent State University Press, 1999), 47–49.
3. Kiper, *Major General John Alexander McClernand*, 87–90; Ballard, *U. S. Grant*, 44; *OR*, 7:182.

4. Kiper, *Major General John Alexander McClernand*, 103, 110, 115.
5. Ibid., 5.
6. Ibid., 121, 124; Ballard, *U. S. Grant*, 60.
7. Kiper, *Major General John Alexander McClernand*, 124–32; OR, 24(1), 22.
8. OR, 17(2), 282; PUSG, 6:288–89.
9. Dana, *Recollections*, 59; Dana to Stanton, April 27, 1863, Stanton to Dana, May 6, 1863, Dana to Stanton, May 24, 1863, PUSG, 8:254–55.
10. Ballard, *Vicksburg*, 331–32.
11. Bearss, *Campaign for Vicksburg*, 3:758–59, 771–78, 799, 802.
12. Ibid., 799–801.
13. Ibid., 802, 814; OR, 24(2), 140–41, 334–35, 24(1), 171.
14. Bearss, *Campaign for Vicksburg*, 3:803–4; OR, 24(3), 331–32, 24(1), 154.
15. OR, 24(2), 140–41; Bearss, *Campaign for Vicksburg*, 3:823–25.
16. OR, 24(1), 55, 172.
17. Ibid., 172–73; Bearss, *Campaign for Vicksburg*, 3:836.
18. Bearss, *Campaign for Vicksburg*, 3:836–37; OR, 24(1), 55–56, 172–73; Sherman, *Sherman's Civil War*, 439.
19. Bearss, *Campaign for Vicksburg*, 3:833, 847, 849; OR, 24(1), 173, 617, 732, 777, 24(2), 67.
20. OR, 24(1), 87.
21. Grant to Halleck, May 24, 1863, PUSG, 8:261.
22. Bearss, *Campaign for Vicksburg*, 3:814–22.
23. OR, 24(1), 165–66.
24. Ibid.
25. Ibid., 162–63.
26. Ibid., 163–64.
27. Ibid., 159, 162.
28. Ibid., 164–65.
29. Wilson, *Under the Old Flag*, 1:182–83.
30. Ibid., 184–86.
31. OR, 24(1), 169.
32. Ibid., 103.
33. Ibid., 157; Fran Swigart, "Vicksburg Campaign," *National Tribune*, August 9, 1888. Swigart was in the 46th Indiana.
34. OR, 24(1), 159, 157; Rawlins, Special Orders No. 184, June 18, 1863, McClernand to Grant, June 18, 1863, Grant to Halleck, June 19, 1863, Grant to Lorenzo Thomas, June 26, 1863, PUSG, 8:385–86, 428–29.
35. OR, 24(1), 167–68.
36. Ibid., 165.

6. Closely Hemmed In

1. Grant to Halleck, June 8, 1863, PUSG, 8:325–26.
2. OR, 24(3), 356, 394, Ballard, *Vicksburg*, 320.
3. Grant to Samuel Casey, June 8, 1863, Grant to Cadwallader Washburn, June 10, 1863, PUSG, 8:331, 336.
4. Grant to Dennis, June 8, 11, 15, 1863, PUSG, 8:326, 353–54, 374–75.
5. Grant to Lauman, June 8, 1863, PUSG, 8:330–31.

6. Grant to Porter, June 10, 11, 1863, Porter to Grant, June 9, 10, 1863, Grant to Gilbert Pierce, June 11, 1863, *PUSG*, 8:333–36.

7. Grant to Halleck, June 11, 1863, *PUSG*, 8:344.

8. Halleck to Grant, June 12, 1863, *PUSG*, 8:345.

9. Grant to Halleck, June 11, 1863, Grant to McClernand, June 11, 12 1863, *PUSG*, 8:346, 350–51, 358; Bearss, *Campaign for Vicksburg*, 3:1010, 1016; Ballard, *Vicksburg*, 392.

10. Grant to McClernand, June 15, 1863, McClernand to Rawlins, June 15, 1863, *PUSG*, 8:369–70.

11. Grant to Hurlbut, June 11, 1863, *PUSG*, 8:348.

12. Grant to Sherman, June 11, 1863, *PUSG*, 8:351–52.

13. Porter to Grant, June 16, 1863, *PUSG*, 8:355.

14. Washburn to Grant, June 14, 15, 1863, *PUSG*, 8:373–74.

15. Grant to Washburn, June 15, 1863, *PUSG*, 8:372–73.

16. Grant to Jesse Root Grant, June 15, 1863, *PUSG*, 8:375–76.

17. *OR*, 24(3), 412.

18. Grant to Julia Grant, June 9, 1863, *PUSG*, 8:332.

19. Ibid., June 15, 1863, 8:376–77; Ballard, *Vicksburg*, 378; David W. Reed, *Campaigns and Battles of the Twelfth Regiment, Iowa Veteran Volunteer Infantry* (Evanston, IL, 1903), 124; Edward N. Potter, diary, 29th Wisconsin, June 3, 1863, Wisconsin Historical Society, Madison; David N. Holmes to parents, June 13, 1863, David N. Holmes Papers, Illinois State Historical Library, Springfield.

20. Grant to George Pride, June 15, 1863, Grant to Halleck, June 18[16], 1863, *PUSG*, 8:379, 382–83.

21. Rawlins to Sherman, McPherson, and McClernand, June 15, 1863, Grant to Herron, June 16, 1863, *PUSG*, 8:384, 383.

22. Grant to Porter, Porter to Grant, Grant to McClernand, June 16, 1863, *PUSG*, 8:384.

23. Sherman to Rawlins, June 16, 1863, Grant to Sherman, June 17, 1863, Grant to Porter, June 18, 1863, *PUSG*, 8:387–89.

24. Grant to Parke, June 18, 1863 (2 messages), Parke to Grant, June 18, 1863 (2 messages), *PUSG*, 8:391–92; Orville Babcock, diary, June 18–19, 1863, USGPL.

25. General Field Orders [June 19, 1863], Grant to Porter, June 19, 1863, Porter to Grant, June 20, 1863, *PUSG*, 8:394.

26. Dana, *Recollections*, 91.

27. Sherman to Grant, June 2, 1863, *PUSG*, 8:396.

28. Grant to Lincoln, June 19, 1863, *PUSG*, 8:395.

29. Halleck to Grant, July 14, 1863, *PUSG*, 8:397.

30. Grant to John Kelton, June 18, 1863, Kelton to Grant, June 8, 1863, *PUSG*, 8:388–89.

31. Ord to Grant, June 19, 1863, Grant to Ord, June 19, 1863, *PUSG*, 8:397.

32. Grant to Porter, June 21, 1863, *PUSG*, 8:398–99.

33. Porter to Grant, June 22, 1863, *PUSG*, 8:299.

34. Grant to Porter, June 22, 1863, Grant to Herron, June 22, 1863 (2 messages), *PUSG*, 8:402, 403.

35. Grant to Ord, June 22, 1863, Grant to Osterhaus, June 22, 1863, Osterhaus to Grant, June 22, 1863 (4 messages), *PUSG*, 8:404–7.

36. Bearss, *Campaign for Vicksburg*, 3:1090, 1094.

37. Grant to Parke, June 20, 22, 1863, Parke to Grant, June 22, 1863 (3 messages), Grant to McPherson, June 22, 1863, *PUSG*, 8:405, 407.

38. Feis, *Grant's Secret Service*, 171–72; *OR*, 24(3), 965.

7. Big Black, Black Powder, Brush Fires

1. Grant to Sherman, June 22, 1863, *PUSG*, 8:408.

2. Grant to Herron, June 23, 1863, Herron to Grant, June 23, 24, 1863, *PUSG*, 8:409.

3. Grant to McPherson, June 23, 1863, McPherson to Grant, June 23, 1863, Grant to Ord, June 23, 24, 1863, Ord to Grant, June 23, 1863, Ord to Rawlins, June 23, 1863, *PUSG*, 8:409–10.

4. Grant to Sherman, June 23, 1863, *PUSG*, 8:410–11.

5. Sherman to Grant, June 23, 1863, Rawlins to Ord, June 23, 1863, Washburn to Grant, June 23, 1863, *PUSG*, 8:411–12.

6. Grant to Porter, June 24, 1863, Washburn to Grant, June 24, 1863, *PUSG*, 8:412–13.

7. Porter to Grant, June 24, 1863, *PUSG*, 8:413.

8. Grant to Samuel Nasmith, June 25, 1863, Nasmith to Rawlins, July 1, 1863, Porter to Grant, June 26, 1863, *PUSG*, 8:425–27; *ORN*, 25:199.

9. Grant to Halleck, June 27, 1863, *PUSG*, 8:434–35.

10. Ballard, *Vicksburg*, 365.

11. Andrew Hickenlooper, "The Vicksburg Mine," in Robert U. Johnston and Buell, eds., *Battles and Leaders of the Civil War*, 4 vols. (New York: Yoseloff, 1956), 3:539–42.

12. Grant to Herron, June 25, 1863, *PUSG*, 8:415.

13. Grant to Ord, June 25, 1863, McPherson to Ord and Grant, June 25, 1863, *PUSG*, 8:415.

14. *OR*, 24(2), 376; Ballard, *Vicksburg*, 367; Jerome Dann to [?], March 3, 1902, 20th Illinois file, Regimental Files Sub-Series, VCS.

15. Ballard, *Vicksburg*, 367–69.

16. Ibid., 369; Grant, *Memoirs*, 1:553; Bearss, *Campaign for Vicksburg*, 3:924–25; Grant to Ord, June 25, 1863 (2 messages), *PUSG*, 8:416–17.

17. Grant to Halleck, June 26, 1863, *PUSG*, 8:431–32.

18. Sherman to Grant, June 24, 1863, Grant to Sherman, June 25, 1863, *PUSG*, 8:421–22, 424.

19. Grant to Sherman, June 25, 1863, *PUSG*, 8:423.

20. Grant to Thomas Hendrickson, June 26, 1863, *PUSG*, 8:432–33.

21. Grant to Absalom Markland, June 29, 1863, *PUSG*, 8:445–46.

22. Grant to Julia Grant, June 29, 1863, *PUSG*, 8:444–45.

23. Grant to Hurlbut, June 27, 1863, Hurlbut to Rawlins, June 23, 25, 28, 1863, *PUSG*, 8:435–38.

24. Osband to Rawlins, June 30, 1863, Dennis to Grant, June 30, 1863, Grant to Dennis, June 27, 1863, *PUSG*, 8:438–39; *OR*, 24(2), 450.

25. *OR*, 24(2), 246–48, 24(3), 449–50, 987; Ballard, *Vicksburg*, 395. Sherman had used similar actions or polices as tactics in Memphis when he evicted a few families in retaliation for Confederate guerillas shooting at Union boats. Later

in Atlanta, he expelled most of the city's civilians so he could turn the city into a fortress. His actions along the Big Black were less severe because, by comparison, few people lived in the sparsely populated area. John F. Marszalek, *Sherman: A Soldier's Passion for Order* (New York: Free Press, 1993), 195, 285.

26. Grant to Sherman, June 29, 1863, *PUSG*, 8:442–43; Charles A. Willison to sister, July 1, 1863, 76th Ohio File, VCS; "A Narrative of the Services of Brevet-Major Charles Dana Miller in the War of the Great Rebellion, 1861–1865," handwritten MS transcribed by Roy Gilman Miller, June 30, [1863], 48–50, Journals, Diaries, and Letters Sub-Series, VCS.

27. McPherson to Grant, July 1, 1863 (2 messages), Grant to McPherson, July 1, 1863, *PUSG*, 8:448.

28. *OR*, 24(3), 456.

29. Ballard, *Vicksburg*, 369–70; Samuel Lockett, "The Defense of Vicksburg," in Johnston and Buell, *Battles and Leaders*, 3:491.

30. McPherson to Grant, July 1, 1863, *PUSG*, 8:448–49; Grant to McPherson, July 1, 1863, McPherson to Grant, July 1, 1863, *PUSG*, 8:449.

31. Ord to Grant, July 1, 1863, Grant to Ord, July 1, 1863, *PUSG*, 8:449.

32. Ord to Rawlins, July 1, 1863, *PUSG*, 8:449–50.

33. Grant to Ord, July 1, 1863, Grant to Herron, July 1, 1863, Herron to Grant, July 1, 1863, *PUSG*, 8:450–51.

34. Ord to Grant, July 1, 1863 (3 messages), Grant to Ord, July 1, 1863 (4 messages), Grant to Herron, July 1, 1863, Osterhaus to Grant via Ord, July 1, 1863, Grant to Sherman, July 1, 1863 (3 messages), Sherman to Grant, July 1, 1863 (2 messages), Sherman to Grant, July 2, 1863, *PUSG*, 8:450–53.

8. Surrender, Clutter, Impact

1. *OR*, 24(1), 283–84.

2. Grant to Pemberton, July 3, 1863, *PUSG*, 8:455.

3. Ballard, *Vicksburg*, 397; *OR*, 24(3), 544.

4. *OR*, 24(3), 544; Badeau, *Military History*, 1:380–31; Grant, *Memoirs*, 1:560.

5. Grant to corps commanders and Herron, July 3, 1863, Grant to Herron (two additional Messages), July 3, 1863, Rawlins to Herron, Ord, and McPherson, July 3, 1863, Ord to Grant, July 3 (5 messages), Grant to Ord, July 3, 1863, *PUSG*, 8:456–57.

6. Grant to Pemberton, July 3, 1863, *PUSG*, 8:457–58; Ballard, *Vicksburg*, 398.

7. Pemberton to Grant, July 3, 1863, *PUSG*, 8:458.

8. Grant to Pemberton, July 4, 1863, *PUSG*, 8:467.

9. Ibid.

10. Pemberton to Grant, July 4, 1863, *PUSG*, 8:468; *OR*, 24(1), 285; Grant, *Memoirs*, 1:565. For more on the surrender, see Pemberton's and Grant's postwar accounts in Johnston and Buell, *Battles and Leaders*, 3:530–35, 543–46; Grant to Porter, July 3, 1863 (3 messages), Grant to Porter, July 4, 1863, Porter to Grant, July 4, 1863, Rawlins to Herron, July 3, 1863 Rawlins to Herron and corps commanders, July 3, 1863, Wilson to McPherson, July 4 (2 messages), Wilson to Ord, July 4, 1863, *PUSG*, 8:458–59.

11. Sherman to Grant, July 3, 1863, Grant to Sherman, July 3, 1863, *PUSG*, 8:460.

12. Sherman to Grant, July 3, 1863 (2 messages), *PUSG*, 8:461.

13. Grant to Sherman, July 3, 1863, *PUSG*, 8:461.

14. Sherman to Rawlins, July 3, 1863, Parke to Grant, July 3, 1863, Grant to Parke and Sherman, July 3, 1863, Wright's report, July 3, 1863, Osterhaus to Grant, July 3, 1863, *PUSG*, 8:461–63.

15. Grant to Sherman, July 4, 1863, and Sherman to Grant, July 4, 1863, *PUSG*, 8:476–78. Edward Everett, a noted orator of the day, delivered a long speech preceding Abraham Lincoln's Gettysburg Address. As his words indicate, Sherman hated the press for the way reporters had attacked his reputation earlier in the war.

16. Ord to Grant, July 4, 1863, Grant to McPherson, July 4, 1863, *PUSG*, 8:473–74.

17. Grant, *Memoirs*, 1:366–67.

18. Fred Grant, speech to Army of the Tennessee union, *Vicksburg (MS) Herald*, November 8, 1907, VCS; Christian McWhirter, *Battle Hymns: The Power and Popularity of Music in the Civil War* (Chapel Hill: University of North Carolina Press, 2012), 51–54.

19. Special Orders No. 180, July 4, 1863, *PUSG*, 8:464–45; Ballard, *Vicksburg*, 414.

20. James H. Wilson to Grant, July 4, 1863, Theodore S. Bowers, circular, July 12, 1863, Sherman to Rawlins, September 25, 1863, Rawlins to Hurlbut, Ord, and McPherson, October 6, 1863, and Bowers, General Orders 64, October 15, *PUSG*, 8:465.

21. Grant to Graham, July 3, 4, 1863, Graham to Rawlins, July 3, 4, July 4, 1863, Rawlins to Graham, July 4, 1863, Graham to Grant, July 4, 1863, *PUSG*, 8:470.

22. Grant to Halleck, July 4, 1863, Halleck to Grant, July 8, 10, 1863, *PUSG*, 8:469–71.

23. Grant to Halleck, July 6, 1863, *PUSG*, 8:484–85.

24. Grant to Banks, July 4, 1863, Banks to Grant, July 7, 1863, *PUSG*, 8:471–72.

25. Porter to Grant, July 4 (3 messages), Grant to Dennis, July 4, 1863, Grant to Sherman, July 4, 1863, *PUSG*, 8:472–73; Grant, *Memoirs*, 1:566; David Dixon Porter, *Incidents and Anecdotes of the Civil War* (New York: Appleton, 1885), 200.

26. Grant to Ord, July 4, 1863 (2 messages), Grant to Sherman, July 4, 1863 (2 messages), *PUSG*, 8:475–77, 479.

27. Sherman to Grant, July 6, 7, 8, 1863, *PUSG*, 8:479–80.

28. Grant to McPherson, July 5, 1863, *PUSG*, 8:483–84.

29. Grant report, [July 6], 1863, *PUSG*, 8:485–523; Wilson, *Life of John Rawlins*, 147.

30. Grant to Jesse Root Grant, July 6, 1863, *PUSG*, 8:524–25.

31. Grant to McPherson, July 4, 1863, *PUSG*, 9:3.

32. *OR*, 24(3), 484, 487. See also 483.

33. Grant to McPherson, July 8, 1863 (3 messages), Grant to Commanding Officer at Bovina or Big Black Bridge, July 8, 1863, *PUSG*, 9:4–5, 8.

34. Grant to Pemberton, July 10, 1863, Pemberton to Grant, July 10, 1863, *PUSG*, 9:9–10.

35. Grant to Banks, July 10, 1863, *PUSG*, 9:17–18.

36. For an account of the fight at Helena, see Bearss, *Campaign for Vicksburg*, 3:1207–45.

37. Grant to Banks, July 10, 1863, *PUSG*, 9:18.

38. Banks to Grant, July 8, 1863, *PUSG*, 9:32.

39. Grant to Banks, July 11, 1863, Grant to McPherson, July 11, 1863 (2 messages), Porter to Grant, July 11, 1863, *PUSG*, 9:31–4; *ORN*, 25:281.

40. Grant to Sherman, July 11, 1863, *PUSG*, 9:35.

41. Sherman to Rawlins, July 11, 1863, Rawlins to James Burdick, July 12, 1863, Sherman to Grant, July 12, 1863, *PUSG*, 9:36–37; Bruce J. Dinges and Shirley A. Leckie, eds., *A Just and Righteous Cause: Benjamin H. Grierson's Memoir* (Carbondale: Southern Illinois University Press, 2008), 298–99.
42. Grant to Sherman, July 13, 1863 (2 messages), *PUSG*, 9:43–44, 47–48.
43. Sherman to Grant, July 14, 1863, *PUSG*, 9:44–46.
44. Grant to Sherman, July 14, 1863, Sherman to Grant, July 14, 1863, Hurlbut to Rawlins, July 11, 1863, *PUSG*, 9:46–47.
45. Grant to Herron, July 14, 15, 1863, *PUSG*, 9:48; Ballard, *Vicksburg*, 409.
46. Grant to Halleck, July 15, 1863, Grant to Schofield, July 15, 1863, Schofield to Grant, July 8, 1863, *PUSG*, 9:50–51, 54–55, 56.
47. Grant to Sherman, July 15, 1863, *PUSG*, 9:57.
48. Sherman to Grant, July 15, 1863 (2 messages), July 18, 1863, Cyrus Bussey to Sherman, July 18, 1863, *PUSG*, 9:57–58.
49. Sherman to Grant, July 17, 1863 (2 messages), *PUSG*, 9:66.
50. *OR*, 24(3), 528.
51. Grant to Porter, July 16, 1863, Porter to Grant July 14, 1863, Grant to W. G. Watts, July 11, 1863, *PUSG*, 9:22, 58–59; Ballard, *Vicksburg*, 418.
52. Grant to Dennis, July 11, 1863, Grant to Watts, July 11, 1863, *PUSG*, 9:39, 22.
53. Grant to J. H. Hammond, July 10, 1863, Grant to Moore, July 10, 1863, *PUSG*, 9:49–50.
54. Grant to McPherson, July 15, 1863, *PUSG*, 9:53.
55. Grant to Banks, July 16, 1863 (2 messages), Charles Stone to Grant, July 18, 1863, Banks to Grant, July 12, 18, 1863, *PUSG*, 9:59–63; *OR*, 24(3), 547.
56. Basler, *Collected Works of Abraham Lincoln, Supplement*, 6:326, 374; Grant to Schofield, July 21, 1863, Theodore Bowers (Grant staff), Special Orders No. 207, July 31, 1863, Grant to Lincoln, August 23, 1863, *PUSG*, 9:88, 102, 196.
57. Simon, *Personal Memoirs of Julia Dent Grant*, 120.
58. Halleck to Grant, October 16, 1863 (2 messages), War Department Orders 337, October 16, 1863, John Rawlins, issued Special Orders No. 1, October 18, 1863, Stanton to Halleck, October 19, 1863, *PUSG*, 9:295–98.
59. Wilson, *Under the Old Flag*, 2:17.

INDEX

Adams, Wirt, 40

Babcock, Orville, 118
Badeau, Adam, 147
Banks, Nathaniel, 29–30, 34–35,
    135, 151, 153, 157, 161–63, 169
Bell, Charles, 126
Benton, William, 95
Blair, Frank, 10, 12, 14, 16, 35–41, 86
Bledsoe, Hiram, 129
Bowen, John, 146–48
Boynton, Henry Van Ness, 45
Bragg, Braxton, 42, 138
Breckinridge, John C., 118
Buckland, Ralph, 130
Buell, Don Carlos, 3–4
Burbridge, Stephen, 18–19, 21
Burnside, Ambrose E., 111, 158, 166,
    169

Cadwallader, Sylvanus, 45–63
Carr, Eugene, 18–19, 95, 131
Carter, Samuel, III, 59
Catton, Bruce, 57–58
Coehorn mortars, 132
Comstock, Cyrus, 155

Dana, Charles, 22, 32, 68–69, 78, 92,
    103, 105, 119, 156, 172
    and Grant drinking story, 43–46,
    51, 53–57, 59–61, 100
Davis, Jefferson, 9, 135
Dennis, Elias, 66–67, 76, 108,
    123–24, 139, 157

Dent, Lewis, 115
Dodge, Grenville, 30
Duncan, Stephen, 168

Eaton, John, Jr., 77–78, 85
Ellet, Alfred, 32, 112, 122
Everett, Edward, 154
Ewing, Hugh, 130

Farragut, David, 109
Foote, Shelby, 58–60, 62

Gardner, Franklin, 157, 162
Garland, Hamlin, 60
Gist, States Rights, 38
Grabau, Warren E., 60
Graham, (George) "Wash," 49, 156
Grant, Fred, 115, 170
Grant, Jesse Root, 114
Grant, Julia, 58, 114, 136–37, 170
Grant, Ulysses S.
    and Nathaniel Banks (see Banks,
        Nathaniel)
    and burial truce, 33
    and drinking story on Yazoo
        River, 43–63
    early attempts to take Vicks-
        burg, 5–7
    enters Vicksburg, 154
    and family, 58, 114–15, 136–37, 170
    goes to Chattanooga, 170
    and Joseph E. Johnston (see
        Johnston, Joseph E.)
    Louisiana situations, 64, 66

193

Michael B. Ballard has authored or edited fourteen books. In December 2012 he retired after thirty years in the Mississippi State University Libraries, where he was university archivist, coordinator of the Congressional and Political Research Center, and associate editor of publishing projects in the U. S. Grant Presidential Library. He lives in Ackerman, Mississippi.